# BRANKO'S RIDE

# BRANKO'S RIDE

*Hi John & Amy!*

*Best wishes*

*Živio*

## Berislav Branko Dujlovich
## with
## Michael Goodreau

Copyright © 2005, 2006 by Berislav Branko Dujlovich.

Library of Congress Number:    2005910193
ISBN:             Hardcover    1-4257-0328-3
                  Softcover    1-4257-0327-5

All rights reserved. No part of this book may be reproduced or transmitted in any form or by any means, electronic or mechanical, including photocopying, recording, or by any information storage and retrieval system, without permission in writing from the copyright owner.

This book is *not* a work of fiction. It takes place over the course of fifty-eight years. My story begins when I was a mere six years old. The locations listed are correct, as well as names of the major characters. Some names and places are indelibly stamped in my memory, while others were arrived at through questioning my family and academic research. *All* of the major events listed herein are true and real to the best of my recollection. Minor character's names, as sharp as their image is in my mind, have escaped me over the passing of decades. Please allow me some latitude in recalling sixty years worth of events, names and conversations.

This book was printed in the United States of America.

To order additional copies of this book, contact:
Xlibris Corporation
1-888-795-4274
www.Xlibris.com
Orders@Xlibris.com
32091

# Contents

Prologue ................................................................................. 9

## Part I—EUROPE

1. The Counting of the Plums ............................................ 15
2. Sljivovica ........................................................................ 23
3. Fleeing Serbs ................................................................. 31
4. The Hungry Window ...................................................... 37
5. Camp Life ....................................................................... 43
6. Milan's Homecoming ..................................................... 59
7. Sandals and Brown Robes ............................................ 67
8. Servants of Saint Francis .............................................. 75
9. Dark Secrets .................................................................. 87
10. Viva il Papa .................................................................... 97
11. Secrets and Bad Habits ............................................... 101

## Part II—AMERICA

12. An Ocean of Change ................................................... 111
13. Dreamland ................................................................... 121
14. Drexel Boulevard ......................................................... 135
15. Saint Joe's Time .......................................................... 143
16. A Summer (or three) of Repayment ............................ 151
17. A Day in the Life of a Newly Freed Man ..................... 167
18. The Daily Grind ........................................................... 181
19. Private D.P. Dujlovich .................................................. 197
20. Chicago—Round II ...................................................... 213
21. Cerebral Vascular Accidents Happen .......................... 223
22. Only in America .......................................................... 231

# *Dedication*

I dedicate this book to my country, the United States of America, and the people that make this country what it is-the greatest place on earth to live. For those of you realizing this to be true, enjoy the read. For those of you that don't it is my hope that by the turning of the last page you will appreciate your country for what is; a land of unparalleled opportunity limited only by your vision.

I also wish to extend a special dedication to my friend and mentor, Mr. Donald A. Manna. No words are sufficient to express my gratitude for his kindness, humor and wisdom-instrumental to my success in business and as a human being.

Few things in life proceed flawlessly from the beginning, and this project was no exception. Though ultimately choosing Michael Goodreau to write this book, I would like to offer a special thanks to Anna Paulos and Mary Ann Cortopassi for their early efforts. I would like to thank my wife Lee, and my daughters Lisa and Pam for their patience and understanding. Also, to my mother-in-law Lil Loess-a magnificent woman whose support and genuine understanding was instrumental in my carrying this project through to completion. Thank you all.

Barry Dujlovich

# PROLOGUE

## The North Sea Port of Bremmerhaven, Germany—1951

Mother was long since gone—a number in the refugee camps of Austria. Father was dead. I became an orphan in a system placing refugee children below the value of a warm bowl of gruel. Along with my home and farm gone were simple pleasures, such as warming by the fire on an icy winter night. My sense of security had long since evaporated, but in the funny way that life slaps with one hand, and caresses with the other; I also gained the world. I can make that claim now, after sixty-five years of caresses and slaps, but if I peel away the years and go back far enough, the fear and loathing quickly set up camp.

Eastern Europe was coming apart at the seams, and I was a puff of stuffing swept underfoot. World War Two consumed Europe a bomb at a time for four years before touching my life directly. Some memories are fuzzy, the blurring of a faded photograph, and yet some seem as if they happened only yesterday.

Tug tug on my sleeve. "Branko, what will we find in America?"
I was silent, conjuring a suitable answer.
"We will find bread, Mirko, more bread than we can eat-with jars full of fresh honey, and more milk than your tummy can hold"
My younger friend looked up at me, silently holding my eyes for a moment, then asked,
"Our mothers and fathers, Branko, will we see them again?"
My throat closed and my eyes hurt. I felt an unceasingly dull ache of pain, almost as much for Mirko as myself. But I had been through a lot and seen so much, that while answering him with compassion, I still provided the unvarnished truth.
"No, Mirko, we may never see our parents again."
A tear, sprung from a pool of thousands, grew in size at the corner of his left eye until gravity took command, slipping down Mirko's cheek. A hand swooped up from below, erasing its existence.
"Then why are we going to America, Branko?"
Replying softly, "There is nothing left for us here." Continuing I assumed an upbeat note, as much for his benefit as mine. "Everywhere people talk of America.

All of the talk is good. *This* is why we will go. They call America the land of the free. You remember the soldiers, how they smiled?" I asked him.

Mirko smiled at the memory. The two of us stood on the concrete dock facing the water as it smacked in angry rolls against the mammoth gray steel flanks of tied off ships, swaying on thick ropes. At last, we were going to America! The land of baseball and laughing soldiers, the place where *anyone* could become whatever they wanted.

# PART I

# EUROPE

# Barren Fields

Where are you going child?
Why are you so alone?
You're standing in a field barren,
Other kids are home.
They're eating mother's cooking
Round a table filled with cheer.
You're beneath the open sky—
Not a living soul is near.
While light dances in their eyes
From Daddy's jokes, Momma's sighs,
You look around your barren hell,
There's no Mom to ring that dinner bell.
And while Daddy tucks them in tonight
With a kiss of love, then out the light,
It's hard to see you so alone,
No Mom no Dad, no love no home.

Michael W. Goodreau

# CHAPTER I

## "The Counting of the Plums"

My early childhood was no better or worse than any other peasant-farmer family surrounding us. We were but one more. Farming didn't make anyone wealthy, at least not in Ivanjska, the nearest village to my family farm. Ivanjska is nestled in low rolling hills near the city of Banja Luka in the country of Croatia, which occupies a portion of Austria's southern border in central Europe.

Joseph Dujlovich, my father, was an excellent farmer, and the soil in this region is very fertile—much like the Croatian women who walked upon it. While nurturing the soils capacity to provide a healthy crop, his gift for producing life extended to other areas as well. Yela Dujlovich produced Milan, Milka, Mara, Anka, Ruska, Regina, and me—Berislav Dujlovich.

My father was strong and coarse; a man who ensured with military discipline that his crops grew and his children worked. Any, and I mean *any* form of rebellion met with the back of his hand or the sting of whipped leather. My mother Yela attended the same school of parenting as Joseph. The differences between them lie not in the length of the fuse igniting their anger, but in the strength of the explosion that followed.

Joseph learned to farm from his father Jozo. Never meeting my grandfather, Joseph did tell me he was not wealthy; he *was* a landholder of above average acreage. My father was himself one of seven children. My father received a portion of the land on his wedding day, as was the custom. He was also a military officer in the *Ustasche*, the military force in Croatia. As a low ranking officer at a military prison not far from Ivanjska, he guarded Jewish, Gypsy and Serbian prisoners. Memories of Joseph are, with rare exception, that of a stern faced man-bestowing smiles with a miser's frugality. Eight hungry bellies to fill on a junior officer's salary was a very serious affair, leaving little time for endeavors not related to survival.

I lived on a working farm. There was some form of food being grown at any given time of year. Of the produce we coaxed from the earth half made its way to our dinner table and the other half to the markets of Ivanjska and Banja Luka. We spent most of our time performing chores essential to our continued existence. Water was lugged a bucket at a time from the well to the house, and firewood was gathered and stored year round.

The rhythmic pounding of rocks signaled washday. I wonder which was harder-Yela or the rocks. Her attitude toward life emitted a coldness seven children's smiles could not thaw. Born poor and wanting more out of life, she knew she would never get it. Yela was an illiterate peasant woman, but she was well aware of the hand life dealt her. She knew that women of means do not give birth to seven children in the same house with the same mid-wife. Poverty and the never-ending demands of simply staying alive crushed her spirit, leaving room for little else. Her rare expressions of love I did see were brief-a bubble of light miraculously surviving all the way to her eyes.

Our home was a glorified barn-nothing more than a room with dirt floors encased by four wood walls. Blankets strung wall-to-wall created rooms. The walls of my "room" shuddered with the opening of the front door. The thick blankets separated our home into three sections. Yela and Joseph shared a corner; the kitchen/dining room/living room took another chunk, leaving us seven children with the remaining third.

Morning began with Joseph rumbling in the pre-dawn murk, grunting as he pulled together his needs for the day. When not guarding prisoners Joseph worked from sunrise to sunset at home. Farming is hard work and hard work requires energy. Joseph took his meals at mid-day and early evening. When he was home sleep was his only reprieve from the plow.

Work did not begin and end with my parents' toils however. Milan was the oldest child and therefore worked the hardest among us all. He was sixteen years old when I was born, making him not so much a brother, but more of an "Uncle". My own chores changed with the seasons. Last year, my fifth season on earth, gathering eggs was my responsibility. This year though my youngest sister Regina roots for eggs in the chicken coops every morning. This year I *milk the cows*! When it came to the livestock, Captain Joseph-commander of Brigade Dujlovich took a very keen interest indeed. As such, I took extra care with the cows. I was more concerned for my own hide than all the cows combined.

We were poor, but we *did* live on a farm. My father's pride and joy was a small, but well tended orchard of plum trees. If inspecting a wagonload of Dujlovich grown fruit and vegetables made him smile, he fairly beamed as he held the glossy, ruby-black plums up to the sun after picking them from the grass. Satisfied with their firmness and luster he set them gently in a basket.

This was a fun time of the year for me, harvesting the plums. All seven kids took part. Milan and Milka shook the plum tree branches letting nature decide which plums were ripe and which ones needed a little more time on the branch. *Thump, thump* dropped the plums, plopping onto the thick grass cushion below.

During plum harvest, Joseph moved with a springiness of step not found in the turnip harvest. He spoke a bit softer, favoring me with a rare smile. I sensed my father's happiness, and it made me happy in turn. The same was true for my siblings, so we naturally grew to look forward to the plum harvest. This was the best time of the year for us since we received more attention and affection than the rest of the year combined. As a few plum harvests came and went I finally grew inquisitive enough to find out *why* our father was so happy to gather plums.

Milan was oldest, so of course I took my questions to him.

"Oh, Branko, you know nothing!" He laughed and rubbed my hair. It always made me happy when Milan called me Branko. I was born Berislav Dujlovich, but my family called me Branko. "You know Papa sells the plums and grapes at market, don't you?" He asked.

"Yes, of course" I answered.

"Think Branko, last year Papa picked fifty baskets of plums, yes?"

"Yes" I replied. I didn't really know, but if Milan said fifty baskets then it must be so.

"And how many did he sell at market? Huh? You don't know. You are so young! He sold *thirty*! There were thirty, Branko. Now, what happened to the other twenty, eh?"

By this time, I was thoroughly mystified. All I knew for sure was that Papa had a *bunch* of plums to sell, but he didn't sell a bunch—he sold *some*.

"What did he do with the other twenty baskets Milan?" I obligingly asked.

"Ah, now *that* is the source of Papa's smile," Milan smugly stated.

I must have looked blank.

"Branko! Surely when you've woken up to go outside and pee you have heard Momma and Papa laughing! They sit at the kitchen table, yes? And what have you seen between them? A bottle!"

"Yes" I muttered. I was afraid Milan would tell Yela and Joseph I had spied on them.

"That bottle on the table was filled with *Sljivovica*. It's brandy made from the choicest plums in the whole orchard. Papa makes the best *Sljivovica* in Ivanjska. Everyone agrees this is so." Softer now. "*Sljivovica* is magic, Branko. Smiles, laughter and happiness are inside it. When do you *ever* hear Momma or Papa *laugh*? I will tell you when! Almost never! *Except* when Papa brings out a bottle of *Sljivovica*-and its true." Whispering now, "I've had it. All your cares *do* go away, Branko."

"You had some Milan?" I couldn't believe it!

"I was fifteen." Milan looked around and leaned into me. "I drank one glass, and felt blessed by God. I drank two glasses, and I was glad to be alive. I drank *three* glasses, and I felt the Devil take me-I felt so strong I could wrestle a snake! I wanted more but Papa said no. Mama would have his head if she knew I had even *one* drink."

*Sljivovica, Sljivovica* . . . I thought of little else. I *had* to drink it! It made Papa smile and Yela laugh, according to Milan. He also said happiness came to those who drank it. I was not unhappy, but nonetheless it became my mission to drink some.

As the time came round to take a wagonload of produce to the market in Banja Luka, I offered Papa my help. I was secretly scheming to be near the plums, and hopefully the *Sljivovica*. To my surprise he told me that I could go with Milan and himself to Banja Luka. Yes! I knew my chance was not far off! I would soon taste this *Sljivovica* for myself. I was lucky-Joseph was in a jovial mood.

There was only a narrow window of time for my father to harvest his plums and get to market to sell them while fresh, still factoring the rest of the produce that had to be sold before it went bad.

We were off to the market in Banja Luka! I had gone many times to Ivanjska's market, but Banja Luka was a *city*! All of my sisters, except Regina, were busy loading cases of fresh corn and plump tomatoes. They stacked boxes of multi-colored peppers and bushels of string beans in the bed of the wagon. The last cases of produce to get loaded were the plums. Ah, yes, of course, the plums. I had been waiting for the plums. I began counting the number of cases my sisters stacked on the wagon bed. I knew we picked twenty-seven cases of plums this year. Milan had counted them and told me. I was sure he told me the truth on how *Sljivovica* was made, but I *still* wanted to see for myself. As Anka stooped to pick up the last crate I stopped counting at seventeen. It was all true!

Papa was cinching the last harness for the four horses hitched to pull the wagon while instructing Yela about this and that. This was always a good time to be scarce. Gone for a few minutes behind the hut I wandered back out front after inspecting an ant colony. I came from the edge of the hut where Papa and Milan stood surveying the load.

"Milan, come with me" Papa said as they converged on the corner of the wagon diagonal to me. "We will sell twelve bottles of *Sljivovica* in Banja Luka so that your brothers and sisters can have shoes, yes?" His face turned to a scowl, followed by the ghost of a smile.

"But we will bring thirteen. One for the cold ride back, eh, Milan?"

"Best to be prepared against the chill Papa" Milan answered, managing an even reply.

I was peeking around the corner of the wagon when I saw Joseph's face sweep into a thunderstorm of anger. His eyes flashed lightening followed by the crack of thunder a second behind.

"Branko!"

"Yes, Papa" I meekly answered, directly behind him in an instant. There was no reason to let the clouds grow stronger or darker. He gave a little jump and barked at me to climb up on the wagon so we could be on our way. Looking around for a place to sit I saw nothing but a wall of wooden crates, spilling color out their tops and between their ribs. I made do with sitting off the back of the wagon. My legs swung inches above the dirt. The horses began pulling us up the rutted track to the main road. The view of my house receded, growing smaller until a hill swallowed it whole.

The steady plodding of the horses' hooves and the clanking of the metal-rimmed wheels seduced me into reverie. I thought back to yesterday afternoon. I had been watching a line of ants work their way about their tiny kingdom. I spent many hours watching ants. The same amount of time was devoted to knowing where the frogs called home in my pond. Snakes may slither and think themselves invisible but I knew every hole they slunk into! But new and exciting things had just happened. I started out this trip contemplating the business of ants and ended it with visions of a completely different existence from my own.

"Berislav! Snap out of it! Quit daydreaming and get off the wagon" my father's jagged voice intruded, bursting the bubble of my vision. What? We are here already? "Start unloading the crates!" he barked. "Stack them so you can see what is in them. Leave enough space between the wagon and the boxes for us to walk through. Move, Branko! We haven't much time." He said the last part with less of an edge.

My mind was still swimming with what I had seen on the road from Ivanjska. It was incredible! A small *town* of tents sprouted along the road. There were so many! I lost count of the barefoot kids running between the patchwork tents and the flickering lights cast by the flames of cooking fires. Shadows danced briefly before them on the tent walls, dispelled in a flash as they moved to the next circle of light. The clothes these strange people wore were not the drab brown I was familiar with. Their pants and shirts were multi-colored splashes of brightness. But why would people camp on the side of the road? Why did they not have homes like Papa, Milan, and me?

The women bore expressions as lusterless as their dresses were vibrant. They were draped in clothing of the reddest reds and bluest blues I had ever seen! Until that day, I thought only birds could have such colors. Around their throats I saw necklaces jumbled with little bells and "jingly-things" dancing a rumba of sparkle and tinkling sounds as the women went about the business of living. I saw at least six different cooking areas spread throughout the camp. At each one of them women stirred delicious smelling stews, steaming and bubbling in large kettles over fires flickering in varying degrees of liveliness. The children sang an unfamiliar song, a choppy sounding melody, stark in contrast to the stillness of a morning glowing by the light of a newly risen sun.

As Joseph, Milan and I drew alongside them the horses pulling our wagon suddenly sped up. They didn't return to their normal plodding gait until the campsite was little more than glowing points of amber light far behind us.

After my father issued his orders regarding the unloading of the produce I ventured to ask him why he had sped up.

"Branko," my father looked down at me and answered, "those people are gypsies. They wander here and there and camp where they please. I have heard they come from India but have been wandering this land for centuries. They have no real home as you do. With no real home, they do no real work. How do they eat and clothe themselves and repair their tents and buy pots and pans when they do no work? If you don't work, you cannot make the *kuna*, eh? If you have no *kuna*, how do you buy pots and pans, eh? They *steal* them, Branko! That is how! If I had gone too slowly they could have swarmed our wagon and taken our food. *You*, Branko, they would have sold into slavery to some *other* band of traveling gypsies. Do you wish I had gone slower *now*?"

"Uh, no papa," I replied. I turned from him quickly and set about unloading the crates. Sold into slavery to a band of wandering thieves! I blessed my father for his wisdom and worked doubly hard to please him.

The Bazaar was a beehive of activity by the time we arrived several hours after sun-up. Apparently, we arrived later than most of the other vendors in the square. Many were already busy hawking wares or produce. Banja Luka was so big! So many people! All of them, if not buying something, were selling something. It seemed they were all trying to do what my father seemed to do better than most. We had arrived late with a full wagon of goods and were prepared to leave with an empty one sooner than anyone else. As my Father sold his last bottle of *Sljivovica* to some haggled-toothed wretch he motioned at me to begin stacking the last of the empty crates for our trip home. I hoped Papa would gallop the horses past the gypsies. I had been thinking about it and decided I didn't want to be a gypsy. I didn't want to be a slave either-good smelling food and bright colored clothing or not.

A frightening noise assaulted my ears. I quickly crouched under the wagon and looked out onto the square. I saw some people (the ones in flowing robes) stop what they were doing—even in the middle of negotiations! They laid down whatever they were holding and put away any money they were waving. They looked on the far side of the square to a large building with a domed roof. The building was at the foot of a tower that was as narrow as it was tall. They began walking across the square, vanishing inside the large doors. Father told me on the way home that the tower is a Minaret and the building itself is a Mosque.

I reached out and tugged my Papa's pants leg.

"Please make the noise stop, Papa. It's scaring me!"

"Why are you scared, child? There is nothing to be afraid of. See that tower over there?" He pointed across the square to the tower I had seen earlier. "The noise you are hearing comes from the muezzin in the top of the tower, called a minaret. It is how they know it is time to pray. They do it five times every day. This is the way of the Muslims Branko. You have nothing to fear by them."

I craned my neck and stared up to the top of the impossibly tall building, but still couldn't see who was making the noise. The tower itself scared me. In Ivanjska the tallest building belonged to our village leader, and that was only a barn slightly taller than everyone else's was.

As the singing-chanting sound continued it grew less terrifying, becoming almost pleasing with the passing seconds. At length it stopped. I asked my father if we could go into the building the Muslims had disappeared inside.

"Yes Branko, but we must hurry. The call to the faithful has ended. Everyone is inside."

Approaching the front of the Mosque rows of shoes, neatly placed side by side, stretched from the front door and down the outside wall. Joseph bent to take off his shoes; Milan and I followed suit. We set them at the end of the closest row then entered the building. Walking softly into a cavernous foyer the light faded to darkness in its upper reaches. The worshipers lined up on the floor just like their shoes outside. Muslims must like rows I thought. Kneeling, they faced southwest towards the back of the building. I followed my father's cue and knelt as he did. Obviously we weren't Muslims. We wore simple peasant's clothing. They wore floor length robes that pooled about them as they knelt in worship. The degree of intensity with which they prayed gave me chills. My family went to church as all the families in our village did. We prayed, but not with the same devotion. They chanted rocking back and forth on their knees with eyes closed and arms reaching for salvation-complete submission to the One they called Allah.

It was a day of realization-the day I learned the world is larger than Ivanjska, indeed larger than Banja Luka itself. I assumed *all* people prayed to the same God as my family and everyone in my village. It had never occurred to me that another God could exist. I was aware of the Jews, of course, since we prayed to the same God. In spite of that, the people I knew were not kind to Jews. I found out gypsies are not liked either. I still didn't understand why Jews and gypsies were treated with such mistrust and contempt. People are people, and I wouldn't recognize a Jew if he bumped into me!

# CHAPTER II

## "Sljivovica"

Arriving home, as the sun slipped further west, dinner came quickly and bed soon thereafter. I was exhausted, as much from the labor of the day as from the infusion of new sights. I went to bed and drifted off to sleep, glowing in the praise Papa heaped upon me at the dinner table to my sisters and mother.

Late that night, as the moon reigned king of the sky, I awoke with an urge to empty my aching bladder. Creeping over Regina I made my way quietly to the door, freezing as I heard Yela *laughing! This* I had to see! Peeking around the corner into the kitchen I saw a half-full bottle of *Sljivovica* on the table between Joseph and Yela. Holding glasses filled to the brim they tapped them against each other.

"*Zivili*" they said in unison, then drained them. My father's eyes sparkled, supported by a satisfied grin. My mother, who rarely smiled, actually *giggled* and brushed her hand upon Joseph's cheek. Such a display of affection was unprecedented!

I crept outside, completing my original task, and crept back to bed snuggling between Regina and Ruska for warmth. Drifting off to sleep I renewed my vow to taste this *Sljivovica*-and soon! If it could make Momma giggle like Regina it must be magical indeed.

With dawn's break I awoke to my father's usual grumbling and was a little saddened. It was back to the cows and women. Since I wasn't old enough to be of any real help in the fields I stayed in the main yard by the house and did whatever tasks Yela or Milka assigned to me. I couldn't wait to get away from them and spend my days in the fields with Papa and Milan.

Milka, as the eldest daughter, wielded the greatest power next to mother when Papa and Milan were not around. She was a hard worker just like her mother. Also like her mother Milka could neither read nor write. She was charged, as eldest, to keep at least one eye on Regina and myself throughout the day. Mostly though she kept an eye on me. It seemed I was always getting into trouble with Milka.

"Branko, the laundry dried hours ago! I told you to take it into the house and give everyone what is his or hers. Why do I have to remind you over and over and over? Where are your brains, Branko?" she asked in an exasperated tone.

"I'm sorry Milka." I usually had some excuse on the tip of my tongue but today I was in a serious mood.

"Yesterday in Banja Luka I saw gypsies and people from other lands. I saw, or heard anyway, a muezzin. Papa told me he is the man who calls the Muslims to prayer. Anyway Milka, you would not believe it! Papa, Milan, and I went into a church where they worshipped another *God!* Bringing in the laundry is not what I'm thinking about." I paused, afraid to ask her the question on my mind, but did so anyway. "Milka, don't you ever think about things that don't involve laundry or keeping the fire going or turnips?"

"Sometimes I do Branko," She said softly. Her face painted itself into a wistfulness that disappeared as quickly as it surfaced.

"My place is here," she said with summoned force "I will marry a farmer like Momma did. I will have many children and work hard every day. This is my life, Branko. This is the way of things. For you also, my brother."

"*Not* for me!" I answered in a defiant jumble. My eyes squeezed and my face grew hot.

"Berislav, look at me!" she commanded. I raised my eyes to her. Milka's face softened. For me she let go of the hardness and tried to make me understand.

"Branko my brother, your dreams are nice, but they will not help you become a good farmer. You must listen to Papa and Milan. This is our *life* Branko, *your* life. You must watch, listen and learn, so that one day you may raise a family and own a farm. It *is* what we do-what Dujlovich's have done for hundreds of years. Nothing can change this."

Milka was wrong.

I wiped my eyes, trying to be older than I was. I turned from her, walking toward the clothes flapping on the line. Milka called out to me, "Branko, you and Regina must take the sheep to pasture this afternoon. And Branko, they must graze all day! Oh, one more thing Branko, Muslims worship the same God as us-just differently."

I nodded and kept walking.

After bringing in the clothes and putting Milka's dress on Milka's pallet, Milan's shirt on Milan's pallet, and so on until my arms were empty, I pushed aside the blanket and entered the kitchen. Mama was placing thick slices of bread and meat on the table for lunch. The rest of the family was coming inside, talking and moving noisily.

I was still troubled. Milka, for all her good intentions, had not dissuaded me from thinking about gypsies or the many things I had seen in Banja Luka. I had no desire to sit through a meal with eight people's conversations distracting me. I needed quiet-I needed a plan. Examining a number of options, I discarded all of them until a palatable one presented itself. I had it!

"Momma, Milka told me to get Regina and take the sheep out to pasture. I was thinking about taking them to the hills over by Marko's. The clover there is thickest.

It's two fields over, so I was hoping we could leave now. Can Regina and I pack a lunch so we can go quickly? I promise we'll be home before dark." I held my breath on her answer.

Yela had not been listening. She was looking at my feet, caked with mud from my laundry gathering efforts.

"Berislav, you are always bringing mud onto my clean floor! Why? Do you have no brains?"

I was used to being scolded and knew how to respond according to the tone of her voice. This was not serious. I hung my head, the picture of remorse.

"Sorry momma, I'll be more careful".

Yela turned away to scold Anka for not washing the *kupus* well enough. She had discovered a worm making its way through the supposedly clean and washed cabbage in the middle of the table. I supposed my request had been ignored and turned away to go wash my feet. As I headed towards the door my mother called out to me.

"Berislav, wash you feet, get your shoes on, find Regina then come back here for a basket of food for your lunches. I want you both back before sunset!"

My mood improved dramatically, but Yela never knew it.

"Thank you momma. We'll be back in time."

I found Regina just outside the front door and informed her of our plans. I told her to fill a container with water. We would be gone all day. My shoes! Momma had told me to get my shoes. I thought about where I had left them and started into the house and down into the *podrum*, or cellar. As I searched the gloom for my shoes I spied the cabinet where I had seen Papa remove a bottle of *Sljivovica* and take it upstairs. Hmmm . . . this was my chance! The cabinet was too high for me to reach standing on the ground so I pulled a crate from the corner and set it beneath. I hoped it would be strong enough to hold me. There was no contingency explanation plan for a smashed crate. I climbed up and undid the latch, then reached inside. My hand explored, feeling the shape of the bottles. Inching my hand upward the bottles grew narrow further up. When my fingers closed around the top of one I removed it from the cabinet. It's mine! The *Sljivovica* is mine!

Furtively, with a thief's mentality, I shoved the bottle under my shirt. Closing the cabinet door I remembered to put the crate back where I got it from then bolted up the steps and outside. Except for Regina my family was all at the table eating lunch. Regina gasped when she saw the bottle.

"Branko, what are you doing? You've lost your mind!" she exclaimed in terror.

"I *must* do this Regina. You can too. Come on, let's go," I urged. Regina was gripped in fear, but followed nonetheless.

An hour passed as we herded the sheep into a manageable group and guided them to Marko's field. The sheep's noses were finally buried in the clover, focused on eating instead of wandering, only then did I relax. While herding them here a portion of my mind engaged in a tug of war. On one side the fear of being caught, and on the other, my vow to drink the *Sljivovica*.

It was not too late to return the bottle I argued.

True, I answered myself, but I've already gone this far so I might as well do it.

The core issues of my debate centered on whether Joseph knew exactly how many bottles were in the cabinet. I concluded since the basement is always dark, unless Joseph took a lantern down there every time he opened the cabinet, the chances were in my favor he didn't know precisely how many bottles there were. Smelling victory the strength of my personal vow surged and fear took a stumble, vanquished to another region of my brain.

I reached in the basket grabbing the bottle of *Sljivovica*. Wrestling the cork free I held the bottle to my lips, tilted it up, and took a mighty swig. Regina's eyes widened as I did it. The clear liquid burned as it splashed the back of my throat. Traveling down, charring a path of molten heat in its wake, it settled in my stomach like so many embers at the bottom of a dying fire. In a few minutes the burning subsided to a glowing. This new warmth soon spread to my limbs. Then the warmth made it's way to my brain.

I grinned, pushing the bottle toward Regina. She scrunched her face in refusal. Lifting it to her I said, "Drink, chicken . . ." and began to giggle.

Regina didn't like being called chicken. She took the offered bottle, not sure about any of this. She held it up, tentatively putting the neck of the bottle to her lips. With eyes screwed shut and mouth a' pucker she swallowed, gagged, and swallowed again what I considered to be an impressive amount of *Sljivovica*. As the plum brandy dimmed our minds and squashed our fears of everything we laughed and laughed at the silliest of things.

I found the morning, or the morning found me. Invisible cows stampeded back and forth inside my skull pounding a rhythm of pain. My eyes cracked open and met the new day's light. The sun sprang into me, a thousand piercing needles aimed at my discomfort. What happened? This was my first thought.

I remembered muttering to Yela that I had a terrible headache. I was relieved to see Regina seemed unaffected by the *Sljivovica*. She had gotten up with everyone else and was gathering the eggs even now. I lay with my eyes shut, trying to reconstruct the events of yesterday afternoon.

Ah, yes! I had kept drinking. Regina had taken the bottle that first round, bravely swilling her share and drinking no more. At some point I saw myself throwing the almost empty bottle into the clover.

Ugly now! Another scene this time, I'm hunched over, leaning against a tree. I see vomit *fly*. Not dribble, but fly! My recollections faltered after that. I remembered smiling and laughing with Regina, vomiting and then . . . nothing.

"Joseph, be careful" Yela's voice floated to me through invisible layers of gauze, making mushy both sound and light.

"Don't worry Yela, the war is almost over" came Joseph's gruff reply. This time, he wasn't off to his normal job at the prison. My father was going to war. His unit had been called to duty on the front lines.

I saw my father's silhouette in the sunlight streaming through the open front door. The sharp creases of his uniform divided the light and dark with unforgiving rigidity. Glancing quickly around his home, my father stepped outside and was gone.

I had heard conversations between my parents. Joseph told Yela the Croatian government was falling apart. As a soldier fighting against Tito's Partisans he was afraid for our safety. The communists were coming, he said. He told Yela tortures and killings were commonplace. The Americans and the British were on Tito's side so Croatia had no friends to count on for support when the communists invaded.

Joseph was gone, the months passed, and life went on. The day came when Milan was gone as well. Tito's soldiers were rampaging throughout Croatia, so every able-bodied Croat was called upon to stop him.

At the top of a small hill overlooking our farm Regina and I were again watching the sheep (this time without *Sljivovica*) and the morning moved along in lazy fashion. The sheep's noses scrunched through snow to the frozen green growth trapped beneath. As Regina and I sat on the ground, dreaming our dreams, I noticed a group of men on horseback turning off the main road and up the track to our farm. They were leaning forward in their saddles brandishing rifles. A leaden gruel of fear settled in my stomach. Regina and I moved behind a bush and watched them thunder into our yard. One soldier barked orders I couldn't hear. The soldiers dismounted fanning out around the cows and the few sheep we had left behind. Two other men dismounted and went inside the chicken shed. Shots rang out as soon as the two disappeared inside it. The other soldiers were herding our cows and sheep into a circled mass of confusion in the middle of the front yard. The officer of the group dismounted and headed towards the front door, which I couldn't see from my vantage point. I whispered to Regina that we should go see what was happening. Praying the soldiers wouldn't see us we slipped in the snow, rolling and tumbling to a stop behind a small dug-in-the-earth building where we stored food the cold wouldn't ruin. As I looked inside through the ribs of the back wall I spied my sisters huddling together in a corner. Fear consumed them. They knew what Tito's soldiers did to females they found on farms. No age was sacred.

I heard a yell and snuck a peek around the corner of the building. A barefoot Yela ran into the yard from inside the house. Heading quickly to the tightly herded livestock she attempted to rescue a cow from the stomping confusion. She screamed obscenities at the Partisans for what they were doing. Several soldiers had remounted their horses and were placing well-aimed shots into the head of every cow and sheep we owned. They methodically slaughtered our livestock with the exception of the healthiest looking horses, cows and sheep. They were already grouped away from the main herd. It was obvious they were planning to steal them. I turned around looking up the slope I had just come down. The sheep Regina and I were watching shuffled in the snow and munched frozen grass, oblivious to the events transpiring at the bottom of the hill. Yela became such a nuisance the officer in charge barked an order. Immediately several soldiers formed a circle around her. Laughing and making guttural sounds they groped her in places reserved for Joseph's hands only.

I could not sit still for this! I am the man of the house! Father is gone, Milan is gone and I, Berislav Dujlovich, will not hide and watch this happen to my mother! In a fury I charged from my spot behind the out-cellar and ran directly toward my Mother's tormentors. I was determined to dispatch them one by one.

"Run Branko, run!" my mother screamed when she saw me.

"Leave my Mother alone! Leave her *alone!*" I yelled at the top of my voice even as a *Partizani* scooped me up as so much nothing, then pinned my arms against my chest in a bear hug that robbed me of my breath. Yela saw what was happening and charged the soldier. She was a screaming woman boiling with rage. Her bare feet had become a grisly contrast of blue flesh and red blood. The soldier ran from her, laughing. This was *fun!* Not looking down while running from Yela he tripped on a jutting rock and sprawled forward to the ground. He lets loose of me to break his fall. Taking advantage I scrambled away. He lay motionless, the wind knocked out of him. Yela appeared immediately at my side kneeling down and hugging me. Relief, fear of the moment, and heaving adrenaline combined forces to smash the floodgate holding my tears at bay. I cried and wrapped my arms around her ample waist. She was my rock!

The steady bang of small arms fire stopped at last. I pulled my head from Yela's skirt seeing the scattered bodies of our livestock lumped about the front yard. All that kept us from starvation now lay dead.

The soldier that had tripped and lost his grip on me had regained his senses and was approaching Yela and I with murderous intent. A shouted command from the officer in charge stopped him in his tracks. He turned to rejoin his comrades. My sigh of relief hadn't fully escaped my lungs when he turned around and quickly advanced on us determined to finish the job. His comrades had enjoyed a good laugh at his expense and he meant to take out the sting of his embarrassment on the source. As he grabbed my collar and yanked me away from Yela the officer barked angrily at him. He held me in the air evaluating his next move. With a look of disgust he threw me to the ground. Turning again he ran back to his horse and swung into the saddle. Herding their stolen livestock together the Partisans left us amidst the thunder of pounding hooves, roiling dust, the crack of gunshots and victorious laughter. Our despair was all consuming and the silence deafening.

Joseph Dujlovich circa 1942

# CHAPTER III

## "Fleeing Serbs"

The Partisans were everywhere now. We heard about public executions. In Banja Luka, the Catholic Bishop, Bishop Platon, was beaten to death and his body thrown from the top of the church into the Vrbas River. Nobody had the courage to remove his corpse so it floated in plain sight for days. The Partisans swept through Ivanjska; farms burned, people died, whole families disappeared.

On a night when the moon chose to hide Yela shook me awake into pitch-black. When all six of us were alert Yela gathered us around her. She wore a sad expression.

"We must leave here tonight. Death awaits us if we stay any longer." She let this sink in.

"But Mother, what of our farm?" I asked in a quiet panic.

She replied harshly, clearly in no frame of mind to field inquiries. I was (as usual) doing the asking. She replied to me in an exasperated whisper, "Listen to me Berislav! The Partisans have killed our livestock. Our neighbors have been taken away. Your father and brother fight the men who did this. How long do you think we can stay here? The wife and children of an *Ustasche officer!* Tito's soldiers will kill us all when they find out. And they will find out. We must leave tonight! We are going to Bosanska Gradiska. Father has arranged for our safety there. It will be a very dangerous trip-Tito controls every town along the way. If we are discovered we will be killed. Now, no more questions!" It was action time.

The march to Bosanska Gradiska began immediately. Yela had packed each of us a bundle of clothes and food. We followed Yela out the door into a frozen Croatian winter night. Branches snapped beneath our shoes, ice crackled in protest. With no moon to guide us we stepped gingerly, and in no time night swallowed the farm. It was all behind me now-my family of frogs, my anthill, my favorite snakes, my pond and my home.

In order to avoid the Serbian patrols we traveled exclusively at night. Our journey took us through a dense forest of giant evergreens. The ground was a smooth carpet of unmolested snow. Green and white, white and green, such were the colors of this place. The only color intruding on this duet of trees and snow were our clothing. The chill was so complete we were never rid of it. It snuck beneath our clothes, beneath our skin, and was only satisfied when it settled in our bones. Yela packed what food she could but the demands of seven stomachs quickly reduced our reserves to precious memory. Hunger can become a living thing in itself. Three days and nights slid by.

At last we reached the outskirts of Bosanka Gradiska. Spying from behind a group of trees on the edge of town I quickly saw that Tito's soldiers were in firm control. They strolled freely through the streets with machine guns nestled in their forearms. They weren't afraid to use them either. Screams floated to us on the wind, only to be abruptly silenced by a gunshot. This went on until dusk. When the sun took its light west Yela led us into town. The Serbs had imposed a "shoot on site" curfew so the going was very slow. A frightened, bedraggled human herd, we crept along the dark streets searching for our sanctuary. Yela pointed first up this street, then down another, then to an alley, until at last we stopped in front of a small blue door. Yela rapped softly on the door three times, then once, then twice. There was no response. No light cast a glow through the curtains. No sound made its way through the door. The normal in-out function of breathing ceased in our lungs, holding out for a response. The journey from Ivanjska and the constant fear of discovery had ravished our minds with the ferocity of wolves. Cold and hunger froze and burned within us-twin furies vying for mental supremacy. The door *must* open.

Exhalation.

A curtain in a small window to the right of the door slid to one side revealing the face of a woman. In the shadows it was difficult to see her in any detail. Fear and caution held center stage in her eyes, which scanned up and down the alley. A sudden swoosh of air and sound, and the door floated inward and we heard her whisper in near panic, "Quickly, in, in!"

When all seven of us were safe behind the closed door Yela went to her, enfolding both of the woman's hands in hers. She said, "My name is Yela, wife of Joseph. These are our children. You have our thanks from our hearts."

"You are welcome, wife of Joseph" the woman replied.

She was clothed head to foot in a dark cloth. From my short time in Banja Luka, I took her to be Muslim. She was very pretty. Her olive skin reflected the soft glow of an oil lamp. Fine cheekbones, full lips and deep black almond-shaped eyes leant themselves in perfect harmony to a delicate nose. Her beauty was framed in flowing jet-black hair that disappeared beneath her *alhigab*.

"My name is Sahar. I bid you and your children welcome. My husband, Hassid, is not here but told me to expect you. I have news for you from Joseph. He has instructed me to tell you to go to Zagreb. A gymnasium there has been converted into a barracks for people fleeing Tito. He thinks you will be safe there, but only for a short time. Your husband has secured passage for you on a train leaving tomorrow tonight for

Zagreb. You need to be at the train station shortly after sunset. You may stay here until then. I have a hot meal for you and your children. You can sleep in the basement when you're done eating."

She paused a moment then added, "May Allah bless you and keep you well."

True to her word, Sahar sat us on cushions around a low table. When we were settled she placed a steaming bowl of meat and potatoes directly in the center. The spices were unfamiliar to me but smelled better than anything I had ever smelled in my life. After we had eaten to near bursting she directed us to the basement. We now had a roof over our heads instead of a winter sky. We had warmth, and full bellies. We slept, woke, and slept again through the night and next day until it was time to go to Zagreb.

When the sun was losing again to the inevitable army of night, we crept forth onto the deadly streets of Bosanka Gradiska. Sahar had fed us again and packed stores for us to eat on the train ride to Zagreb. Tito's soldiers prowled about. Bosanka Gradiska was newly occupied. The soldiers were looking for Croatian soldiers at this point, not women and children. That would come later, but with the vigilance of conquerors they were always on the lookout for any reason to exercise their authority without consequence. We walked slowly, keeping our heads down. This was the advise of Sahar.

Approaching the station we saw a caravan of at least twenty flatbed trucks parked bumper to bumper. All of them packed with people. Mothers held screaming babies. Boys and girls my own age fidgeted in their confinement. Old ones stared beyond us all. Not far in front of us one of the trucks crammed with refugees exploded into a fireball, lighting up the night. With a whoosh and a roar a rain of metal, fire, fabric, blood, and body parts plummeted all around us, clanking and wetly thumping, depending on the object.

"Mama, Mama!" we all screamed. Yela was as horrified as us but kept her wits and gathered us about her barking commands.

She herded us toward the train, hissing as she jostled us forward.

"Stop staring! Start walking! We will miss the train and miss seeing papa. Move!"

The train ride to Zagreb was an uneventful affair. Aside from the never ending cold we clickety-clacked until reaching the safety zone of Zagreb. Tito's forces had not yet taken my country's largest city. For the first time in weeks we breathed the air of freedom, such as it was. War was on our heels though. As best we could we settled into the building we were directed toward, entering a large, gloomy, cold, smoky, smelly room. What little light fought its way to the middle of the room was rendered joyless in the thick haze of cigarette smoke. The bunk beds swayed precariously, seven beds high and fifteen feet up. Yela led us about the room and when she found a spot that could sleep all of us in a somewhat defined area we dropped our bundles, sinking to the floor in exhaustion. Night found us quickly and we embraced the darkness. Two weeks of cramped misery rolled upon each other, creating a pile of fear and anxiety.

I opened my eyes to see Joseph caressing Yela's cheek as the windows hinted at dawn's first breath. He looked so strong and proud in his *Ustasche* uniform. He reached out for us, leaning down and hugging my sisters one by one. When Joseph came to me he knelt down and looked deep in my eyes.

"Branko my son, you must obey your mother as a child, but help her as man. Danger is all around us. You must watch out for her and your sisters. Milan is gone and you are the oldest male Dujlovich left to guard our family. So! You must be the man. Your days of talking to frogs and looking at ants are over. Now you must watch out for things that are more serious. You are a Dujlovich. Make me proud."

"But Papa," I sputtered, "When will we go home? You won't be gone long, will you? I want to go home!"

Tears welled in my eyes and I reached out to be held.

"Stop your whining, Berislav. Be a man!"

With a shove he sent me flying into the arms of my sisters, disgusted at my lack of control. He abruptly turned from me motioning Yela toward the corner of our area. I crept away, my face burning with shame at letting my father down. But I wanted to hear what Joseph was saying so I crept close enough to hear him speak.

"Yela," I heard Joseph say softly, "I have to go to Maribor. The Partisans are approaching the outskirts of the city and my unit has been ordered to defend Maribor at all costs. If we win I will see you soon. If we don't," he paused, "you may not see me again."

"No! Joseph, my husband, don't say such things. This will end, and we will go back to our farm. It *must* be this way!" Yela said this in a rush, her agony a visible thing upon her face.

He transformed, harder than granite.

"Yela, you must be realistic. Tito is winning. Croatia is falling town by town. Hitler is done and the Americans are going home. But Tito remains, and the Communists will not be satisfied until the Independent State of Croatia is no more. I took the oath of an *Ustasche* officer and I will honor it-even if it means my life. Take the children to the refugee camps in Austria. I will try to come to you. Until then, goodbye, my wife."

A single tear, the first and last I ever saw from him, slid down his cheek.

He hugged her a long moment then broke his embrace. Looking slowly at each of us, his children, he absorbed every detail of our faces. Pain and love danced tightly all about his features and within his eyes. His lips quivered, his nostrils flared. Joseph knew this was the last time on earth he would see his children. With the resolve of the military man he was he stood and did a swift about-face. Striding quickly toward the door, the smoke gave effort to swallow him. He went through it and was gone.

# CHAPTER IV

## "The Hungry Window"

Scars of the flesh, sometimes visible forever, will in time heal. In doing so they become a nerveless band of skin. I only wish my mind healed with a similar ability to feel no more pain.

Winter 1944 found me departing Zagreb for Austria. This was Joseph's last request of Yela. Another week had ticked away in the hazy gymnasium. We stepped out of the building beneath a low gray winter sky sweeping above. A freezing wind found its way beneath my coat, staying there. The buildings closed in above us, gray silent monsters intent on swallowing us whole. Children's screams split my ears. Mass confusion reigned. Fear was in the air, and we all breathed it. Yela had told us this morning the Partisans were but a day away and there were not enough soldiers to keep them from taking Zagreb. I knew if we were still here when they arrived I probably would be killed. My sisters would more than likely be raped and then killed.

We made our way to the train station. The seven of us linked hands against the thickening mass of people. Fighting their way to the station platform a sea of desperate people swept up the ramps and into the rectangular mouths of the boxcars. Jostling and being jostled we seven boarded as a group and held a corner of the boxcar our particular human wave had squeezed into. I elbowed, groped and crammed in order to stay with Yela and my sisters. It paid off. All of us were together.

The train started with a jolt-then nothing. Then, jolt! Another, and then another followed yet faster on its heels until they flowed upon themselves taking us away from Zagreb.

The rolling motion continued without pause, hour upon clackety hour. A night passed without a source of light save the occasional grace of the moon. Dawn found us slowing, and then stopping altogether. What was going on? I heard muffled shouts through the closed doors of the rail car. At length the doors rumbled open and the muffled yells became clear instructions to disembark.

Anxiety bear hugged me. We gathered in tight groups, shivering in the icy dawn of a dead field. Metal skeletons lay where they died. The cab of a green truck with a red star on the door rested in the snow on its roof, while the bed of the truck was intact on its tires a few feet away. I looked forward, beyond the locomotive. The tracks our train had labored on from Zagreb were no more. A crater in the middle of where they ran put an end to our trip-at least on *this* train.

Not informed of our next move we hovered in the pre-dawn field. We remained this way throughout the morning as the sun crested the sky on its way to handing us over to night. At last we were ordered to grab our belongings. The guards said another train waited ten kilometers east. The old ones groaned. Many of them were injured from the war, or an even more powerful foe-old age itself. I began walking, my shoes adding to the multiple crunches of frozen grass and pops of hollow ice. Not the first one to reach the train, but not the last either, I dropped my bundle to the ground. Many others hadn't yet arrived, but I wasn't thinking about them. I was thinking about curling up inside one of those rail cars and not having to stand. Getting off my feet was my ultimate goal in life at that moment. Men strolled back and forth in front of the train toting machine pistols. As they turned toward us their machine guns turned with them. They sporadically yelled at us to stay back. The sun grew weary of our patch of sky, succeeding at last in its hasty retreat to the west. When the light faded to shadows we were allowed to board. Without the benefit of a platform getting inside the boxcar was rough on the very young and very old. Yela coiled her body, springing up and into the boxcar, vanishing into the murkiness. She reappeared a few seconds later. I reached for her outstretched hand. Whoosh! I was in! Yela and I—whoosh!—Yela, *Regina* and I were the only ones inside. My sister and I went to the corner Yela pointed toward. Safe at last! Finally, I could give my feet a rest. I glanced around at my new accommodations.

When I realized what I was looking at piss ran down my leg, joining the urine already soaked into the floor. The stench gagged me. Black patches of blood splotched the soaked, rotting wooden floor. Gouges scored the planks of the walls. On the opposite side of me by the door I spied something sticking out of the wood. Two steps later I looked up, focusing on it in the dim light. It was a fingernail. I looked closer and saw dozens of them wedged into the cracks of the planks. The truck that blew up in front of me with all those people in it had scared me—but *this!*

To my relief, people soon replaced the walls and floor with themselves. When the last straggler clamored aboard the train chugged itself into a now familiar rhythm. The sound droned on and on and on . . . My eyes closed to everything. I drifted with the rhythm of the rails. Were we being transported to a secret death camp? It could happen! At the gymnasium I had heard stories of killings, of mounds of dead bodies. That could be me! As sleep took over, protecting me from the horrors of reality, my terror slipped through the net and followed me into my dreams.

I'm naked at the edge of a pit filled with the living, dying and dead. Blood coats them. The wide pit stretches to either side, fading into a bank of smoke. Moans meet bullets and moan no more.

Soldiers place bets on the movers in the pit.

"See that blond with the nice ass? Ten *dinars* say you can't tag the kid she's holding." Chuckles and inhaled breath—a gauntlet has been thrown.

"You're on." the quick reply from the faceless challenged soldier.

Five seconds later the baby's head blows apart in the mother's arms. Two seconds later the mother's agony is no more. The guards turn to the line I'm standing in. A quick order from the officer results in a grumble from a machine gunner, crushing the last bit of life from his cigarette. He checks his ammunition—time to get to work.

I'm going to die! The moment is so close!

Pooph! I'm back to reality, only a little less terrifying than my dream. A small, unremarkable man bumped against me while hitching up to peer out an opening on my left. The small window had no glass or screen. It was wide enough to climb through, but no larger. Pushing his face into the wind his hair swept behind him. He withdrew from the window quickly. I saw a telegraph pole flash by. It couldn't have been more than a foot from the train. He peered outside with more caution after that. Then, without warning, he hitched himself up and propelled his upper half outside the window. THUMP! His body became a spineless rag doll. The window consumed him and he was gone. Blood and body matter seeped between the planks dripping down the inside wall. I screamed. Other screams erupted around me as people standing next to the man realized what just happened. The wife of the man, suddenly a widow, sagged to the floor. Her children wailed, crunching their bodies into hers-their last resort from madness. The mood turned black. By way of escape I went back to sleep, reliving select moments of my life in Ivanjska. The farm was a paradise!

What this rail car lacked in appearance, it made up for in endurance. It didn't stop, leaving us no choice but to urinate inside the boxcar. I took aim between the cracks of the planks with the rest of the boys and men. We were semi-successful. The women and girls were denied our genetic advantage. They went to a designated corner where peasant women of wide girth and voluminous skirts formed a circle in which the girls and other women conducted their affairs in relative privacy. Fecal matter, both male and female, was scooped off the floor and thrown through the window, sporadically fertilizing the fields of northwestern Croatia.

This boxcar carried the dead. There were no Jews this time, but dead is dead. Too old, too tired, too hungry, too sad—who knows? A number of people in our boxcar looked around, closed their eyes, and opened them no more. Their bodies were set in a corner.

Death is but a hiccup in the circle of life. A young girl lay panting on the filthy floor. Her belly was taut, swollen with life. Sweating profusely, it ran in rivulets down her face. Whimpers of pain made their way grudgingly through clenched teeth. She laid on her back, propped up on elbows, with her legs spread wide, vanity forgotten in her pain. While women wiped the sweat dripping into her eyes and pushed back her pasted hair from her forehead she listened to assorted suggestions and complied as best she could. When a woman hunched between her legs told her to push she did just that, and a short time later was rewarded with the wail of a new refugee.

After the darkness of the Hungry Window this was a breath of life! Happiness and laughter set up camp. The babushkas had both mother and child cleaned up and settled down in short order. Snuggled in a blanket the newborn was placed in his mother's arms. When a babushka handed the baby to the girl she turned away from both her child and the old woman offering him to her.

Why does she not smile? Why does she do nothing? I wondered to myself.

At length she turned back to the woman accepting her newborn child with cold indifference. Her son could have been a loaf of bread for all the emotion she displayed. The girl's eyes flickered with something that had no place in this time. Her breast not offered, she denied the baby her milk. Happiness pulled up stakes, broke camp and fled.

My mind shut down at this new atrocity commanding me to sleep. Deep in the night I awoke. I stood up and looked out through the Hungry Window. We were clacking through fields and towns devastated by the war and made no softer by the moonlight. Hearing a noise I turned around searching for the source of the soft crying. The new mother was struggling to her feet. Slatted silver light revealed the newborn in her arms, still a loaf of bread. I sank to the floor with my back against the wall. The girl turned toward me, stepping gingerly between this flung arm and that sprawled leg, until she stood directly before the opening. I looked up at her. She was staring into the blackness. Tears flowed down her cheeks and before I realized what she was doing she pushed her newborn son through the opening, bringing her hands back inside the train only when they were empty.

The Hungry Window ate again. Horrified screams split the night. Her searing cry pierced them all. A primal, wounded wail trivializing the cries of the onlookers. She sank to the floor beside me. I had a difficult time even looking at her, so horrible was the moment. It was the same for everyone else. They moved as far away from her as space allowed so she sat alone, except for me. She became a displaced person in a group of displaced persons. She stared into nothing, or everything, and the night consumed itself. Eventually the thumping rhythm lulled me into the realm of dreams. A nudge on my shoulder brought me back. We had caught the sun, or the sun had caught us-I don't know which. Yela handed me a cup of water and a chunk of black bread. Oh goody, black bread.

The girl had returned to her patch of floor. As my fellow travelers began to awaken and gain their bearings their faces hardened as last night's memory clicked in. Yela, ever the direct one, made her way to the girl. Towering over her, hands on hips, she demanded an explanation.

"Why? Why did you kill your baby? How could you do such a thing? *Your own child!*"

"That was *not* my child! It was a thing of evil!" She screamed at Yela. A fit of tears took her. As she sobbed uncontrollably no one offered a hand to hold or a shoulder to cry on. She had murdered her own child. When her chest heaved less she resumed. Her choked voice was the only sound beyond the disinterested rumble of the train.

"You want to know why I killed that child. I will tell you." She stood up and faced Yela. There was no fear in her eyes. Gathering her wits she told her tale. She had the undivided attention of every person present.

"My name is Andrija Borovich. I come from Mostar. The Serbs came to our town. In the middle of the night they busted into our house and took Papa and all three of my brothers. They went to every house in our village, taking every man and boy. Then they took them to a field outside of town and shot all of them. Papa was killed. My brothers Anton, Vlado and Toma were also killed. A few days later the Serbs brought in bulldozers. They dug a trench and pushed all of them into it. The bulldozers shoveled the earth over them, but soon after they departed the ground where they were buried began moving. Then it split open. Their bodies came up from the ground! I saw my brother Anton pushing up from the earth!"

She stopped speaking. The demons of her memories dictated her words. She looked into the ring of hostile faces and resumed with greater focus—she knew she had to account for her actions. She *had* just killed her own child.

"The same night they killed my father and brothers the soldiers came back into Mostar. The Serb pigs searched all our homes one by one. When they got to mine they found mama and me in the cellar. There were ten soldiers. When they saw me in the corner they got quiet. Then they came at me all at once, tearing my clothes off until I was naked. Their leader grabbed me by my hair and threw me on a table. He flipped me on my stomach and jammed his thing into me from behind. I saw the men in front of me unzipping their pants. They tried shoving their things in my mouth. I bit the first one that tried. He got so mad he cut me." She pulled down on her dress, exposing a long angry scar running from her right shoulder to her lower left back. She continued after rearranging her dress.

"Mama screamed at them to stop. They told her to shut up and watch. She begged them. She told them I was only thirteen; they laughed and said in that case they would be back next year as well. All ten of them left their seed in me. They forced my mother to watch. They joked how they were making soldiers for Tito. Always one of them held a rifle at mama so she could do nothing. When they were finished with me they turned toward her to continue. But after they ripped her clothes off the leader said she was too old, and therefore useless. The soldier pointing the rifle at Mama told everyone she was too old to screw. He said that's the only thing a Croat woman is good for, and if she wasn't good for that then there wasn't any reason for her to live. He put his rifle to her head and pulled the trigger. My mama's brains splattered all over me! She died looking at me." Andrija choked, and it seemed her sorrow would rob her of life right before my eyes. "And so they left me with child. My papa is dead. Mama is dead. My brothers are dead. Why didn't they just kill me?" She slumped in a puddle to the floor, the trial concluded before it began. There were no more questions after that.

    I could hardly stand it. Some could not stand it *any longer*. Gripped in the madness of this hell a number of people escaped from the boxcar through the Hungry Window. This was my spot for the entire trip, so I saw every one of them climb up, look around and push forward. They were not trying to kill themselves, just get clear of the tracks. Some would make it and some would not. We felt the "brumph" of the wheels over the bodies of the ones who didn't. Those who succeeded in clearing the tracks rolled down the embankment only to be shot dead by soldiers perched on top of some of the railcars. I was just shy of insanity when the guardhouses at the Austrian border slid slowly past our view.

# CHAPTER V

## "Camp Life"

Austria, Austria. Safety, hope, rebuilding, heaven—Austria meant all these things to us. It was not part of the conflict devouring Croatia. Gunshots didn't stutter us. Screams didn't tear at our minds. Once inside Austria a breeze of hope swept our railcar. Chatter broke out. I heard we were headed to a refugee camp near a town called Braunau. I heard a man tell his wife the British ran the camp. He said they would be able to settle in and get some order back into their lives. He kept mentioning the British ran the camp. I took this to be a good thing. The train, by gradually lessening thumps, eased its way to a halt at the Braunau station.

Yela growled at us to stay near her as we disembarked and made our way down a dirt road leading away from town. The guards informed us the camp was a two-hour walk as they pointed up a gravel road leading over a hill and out of sight. A young couple plodded ahead of us-backs, bundles and moving legs. The wife was complaining to her husband. It turned out he was the same man I had heard go on about the British while still in the railcar. I was amazed as she went on and on. It seemed a person has to breathe at some point.

"Your Uncle Stefan was supposed to meet us at the station! We were told in Zagreb that we could settle in Braunau. Now we find out it's only a staging area! We *weren't* told we had to walk forever to get to the camp. Why don't you do something? Ante, are you listening to me?"

She threw him a sharp look assuming he was paying her no attention. Indeed, he did appear engrossed in his own despair.

"Ante! Listen to me!" she said in exasperation.

To get her point across she pushed him with a bundle of clothes she was carrying, causing him to slip and fall in a pile of person and belongings. At that point he gave her the attention she was seeking.

"Ivkovich, stop it! I'm sure Uncle Anton has a good reason for not meeting us at the station."

A few words *did* get through I suppose. He stood up and glared down into her face. We took the moment to rest.

"Why are you taking your anger out on me?" He snarled. "Leave me be woman! The next time you push me I won't be so forgiving!"

Ivkovich apparently got his point. The rest of the way she stayed a bit behind him.

Two words stuck in my head from the entire conversation between them-"staging area". What's *this* all about? I thought this was the camp where we were going to live- a place to rest. Through the dawn mist of a fallow field I spied the familiar silhouette of tall posts and barbed wire fencing. My spirit slumped and fear gripped me. It's true! We *are* being taken to the camps. Not "a" camp, but "the" camps. Death awaits us! In a panic, I turned to Yela. "Mama, they have barbed wire just like Papa's camp. What will happen to us?"

Yela replied harshly. "Branko, you are weak! Fear rules you. This is a staging area. All kinds of people are here. There are Serbs, Slovenians, Croats, Muslims, Gypsies, Ukrainians, Poles and Russians staying here until transferred to a camp for their own kind. I spoke with a Croat at the train station. He said when we get to the camp we should ask for a man named Perinic who may be able to help us." Glaring, she leaned down, jutting her face within inches of mine.

"Berislav, when we get to the camp you must stay with me. God help you if you get into trouble!" A ringing slap to the back of my head followed her warning. Why did she hit me? We trudged through the camp gates into the main square. Many hundreds of people wandered about the large open area of packed dirt. The milling of thousands of feet swirled dust all about. Many people yelled in languages I had never heard. They repeated the same thing over and over. It sounded like they were calling out names of people, which made sense. We entered the camp in a long, disjointed line. Nevertheless, straggled line or not, we were grouped together by the authorities as the latest trainload of refugees. A man speaking Croat yelled out for all Croatians to gather to his right. He pointed to a small group of people growing in number even as I spied them. We added seven to its strength. Walking toward our group I saw other men by the front gates performing the same service our Croatian guide had done for us. The other men pointed to different areas in the square. There were four or five of them, all repeating themselves in different languages. After a time the British showed up at our group. With the help of interpreters they directed us to a row of barracks. My family was pointed toward the front of a long low building.

It was identical to fifty others stretching away on either side. The camp was an enormous place. On the side of every building small windows punched light through the wall, the bottom of which began where the top of my head ended. There were many of them, evenly space from end to end. Fifty Hungry Windows stared into the square. The buildings were very similar to the boxcars-just wider and longer. The same weathered wooden planks passed for walls and the same dismal air lazed about inside. Stepping up on the porch and through the front door of our barracks I viewed the beds in the gloom. They were spaced two feet apart, stretching in a dormant row to the end of the room. Against the back wall a picture of a toilet hung above a single door. There was no area just for females and another just for males. Modesty was a luxury we did not possess.

Yela pointed at an area for us to claim. She chose the area closest to the cooking center yet equidistant from the front door and the toilet area. Her choice resulted in us occupying the spot with the least amount of cold and bathroom smell, but closest to the cooking fire.

Yela sat on her bed watching us until we all claimed a bunk. She gestured for us to gather around her. We gathered in a loose half circle. She began in an all too familiar format.

"Branko, you better not get into trouble! If you misbehave I won't be so easy on you anymore."

"Anymore?" I thought.

Transferring her glare from myself to her daughters her consternation evaporated. She looked into their faces.

"This place is called Andorff. It is the main staging area for all refugees coming from all the countries around Austria. The town we walked from is called Braunau . . . we are Croatian. You must stay with fellow Croats. If Serbs or Russians find you, they will beat you to a pulp and maybe even kill you. Don't forget Andrija from the train–don't wander off!"

She said this looking at her daughters. It was not a glance of concern, but a granite glare of warning. Such was Yela.

"*Stara babba*," I muttered in my mind. Old bag.

The first few days were little better than the train. More room to move about and no clacking-that was the only difference. There was still no food. Hunger ruled and fueled our thoughts. The wood planks of the barrack walls allowed the freezing wind partial access to our bunks. So essentially, we were still hungry and cold. This place of confusion and fear squatting in a field in central Austria was an empty stomach. For the hundredth time thoughts of home consumed me. I missed it with painful awareness.

Days passed. I was a boy, and boys wander. One morning a convoy of trucks pulled into the main square as I wandered in that area. Painted a flat military green they each had a big red cross painted on the side of the doors. As I saw them being unloaded I realized the trucks were full of *food!*.

Yela had mentioned that the Red Cross oversaw this camp. She told me the Red Cross was an organization from America that helped people in trouble. Someone else had mentioned a woman started it, but I knew that couldn't be true. Women did nothing but work at home.

Our food, and many of the other supplies we received at the commissary, came from the Red Cross. Men unloaded crate after crate of food—peaches, peas, carrots, canned meat and many other delicious things formed a small mountain of cases. It looked *so* good! It *would* be good if I could actually eat any of it.

It was in Braunau that I first learned the meaning of corruption. Before then I didn't know what a payoff was, or a bribe, a kickback. All I knew was that food brought into the camp for us didn't seem to make it to our bellies. Between the British who ran the camp, the Red Cross drivers who brought the food, the clerks who ran the commissary and the "go-betweens" representing each ethnic group, what food did trickle its way to our cooking pots was but a morsel of the original allotment.

The ethnic representatives were the worst sort of men. They were men, having the good fortune of being well educated and bilingual, who acted as liaisons for the British and the refugees. Yela mentioned Perinic earlier. She said he was the Croat liaison. I heard a few stories about him and none were flattering. But when hunger ravenously eats at your mind the flimsiest straw of hope grows into a mighty oak. Perinic and those like him oiled their way into the good graces of the camp administrators. Yela told us that Perinic, as evil as he was, was still essential in helping us get what little we did receive. Andorff was a staging area, not a permanent camp. Thankfully, the British were aware of the bitterness between Serbs and Croats and wisely placed us on opposite sides of camp. Serbs and Croats were but one pairing of animosity. There were other fighting factions in addition to ours. Andorff was a cauldron of hatred.

A few weeks into the dreariness a new day found me sitting on the ground with my back propped against the front wall of the barracks. My mind was far away-I was playing with my frogs on the farm, counting how many new babies swam behind mama . . .

Loud whispers brought me back in a flash. They came from around the corner of my building. Each barrack is spaced about twenty feet apart; so what little ground that lies between them is dominated by shadow, save for a midday sun.

"Meet me by the south fence after lights out," a voice said. "I know where we can get things to make slingshots."

Slingshots! Yes! I must go with them! I could use a slingshot for, well, heck . . . I could use a slingshot. As the sun winked into night I waited impatiently for lights out. At last, the camp gave itself to blackness. Yela settled in, and when all was still in the dormitory I crept silently from my bunk into the night. I made my way through the blackness to the south fence. Creeping upon the huddled forms of the boys excited whispers floated to me on the night. Moving slowly to the edge of the gathering and hunkering down behind a broad back I tuned in on the plans. *Now* I was just one more cohort on this mission-I hoped. The oldest boy (I recognized his voice from earlier in the day) was explaining his plan to the group as he snipped the bottom strands of barbed wire. Nothing changed, and then everything changed. A yank on my shirt collar and I was lifted off my feet. Swung about, I was deposited in the center of the group.

"What are you doing here?" the leader hissed. "You are too young! Go home to your momma!"

Shoving me to the ground he wound his leg back to land a mighty kick in my gut, or worse. Good fortune deposited me directly in front of the opening he had cut. There was only one way to go to avoid his foot and I took it. Scampering between the cut strands of barbed wire as quickly as I could. His foot swung and met air. I was through! He can't send me back now, I thought.

"Get back here you little bastard!" he whisper-yelled. It was too late, and he knew it. Putting me out of his mind he directed the rest of the boys through the opening. When all of them were on my side of the barbed wire the leader appeared out of nowhere and bent down within an inch of my face.

"I should kick the shit out of you!"

My knees grew weak but I stayed the course staring right back into his eyes. I was no stranger to beatings. Ten seconds, or perhaps an hour, we stared at each other. He stared down at me—I stared up at him. He broke first.

With a disgusted sigh he told me, "Well, you're here now. What you did takes guts, I guess. Stay close to me and keep your mouth shut. If you mess up *I'll* beat you first, and then let my friends use you for practice. Do you understand me?" he asked.

He was speaking Croat. I understood with remarkable clarity.

"*Da, da*" I replied.

Victory! I was allowed to stay, *and* I was going to make it without a beating. With the rules established we stole across a dark field leaving the glow of the camp's lights for complete blackness. I was literally and figuratively in the dark. I had no idea where we were headed *or* what we were going to do when we got there. Ten minutes of moonless trudging provided an answer to both questions. Rising in front of me, blacker than black, piles of metal skeletons lay randomly, the droppings of truck eating giants. There were other, softer edged piles. Tires rolled upon themselves twenty feet high, the discarded rings of these giants. It hit me! For every tire, there is an inner tube. I remembered Milan telling me this. Inner tubes are made of rubber! The sling in slingshot!

We set about our task. When we had cut up enough strips of rubber to satisfy our thirst for weaponry we returned to camp. Buoyed by our success we whispered in rushes what we would accomplish. No deer was safe. Pity the pheasant to come across us! If we had been in the mountains of Croatia the wolves themselves would have scampered at the sight of us!

Safely back in the barracks and wrapped in my blanket I rode upon a euphoric wave of success. In my haste to get beneath my blanket I had carelessly set the slingshot under my bed. Not hidden, it was just laying there for the entire world to see.

A brutal rap on my forehead propelled me into wakefulness. Reaching up, my fingers came away smeared with blood. Yela towered above me.

"Branko! How did you get this? What have you been up to? I told you I would beat you, did I not? I will beat you more unless you explain yourself *right now*!"

Yela leaned over me, the slingshot in her right hand cocked above her head. She was itching to crack me again. I had found a sturdy piece of wood, very sturdy, it turned out. Racing from the fog of sleep, the mental wheels in my head rolled into action. Options and consequences presented themselves in a rush. If I told Yela the truth-that I had crept under cut strands of barbed wire to get out of camp, then raided a junkyard and made the slingshot, I would be beaten within an inch of my life. If I told her I found it she would *know* I was lying. Slingshots aren't discarded for some fortunate passerby-it was a useful tool. If I told her I stole it then it was back to the "Branko is beaten" scenario. Therefore I offered the only safe, yet logical explanation I could conjure up in ten seconds.

"One of the older boys gave it to me" I stammered. Picking up the thread and running I continued, "He said it would help so we can shoot birds for dinner. 'Us Croats must stick together' he said. So I accepted it. What else could I *do*? I'm sorry."

I answered perfectly, I thought. Then I had a stroke of genius. She couldn't possibly stay mad . . . .

"I can return it Momma," I sheepishly offered.

I looked into her eyes. There was no hint of a smile. Her mouth was a line of anger. I hoped for the best. The seconds ticked an hour apart. At last her lips deigned to give up a sliver of air.

"If I *ever* hear of you fighting or getting into any trouble over this you will regret you were born Berislav."

*Yes!* I was going to make it! A*gain*! I breathed a sigh of relief. Just when I thought I was home free Yela swung. She did not lightly rap my skull. She hit my head with vigor. Blood flowed from two spots. Love dies a swing at a time and Yela was using her allotment with reckless abandon.

Dismissing me, she turned away to scold Ruska. I sat on the edge of my bunk, trying to hold back my tears. These weren't tears of shame, oh no! These were tears of pain and anger. I wasn't a little kid-I was almost *eight*! Regina sat down beside me. She always sensed my feelings more acutely than my other sisters did . . . perhaps she just cared more. Words were poor company in our misery. Except for my occasional constrained sob we sat in silence.

A room forty feet wide by sixty feet long held ninety to one hundred Croatians under its roof-or Jews, or Serbs, depending what roof you were under. Regardless of who inhabited the barracks all of them possessed a large wood burning stove in the center of the cooking area. The stove was the source of warmth and food, of gossip and life. Winter was easing its grip, but grudgingly. Warmth was still a sought after commodity. There were no free rides in Andorff. To have warmth, there must be fire. To have fire, there must be wood. Basic logic dictated those who go out in the cold and gather wood should be the ones to benefit from the heat their labors generated. Perhaps other camps had their wood delivered, but here in Andorff we fetched it the old fashioned way-an armful at a time. Wood was life. It was the difference between seeing your breath in the moonlight or not, between cold gruel and warm soup. Between numb fingers and blessed, blessed heat.

Yela was ever the military wife. All six of us were on a strict rotation of wood gathering. The Dujlovich clan never lacked a healthy pile of wood. Neatly stacked beneath our beds it was a source of envy and longing from many around us.

I was still smarting from my encounter with Yela. Regina and I sat on the bed saying nothing, yet sharing everything. I looked to my left. A thin, worn out looking woman grabbed my attention. Her peppered gray hair capped off a lackluster dreariness. Two bunks down from mine, she was kneeling and loading her arms with Dujlovich gathered wood. Yela spotted her theft as she turned from scolding Ruska. Her back arched and she immediately moved towards the woman. Her mission was unmistakable. In five short steps she was at the thief's side. She grabbed a piece of wood from the woman's arms and beat her over the head then started whacking her sides with it. She got in several blows before the woman dropped her ill-gotten booty. She dropped all but one that is, swinging at Yela's head with it. *That* was a serious mistake. Yela screamed in anger. She dropped her piece of wood and attacked. The thief scratched Yela's face, her piece of wood also discarded. The room was forgotten. The camp, the war, Austria-all forgotten. Months of starvation, cold, dirt, tears, pain and loss boiled to the surface in both of them and they fought as if to beat out the sorrow of their lives into the other. Yela had greater stores of misery, since it didn't take long to pound the thief to the floor. Only when the woman lay unmoving did Yela stoop and pick up every piece of wood she had attempted to steal. Her arms bulging with firewood she wound back her right leg and kicked the woman in her gut with all the energy she could summon. When Yela's foot connected the desperate mother-turned-thief whooshed, moaned and scrunched into a fetal ball. Yela glared at the circle of spectators. She didn't need to say a word. Every person in the room got her message loud and clear. She returned to her bunk and calmly (as if nothing happened) began replacing the wood in a neat pile under her bunk. Her detachment frightened me. I wasn't a stranger to her temper, but this scared me. Such were the harsh realities of staging camp Andorff.

Wood and food weren't the only things in short supply. The shoes carrying me from Ivanjska to Bosanka Gradiska to Zagreb and now to Andorff were finally protesting. Expressing their dissatisfaction they literally were coming apart at the seams. An Austrian winter is no place to be shoeless. I had seen more than one set of feet with frostbitten toes. They were black, ugly things, and not always in a full set of five. I went to Yela with my problem.

"All of our shoes are just like yours. Stop whining! You're the one complaining so *you* solve it!"

With no help in the maternal quarter I resolved to do just that.

Ding! Ding! Ding! I would sneak out to the junkyard where I had cut up inner tubes for my slingshot. I would cut up some of the tires and get pieces to make new soles for my shoes. I would sew them together and voila!—I would have new soles on my shoes. When night fell I made my run. I was successful. When the sun winked an orange eye upon the new day I industriously set about my task. Before going to bed I had asked Regina to get some needles and strong thread. This was never a problem in a refugee camp.

Yela had woken, turning over and saw me from her bed. My stomach flurried, home to a bumper crop of butterflies. This could go either way. She stood up and plopped her hands on her hips, cocked her head and stared at me for twenty seconds or so, then turned away and set about something else. I beamed at Regina and she beamed back. This was a success!

Yela had essentially said,

"Good job, Branko. I see you take care of your problems. I am proud of you."

When finished I held up my shoe. Re-sewn and possessing a thick rubber sole, it was a dramatic improvement. As I was admiring my craftsmanship, Yela came and stood above me.

"Branko, that is good thinking. Get more of the rubber for your sisters. And be careful!" I was officially exonerated.

Necessity truly is the mother of invention. My shoe trick was but one among many variations of the same. One day a pile of discarded Nazi flags were discovered behind my barracks. Babushka's quickly scooped them up and with a snip snip snip, sew sew sew-poof!—they became children's undergarments. At last, a useful purpose.

The moon had gone from half to partial to nothing to pregnant. Diminished by hunger, beaten by cold and crushed by despair our thoughts and actions were directed toward one thing-survival. Families made alliances-proposals were ratified. "We will gather wood if you will stand in the food queue. We will watch your back if you watch ours." Serbs found Serbs. Slovaks found Slovaks and Croats found Croats. My barracks had its percentage of young boys, the same as any other. We got together with other Croats in other barracks. I spotted Vlado, the boy in charge of our slingshot expedition. The one who tried to gut-kick me. He remembered me and spoke up on my behalf, saying I had guts. Vetted by a leader I fit in with my new group quickly. Most of our fathers fought in the Croatian regular army or in the *Ustasche*. All of them fought the Serbs. There were Serb groups (just like ours) on the other side of camp. They were like-wise fatherless; *their* fathers busy fighting *our* fathers. So naturally we fought each other. We met behind the camp in an open area behind the last row of barracks. We used our slingshots and threw whatever was handy. *The sins of the fathers are not passed to the sons, but the hatreds are. From these hatreds, sin is born anew.*

Since Andorff was only a staging area we were to be here a short time before relocating to a camp comprised exclusively of Croats. The same was true for Serbs, Jews, Gypsies and so on.

Shortly after arriving Yela had gone to the administration building to register the Dujlovich clan. The system for arriving at food quotas was arrived at on a very basic criteria-how many mouths required food. Yela answered seven. The man wrote her answer in a ledger. Among the staples we received I most often saw coffee (off limits to myself and Regina), chocolate powder, lard and black bread. On rare occasions we ate Spam. I wasn't sure if Spam was a punishment or a blessing. My stomach didn't care. More often than not though dinner was black bread and lard. Yummy. As the weeks slid away my good health chose to slide with them. By degrees I became thin and sallow. I quit playing outside with the others and took to lying in bed and staring outside . . . never enough energy these days.

One morning while changing my shirt Yela grabbed me from behind, spinning me around to face her. What now? My shirt hanging limply at my side I looked into her eyes, gauging the amount of trouble I was in. There was no anger. No maternal warmth either, but thankfully, no anger.

"You don't look so good Branko. Your chest bones are sticking out. You must have more food. I will talk to Perinic. If he can get us food then I must do it."

She turned away. Apparently, I was dismissed. So far Yela had covered our needs sufficiently so that Perinic had not yet been required.

I had heard stories about Perinic. He was a Croat of fighting age but had managed to avoid military service. He was college educated, and had been a reporter for a wire service during the war. He had traveled throughout Europe, moving in and out of Croatia during the war. I was told he maintained a mysterious relationship with Rome. Through some twist of fate he ended up in Andorff. Educated, he quickly found a spot working in the commissary as the Croat liaison. Within a short time he was forging requisition reports, then hoarding food and supplies for himself. Why give away something that people will pay for? His greed grew so great we received but a miniscule portion of what was designated for our consumption.

Perinic made deals.

The next day, while leaning against the front wall of my barracks, I spied Perinic making his way down the row. Six strong, healthy teenage boy-men formed a loose circle around him. Well fed and more than ready to protect their food source Perinic was never without them, even in sleep. Unprotected he would have felt the cold steel of a Croatian blade within a sun's dying and resurrection.

Yela saw him from inside the barracks and rumbled past me calling his name. Perinic's circle drew tighter as she approached.

"Mr. Perinic, I must speak with you about my son, Berislav. He is very sick. He needs more food. Can you help us? I will give you what I can."

Perinic slowed his pace as she talked, but when an offer appeared he stopped and turned to face Yela.

"What do you have I would be interested in?" he asked.

"My husband will give you money when he comes for us. He is an officer with the *Ustasche*. He fights Tito at Maribor."

"Then your husband is a dead man," he barked, turning on his heel to leave.

"Wait, Mr. Perinic! You can have my son work for you!"

Yela was a defeated woman. She sagged, her pride fleeing as surely as my stomach growled.

"*That* whelp?" He pointed at me, laughing. "I could have a dozen of him! Do you have anything of *value* to offer me?" he asked with an oily grimace. His eyes drew close and his meager lips pursed together.

"Only my gratitude," Yela replied.

"*Gra*titude! Gratitude will not line my pockets. Perhaps you can feed some gratitude to your son."

He guffawed at his jest, and his lackeys cackled in echo. Yela turned away from him, storming onto the porch of our barracks. Anger and shame fought a pitched battle for dominance of her expression. She didn't look at me as she disappeared inside. This would be, I decided on the spot, a good day to stay outside.

I became a criminal. Vlado told us of some fields he discovered that were overflowing with melons. Our taste buds burned for the taste of fresh, juicy melon. That very night we snuck under the wire, gorging-like so many naughty raccoons. We were sluggish from the melon careening in our stomachs but it was time to think of our families. Not satisfied with just a few, we loaded our arms with as many as we could carry. We were limited only by the confines of our respective strength and reach.

These midnight raids went on until the harvest was completed for the year, at which point the farmers took note of their diminished yields. They were fed up with us draining their income. Shortly before the next harvest they hit upon a logical resolution. Rather than be thieved upon by hungry refugees why not hire and pay them (in part) with that which they would steal anyway? On a fine early spring morning all of us, from young to old, were instructed to line up in front of our barracks. A group of farmers walked the rows, inspecting us with the eye of a rancher at a cattle auction. When they came upon a healthy male a farmer gestured to the closest guard, and the chosen was singled out to stand in a separate group. Girls were chosen according to a different set of criteria, so Milka, the most attractive of my sisters made the cut. At night, after twelve hours of bending and picking, bending and picking, bending and picking, Milka came back to the barracks with a bag stuffed with fresh produce. We were profoundly grateful. I was ashamed I wasn't the provider, but not so much that I ever turned down a plate of food.

Days stumbled upon themselves, and when seven tall, weeks were born the winter sun had given over to its warmer spring brother. We still took turns getting up at four o'clock in the morning to wait in line for food. We still guarded our firewood. Some things don't change.

Living in such close quarters, it was impossible not to get to know the stories of the people in the barracks with us-how they came to be here, where they were from. Did they lose anyone in the war? Falsehoods were quickly uncovered. We had monsters among us! Germans, passing themselves off as Croats, were seeking to avoid the end of a noose. We had all heard of The Death's Head Brigade of the SS. They had numbered in the hundreds of thousands, and were the Nazi's angels of death. Their orders were to seek out and destroy certain races that could taint the Aryan bloodline. They were wanted men so they sought escape in the anonymity of the refugee camps. Never imagining a tattoo could mark them for death at some point in the future, members of the Deaths Head Brigade received a small swastika on the inside of their armpits upon being sworn to service. Searches were becoming more frequent as the British stepped up efforts to apprehend fleeing war criminals.

One night after lights out I lay awake on my side. I hadn't any luck falling asleep on my back or stomach. I saw a man about ten bunks down, sitting on the edge of his cot. He removed his shirt. The moonlight cast ghostly silver on his skin. He sat directly in front of a window, to better gain the light. He raised his arm above his head, exposing his armpit to the light. I gasped! A small tattoo of a swastika was clearly visible. He placed his knife below the tattoo and with a steeled grimace began carving away the flesh around and under the tattoo. Blood flowed freely, creating a delta of red tributaries down his flank.

A week later British soldiers stormed the aisles of our barracks, pounding metal trashcan lids together. When everyone was standing in front of their cot the officer spoke strongly, his commands echoed by Perinic.

"All men, remove your shirts, and raise your arms above your head. All females expose both of your armpits for inspection!"

When everyone had done as the officer commanded the soldiers moved down the line, carefully inspecting every presented armpit. A week was not long enough. The SS soldier I had seen knew this and shivered in fear as the British worked their way down the line towards him. The gouge he had inflicted was a leaking mess of infection. When the officer inspected his armpit he barked a command and immediately two soldiers posted themselves behind the man. I saw his face as he was handcuffed and led up the aisle. His mouth was set in a resigned line, but his eyes swam with emotion-twin pools of sorrow, fear and anger, a boiling cauldron that in time reduces itself to regret.

The day came when we were told to pack our belongings and prepare to go to more permanent lodgings. All I knew was that it was still within Austrian borders. It didn't take long to gather our things. There were no last looks of fondness, no memories we cared to absorb. Arriving in the dead of winter, and leaving in late spring, starvation had thinned our bodies and spirits to where one could hardly prop the other. Not one among us was sorry to see Andorff fade behind us. I was glad to be done with this barren place, this empty stomach.

We clunked north, this time in open-bed military trucks, chugging along the Austrian border, staying ever inside it. To the southeast, war's cancer was eating Croatia from the outside in. None of us wanted to be there, so we were relieved to see the occasional road sign written in German. This meant we were still safely in Austria. Being in Austria meant we were not in Croatia. Croatia was death-Austria was life. Our new destination was St. Martin. I heard the camp was built by the Americans to house their soldiers toward the end of the war. As the trucks came to a stop a now familiar site greeted my eyes. Row upon row of wooden buildings, low and long. All featured identical windows about four feet off the ground. An air of despair clung to this place. The main area of the camp was a huge square of well-packed gravel. The tires of the many trucks rolling in and out of camp left little more than a slight swirl of dust for all the tons rolling on them. With the commissary squatting on one end of the square, and the administration building on the other, Yela, with her usual display of intelligence and efficiency hustled the Dujlovich clan to the last building closest to the commissary. When we were inside the barracks she had selected she turned to her left and dropped her bundle of clothes and supplies on the bed closest to the wall. Gesturing for us to do the same we walked down the line of identical bunks, plunking our belongings on the beds in front of us. With Yela anchoring one end, and Milka the other, we were home at last, such as it was. Yela had chosen our beds as far from the toilet area and stove as possible. As much as we craved the warmth of fire in winter, so did we wish to avoid it in the heat of summer.

This was a new place; hence, Yela had new rules. She gestured for us to gather 'round her.

"We will be here longer than Andorff," she began, and in her usual brusque manner got directly to the point. "Milka, you will go to the administration building and register us. You must ask for an interpreter. Make sure they know how to read and write. And Milka, make sure it is a Croat who helps you. Mara, Ruska and Anka, you will go out beyond the camp and see if any farmers are in need of field help. Berislav, you will find firewood. I want you to find the best area, and then come back for Regina. Both of you get enough wood to fill the underneath of all our beds. There will be a time to relax. First, we must get organized. First we work—*then* we rest." She paused for a moment, and then added, "This is how your father would have it."

Father. I thought about Joseph on and off. He *was* my father and I loved him. I was also very scared for him. I remembered what Perinic had said about Maribor, and what was going to happen to the *Ustasche* fighting Tito. News of the war came to us with newly arrived refugees. Fresh from areas being overrun by Serbs they brought with them stories of death-villages burned to the ground, decapitations of soldiers, babies slaughtered in front of their mothers.

One woman told us how the Serbs came to her village and gathered some of the women with young children. She said they tied some of the women to stakes in the ground and then cut holes through their breasts. Grabbing one of the mother's children they pushed the child's hands through the holes they had cut, tying the children's hands together. This was one story among many I heard. While these horrors were relived some people cried, some ran off. Many more listened in stony silence. We were not strangers to death and brutality. It did remind us, though, that even as we slept in relative security here in St. Martin, brothers, husbands, and fathers fought to the death defending our homeland.

The sad plodding of a tired horse mirrored the passing of our days. These stories took their toll on us. However, youth is, among other things, resilient, and I was more resilient than most of the kids I saw lounging throughout camp. I felt a lot better about St. Martin than Andorff. I could walk around safely here. The majority of St. Martin's fifteen hundred inhabitants were Croat, and there weren't *any* Serbs.

A "mop-up" company was all that remained of the thousands of American soldiers stationed here. These Americans had come from across the sea! They had fought and beaten Hitler. Now they were going home. Even as we trundled in lugging cardboard suitcases and bundles of clothing, the Americans were industriously packing the last of their property and leaving. Home to America!

The American soldiers fascinated me. In my world laughter was a rarity-a pebble dropped in a somber pond. These Americans laughed all the time! Smoking cigarettes they stood in loose groups, joking, smiling and laughing. America must be a great place I thought. If these soldiers, so far from home *and* fighting a war, could laugh *this* much then America must be a very happy place indeed. At some point while watching them I realized *I* wanted to go to America. Over the course of the next month, as the last green truck rolled beyond the gates, this desire crystallized into a vow. I would get to America, *no matter what*!

One thing became quickly evident, and it was a very good thing. We ate better here than at Andorff. Steaming kasha became our morning staple. There was sugar to put in the hot porridge, and the sweet heaviness in our bellies dispelled the morning chill. It was late summer, with autumn hinting at her arrival. Months slid by and the routine of camp life had become just.

However, in late fall, while on a wood hunting foray the humdrum was dispelled in an instant. I discovered the mother-load of firewood! St. Martin was a half-hour up the tracks. Ambling along the bottom of a railroad embankment I spied a rusty pile of old train wheels. I didn't think much of it. Steel doesn't burn. I decided to inspect them anyway. When I reached the wheels I noticed in the middle of every one of them was a chunk of wood! The wheels were as wide as my arm was long, and at least two inches thick. The wood in the middle was pounded into the center hole. I learned later they were "hubcaps" on the huge train wheels. The Germans who built them only used the hardest wood they could obtain, the better to keep them from rotting. They were dry as a bone and had the feel and look of long burning wood. I pounded and pried on one of them, wedging it free only after working up a serious sweat. I wanted to take it back to Yela as proof of my discovery. I reveled in the praise I was sure would be heaped upon me. These thoughts fueled my walk all the way to back to camp. When I showed it to Yela she nodded a curt approval, harshly instructing me to get them all and hide them in a dry spot near the camp. She told me to hide them very well. My excitement evaporated. As I walked back towards the door Yela called out to me to keep my mouth shut or I would get a beating. I kept my mouth shut. So much for praise.

As chilled air became more familiar and warm air increasingly a stranger the inevitable snow heralding Austrian winter made its début. As Yela correctly surmised wood for the stove became an increasingly sought after commodity. Thanks to my find, and Yela's wisdom, the Dujlovichs' never lacked for firewood. A vacancy in our barracks rarely lasted beyond a day.

Winter's icy fingers thawed in the heat of a new spring. Thoroughly settled in after so much time news came to us that we were being moved again. This announcement was met with groans and outbursts throughout the camp. However, no longer having a country to call our own, and no influence on the people deciding our fate, we prepared ourselves for the move. The camp we went to was called Asten. It was still in Austria, but north and east of St. Martin. Asten was not far from a large city called Linz, only fifty kilometers or so from the German border. The move from St. Martin to Asten was much the same as the move from Andorff to St. Martin, or from Zagreb to Andorff–the trucks or trains, the milling, the confusion, the unknown were all present and accounted for.

Once again, we settled into a new camp. Asten was pressed from the same mold as our previous abodes. Not surprisingly Yela kept us organized and we quickly adapted. Beyond the physical moving from one place to another, life went on just as before. We were very close to Linz so there were more supplies available. We were glad, since it lessened our reliance on the British and American authorities for our day-to-day needs. However, Asten was a very crowded camp. There were too many people and not enough beds. As such, we were forced to sleep two to a bunk. Spring's warmth ruled the days, but the chill of a stubborn winter still held firm grip on the nights. I lay scooped against Regina in the dark. A rickety frame and thin mattress held our shivering bodies under an inadequate blanket. I listened to the harrumphs of snores, and the gasp of breath as some sleeping unfortunate relived some fear. I heard (and felt) the icy whistling wind, hungry to enter our bones. The madness of my life was held at bay by the rhythm of Regina's even breathing.

News floated in with the arrival of ever more refugees. The name of a town on the Austrian border had crept into conversation with greater regularity in the last two weeks. Something had happened in a field outside of a town called Bleiburg. Something bad. We learned bits and pieces, related to us in tattered sobs by wives and children of Croatian soldiers. Most of them were now husbandless and/or fatherless. We had yet to hear a first-hand accounting. The vast majority of the Croats who were there to see it were now dead.

Late May 1945. The dreariness of refugee living gnawed with invisible tenacity into the core of my perception of life. My clothes were threadbare shadows of their former well-worn glory. My stomach, though better attended here in Asten than our previous camps, persisted in demanding more, more and ever more! Never satisfied. Never satiated.

Regina had provided comfort and warmth in the winter, but as summer's stickiness seeped down my spine she became an unwanted ember I couldn't escape save sleeping on the floor.

# CHAPTER VI

## "Milan's Homecoming"

On no particular morning, as I went about my chores (this morning I had to sweep under all of our beds) I heard a cry of joy from my sister Anka. She was standing near the front door, and even as I turned, she was already outside.

"Milan! Your back!" Anka yelled.

As one we turned and ran to the front door, jostling each other in our haste. My heart stopped as surely as my feet when I saw him. Milan was no longer Milan. The older brother that rubbed my hair and called me Branko was but a ghost. The half-smile, half-smirk I had grown up with had been wiped clean by the tightrope that was now his lips. His eyes, once a laughing pool (on a good day), were now two dark spots of agony.

Both of Milan's thighs sported twin bullet holes, uncanny in their symmetrical placement. Bright red blood flowed freely over the blackened crust of dead blood. Were it not for a man propping him up Milan could not possibly have walked a step on his own. As we brought him inside and laid him on a bed Milan looked around in a fevered haze. No smile broke his lips, and his eyes regarded us with a miserly portion of recognition. However, his feverish gaze upon his family was enough. With a sigh and a nod he drifted into his dreams. Yela and my sisters tended his wounds as he slept.

The bullets had passed through the meaty part of his thighs thankfully missing bone, but the devastation was nasty looking. Pussy, yellowish ooze flowed from both holes. When he moved the cracked surface of blood would break, and like lava, new blood seeped out. When all of the blood, new and old, was washed away, and the bullet holes revealed they appeared as angry intrusions into his flesh. Unhealthy blackness ringed both holes. Even at my age I knew this was serious. Milan could lose both of his legs! Yela turned to Milka, reaching in her apron and pulling out a crumbled wad of currency.

"Milka, go to Linz and get medicine for Milan. If he doesn't get antibiotics soon he will be legless before the week is out. Hurry!"

Milka took the money from Yela, gestured for Anka to come with her, and sped out the door. Three days passed in a fevered, semi-comatose hell of fits and starts. As the antibiotics worked their magic, Milan at last came around to the living. When he could finally sit up without listing to one side or the other, when he could look Yela in the eyes and know this was his mother-only then did we gather in a circle around his bed, asking the question burning in all of us.

"What happened?"

Milan's gaze traveled slowly, from sibling to sibling, at last resting on his mother's impassive stare. I looked down at his hands. Once strong and sure, plucking plums from the branches in our orchard, now they were trembling, unsure things—frail in the whirlwind of his thoughts. They moved nervously of their own accord, a victim of memory and shock. When he spoke, it was soft and halting. His voice lacked both conviction and purpose.

"My unit fought all over Croatia. We were at Pakrac. Many of my comrades died there." Milan heaved and covered his face. Somewhere buried beneath his forearms, savage exhalations escaped. Granting him the time he needed to compose Milan resumed in the same eerie monotone.

"When Zagreb fell my commanding officers pushed for us to go there and throw out the Serbs. The Partisans had control of every town between Zagreb and Vitrovica. It was a suicide mission, but we went anyway. We had nothing to lose. More than three quarters of our battalion was dead. We lost so many at Pakrac . . . As we began our journey to Zagreb, traveling only at night, we saw what the pigs did!"

His face came alive. Anger and hatred dueled for supremacy in a battle raging from eyes and flaring nostrils to the thin redness of his lips.

"They killed everyone! Women, children, the old ones . . ." he looked beyond us to villages only he could see.

"Milan, my son, please tell us what happened." Yela laid a hand upon his shoulder in an attempt to bring him back to us.

He came back from wherever he had been and saw Yela in full focus.

"When the officers saw what happened in the villages, how they murdered even the children, they decided we should surrender. The longer we fought, the more Croats they would slaughter. They heard from Central Command that the British were accepting the surrender of Croatian Regular Army soldiers. We would be placed in refugee camps if we laid down our arms."

At this point the man who had literally carried Milan into camp appeared at the edge of our family circle. Milan looked up at him, and for the first time since staggering back into our lives he smiled.

"This is Drago. He is my savior. Without him I would not be alive. He is the reason I am here today. He is also very wise and knows many things about the Partisans and the British. He was a professor of history in Zagreb before the war."

I turned to look up at him. He was a tall man. His nose was thin, coming to a definitive point much like his chin. His face was a study in angles and planes and the swarthy coloring of his skin pointed to Turkish blood, but many generations removed. His eyes, buried beneath a peppered bush, burned with the fire of knowledge. He was obviously an intelligent man. His hair had given its color to the years, leaving a trailing wisp of silver playing a halo about his face.

He said nothing. He looked at Milan with affection, paying scant attention to our stares. I turned back to Milan. He was returning Drago's look. The two of them exchanged a ghost of a smile, and their eyes held the same sorrow.

Yela again gestured for him to continue, this time a bit more forcefully.

"Milan, tell me of Joseph! Is he safe? Did you see him? Is he at Maribor?"

He looked at Yela. No longer did he have an air of obeisance about him. Milan had returned a man. He dismissed her questions curtly.

"I will tell you what I saw. First, I must speak of Bleiburg."

Bleiburg. The name of the town I had heard so often lately. A chill crept down my spine. My hair stood to attention at the base of my neck.

"Tito's Partisans were killing everyone in their path," he began. "We heard the Nazis had surrendered, and the British and Americans both said that if we laid down our arms we would be given refuge in Austria. When the news came to us our officers decided to surrender. We were instructed to go to Bleiburg, a town on the Austrian border.

When we arrived there must have been at least a hundred thousand people there. There were *Ustasche* and Croat Regular Army, families, and old people. *Everyone* wanted to get into Austria before the Serbs got us. The British seemed to be in charge. As our group grew larger, we far outnumbered the British, and they became afraid. We were there to surrender! They treated us like criminals! They moved among us, yelling for us to lay down our weapons."

Milan looked up at Drago and then continued.

"Drago didn't trust the British. Before the British soldiers got to us he pulled me towards the edge of the crowd near the river. When were as close as we could get to the river without leaving the group itself we made our brake, running fast and low. It was fifty meters or so to the River Drava, and when we reached it we hid in the brush on the bank. From where we were we could see the entire field of our countrymen. When the last of our soldiers had surrendered their weapons the British began herding the group towards the border-*away* from Austria and into the area under Tito's control. There was a sea of people, and now they're all dead . . ." Milan's voice trailed off into misery, not capable of going on.

Drago's surprisingly deep voice took up the story when Milan couldn't continue.

"The British turned our people back over to Tito. He had a battalion of soldiers waiting to kill us all. Nests of machine gun crews pushed aside tree branches firing into the field. Our people fell in the thousands, in the tens of thousands. The British knew all along. It was a *trap*!" Drago choked on his emotions, himself now unable to continue.

Milan regained his voice.

"They killed everyone. The bodies piled over one another as far as we could see. The machine guns went on for hours, then days . . . the screams will never leave me."

"Joseph! What of my husband?" Yela was consumed with having news of him.

"We made our way to Maribor," Milan continued as if Yela had never spoken. "I heard Papa's division was defending Maribor against Tito. We traveled only at night, but when we got there the fight was already over. All of our soldiers had given up. We watched from the edge of the forest. The line of *Ustasche* was miles long. There were so many it took all day for them to pass us. I looked for Papa the whole time. Tito's soldiers kept pace with them on the edge of the column, one about every ten meters or so, machine guns pointed at them every moment. There were children and mothers. If a child could not keep up the Partisans dragged the child away, a gunshot silencing the screams of the child. If the mother went crazy, they shot her also. If a soldier stumbled and fell they would shoot him and leave his body for everyone to walk around. I looked in every soldier's face, hoping I would see Papa. Toward the end of the line I finally saw him walking with a group of *Ustasche*. He was tired and sad looking. I wanted to run out to him, but Drago held me back. He told me I would die with him, and Papa would not want that."

Milan's tears flowed freely now. He was seeing his father again. Over and over he would see Joseph this way. *My* last memory of him was of a proud officer defending his country in time of war. Milan's last image of his father was a beaten, broken man walking to his death. Drago spoke again, his voice as deep as before, but even more sorrowful.

"When the soldiers and civilians were marched to a field far way from the nearest town they ordered everyone to stop. The edge of the field gave way to deep ravines leading down to the river. The Serbs grouped everyone into a tightly packed circle of people. Some of the soldiers did the herding, while others set up machine gun stations. When they were done and set up in a half circle around the group the Serbs who were keeping everyone corralled stepped behind the machine gunners. The machine guns opened fire on the soldiers, women and children. Thousand and thousands were killed. After hours of this the Partisans decided they were wasting too much ammunition. A group of officers had been talking. I saw them looking towards the river, pointing at the ravines while gesturing with their arms back and forth. The bastards figured out a *much* more effective way of killing our people. After a short discourse they nodded their heads in unison. With a terse set of commands from the lower level officers that were part of the conferring group the enlisted men began herding the remaining Croats toward the ravines. There were still thousands. They had to step over the bodies. While they did this some of the other soldiers were busy placing long boards across the gaps of the ravines which were about twenty feet wide and thirty feet deep. The soldiers spaced twenty of these boards fifteen feet apart on down the line. After the boards were in place over the gulch they selected a group of six and tied them together around the waist with about a foot of slack between each of them. Some started screaming and tried to run. Machine guns sprayed into any area of noise and panic, killing twenty or thirty people in just as many seconds. Many people died because one person panicked . . . but they all died anyway. When the guards tied a group of six together they forced them onto the board over the ravine. When all six were on the plank they crushed the last person's skull with a rifle butt. His dead weight dragged the other five off the board with him. They always grabbed the children for the front and always selected a large man for the last. When there were two or three thousand people in the ravine the Serbs threw grenades into the trench and blew up the remaining living. They screamed on a thick pile of blown apart corpses and ocean of blood . . . no one was left alive."

Retelling this had drained Drago. His eyes were hollow and his cheeks swelled in and out with the labored breathing of his chest. Sweat beaded his brow. Drago turned to Yela, resting his hands gently on her shoulders. His breath caught, and took itself back. Tears beaded the corners of his eyes, and the sadness that had taken such wretched toll of his face was not quite done.

"I saw your husband die." He looked directly into Yela's eyes. "He died in the ravines. He was the sixth."

The hollowness in Yela's eyes discovered a new depth in which to plunge. She sagged against Milka, an oak tree no more. Her anguish was not so different from the woman on the train from Zagreb to Andorff—the young wife and mother of the Hungry Window's first victim. One minute, a wife—the next, a widow. Yela's loss was complete; I could see it in her eyes. They fluttered from sorrow, to acceptance, to resolve, to ice. Coldness had always been her heart's answer to pain.

I floated in a vacuum. My father was dead. My mind ran a slide show of memories. I saw him bargaining in Banja Luka. I heard him whispering to Milan about the *Sljivovica*. I watched him striding magnificently through his plum orchard. I relived the sight of his back, confident and straight as he left the gymnasium in Zagreb. I pictured him walking out on the plank, resigned to his death. I saw his head crushed, falling with him into the ravine.

Weeks passed, and Milan became stronger by the day. His legs were still a constant source of pain, but they were no longer infected. I wanted to be near him. To me, he was the closest thing I had to an adult I was sure *really* loved me. Too much had happened to him though. Milan couldn't recover from the horrors he witnessed. He kept me at a distance and wouldn't sit and talk with me the way we used to. He was detached from the living, but fortunately he met a girl in the camp from Linz named Matilda. As the months became a rolling wave of time he regained his light in the warmth of her embrace.

But once, many months later, I spotted him sitting alone on the edge of camp. Hunched over, his head rested in the cradle of his arms. Softly at first, his shoulders sagged up and down, up and down, then thrust upward in a spasm, just as quickly retreating into ragged gasps. He cried with a ferocity I had heard only once before, from the mother who had thrown her baby through the Hungry Window into the freezing night.

Loss and death were nothing more than scavengers, drawn to the smorgasbord of anguish that war served up. But the simple act of living, of opening ones eyes to another day and living it . . . this heals even the most wounded spirit. Wedding bells were in the air! Milan and Matilda were to be married. While Milan was still distant to me over the last year Matilda had found his smile for him again. We were all very excited. Milan was our brother! This was to be a joyous time! As preparations for the wedding began, I stayed out of the way as best I could. Regina and I wandered around the camp and made new friends.

Once, while walking on the other end of camp, I reunited with an old friend. Vlado was leaning against a railing, idling the day away. He had always been larger than the other boys his age, and a year and a half had favored him with even more growth. He was only thirteen, but already looked down upon the heads of most people he stood next to. When he spotted me he ran down and gave me a quick hug.

"How are you, Berislav?" he asked.

"My father is dead. He died at Maribor," was all I could manage.

His smile fled, and he answered, "My father also died at Maribor."

We looked each other in the eyes. Saying nothing we embraced, holding each other against this crushing wave of sorrow we called life.

As we pulled apart I told him, "Goodbye, Vlado."

Looking in my eyes he replied, "Good bye Branko. I'm glad you went through the fence that night."

We smiled at each other then turned away. He went back up on the porch, assuming the same unambitious slouch. Regina and I started back to our barracks. I never saw Vlado again. We shared a common sorrow his very presence could only remind me of.

The wedding day drew close! We had no wedding clothes. There was no fancy cake, no floral arrangements. However, we had cookies! Yela and some of the other women in our barracks had made dozens of shortbread cookies. Sugar and butter aren't given at the commissary every day. All of them must have donated a month's supply of both to bake that many cookies. The smell of them drove me crazy!

This was not paradise I lived in. Hunger announced itself daily with the rumbling of my belly. Sweets were a distant memory of other times. So-I was driven to distraction by these cookies. I must have some! I must! It was the *Sljivovica* all over again. I became an agent of sinister intent, my mission-to procure those cookies at the earliest and safest moment. The day before the wedding the trays of cookies were set out on a table. This "table" was a refugee's marriage of a door and two barrels. The trays of cookies were covered with cloth to keep the flies off. I was vigilant! I waited patiently and finally the moment came. All of the women had left the barracks. There was no one inside except an old babushka too tired to care what I did-too tired to die even. I crept up to the table, lifting the cloth. Piles and piles of shortbread cookies! My mouth watered. With a furtive glance around the barracks I whisked a cookie from the tray directly to my mouth-done in a flash! Stuffing it in, I chewed, loving every crunch.

"*Branko*! What are you doing?" Milan bellowed from the front door. His silhouette made mockery of a robust posture. He was hunched over, leaning on the doorframe. The wounds had not healed properly, and permanent damage had occurred. The silhouette vanished as he limped towards me. His face, moments ago cloaked in shadow, now emerged from black into murky gloom, radiating pure rage. I froze. He grabbed my hair throwing me to the floor.

"Why did you steal the cookies? *Why*?"

Milan became someone else. *I* became something else. To him I was no longer his little brother. The cookies really didn't matter. I became the horror, the fear, the hatred, the death, the tears, the loss, the betrayal, the pebble that let loose the dam. He screamed over and over.

"Why? Why? Why! Why!"

Punching my face and kicking my stomach he kept screaming "Why!" I was eight years old. I didn't stand up well to his beating. I fell to the ground, my view skewed and blurry. The shoes of the people drawn inside by the yelling were huge and close at floor level. I tried to concentrate on them as they swam in and out of focus. The sea of shoes parted. Looking up, Matilda swam into view, making her way to the inner row. When she saw me on the floor, and Milan poised above me ready to deliver another kick her eyes widened to saucers of disbelief. Staring at Milan as if he were a stranger, the look on her face spoke more than any words could. "This man, this man to whom I am to pledge my life? This *monster* that beats a child?" Her eyes were huge and swimming, on the brink of floods. Her lips had drawn into themselves and her flushed features gave way to the heaviness of her breath . . . . This was her speech. No words were spoken. None were needed.

She backed away from him as he limped towards her. His eyes, now reservoirs of remorse, were met by the stony gaze of hers, two freezing ponds. Calling her name as she turned in revulsion he followed her and they both disappeared through the front door. They were gone all that day and night, showing up a scant hour before the scheduled time to be married. They were.

Regina wiped the blood from the cuts on my lips and above my eyes. I burned with a hatred I had never known. *Milan was no longer my brother*!

Yela had plans for me. A school had been formed by a group of literate Croatians in Asten. Yela insisted I attend. I hated it from the first minute. My friends were running around, finding neat things, doing neat things. I was stuck in a stuffy room with droning bores. No books. No paper. No nothing. Wait! There *was* an old chalkboard. Chalk *itself* was a rarity. In spite of my attitude the teachers told Yela I was a promising student. They in turn told the Croatian priests in the camp.

A day came when the chance to play hooky was dangled in front of me. It was an opportunity to skip class so I *took* it! My friends and I went to the river and fished all day. When I arrived at the barracks that evening Yela was waiting for me on the front porch. Her look left no room for any other interpretation-I was a cooked goose. She knew I had not been to school. The gnawing feeling rumbling in my gut all day came into its own. Yela said nothing. Grabbing me by the back of my shirt she dragged me inside. My feet didn't so much walk with her as they were dragged to the nearest bed. Yela's face was a mask of iron. She pushed me on the bed, harshly telling me to stay there. I stayed. This was no time to argue. She turned her back to me then reappeared with a length of wire in her hands. Grabbing my arms she wrapped her hands around them, sliding her hands up to my wrists. When both of my wrists were firmly in her grasp Yela wrapped a stand of the wire around them, securing the other end of the wire to the bed frame. She did the same with my feet to the other end of the rusty bed frame. Only when I was trussed to the bed and unable to move did she speak.

"Berislav, you are a wicked child. I have been too soft on you."

She began beating me with her fists. This time I was the Joseph who would never reappear, the life that would never be regained, the farm that would never grow our crops again. Yela beat me, punching my face, my arms, and my chest. Blood flowed. My face, just now healing from Milan, took yet another assault. The more I tried to move away the deeper the wire cut into my hands and ankles, adding to the red stains soaking the blankets. The wings that held love aloft dissolved. In my heart, at that moment, Yela ceased to be my mother.

A year passed.

# CHAPTER VII

## "Sandals and Brown Robes"

My schooling continued. More learning materials were made available to us as the weeks and months opened and closed on each other. Chalk was secured, basic skills were taught. After a year of lessons the priests had become a familiar presence in the classroom. At some point the priests went to Yela. They informed her they considered me to be a prime candidate for the priesthood. They told her they had the permission of Rome, the British, and the Italians to take a number of children to a monastery in Italy to train to become priests. They also wanted young girls to become nuns. Yela seized on this. She informed Ruska and myself that we would go with the priests to Italy.

"I don't want to go!" I yelled.

"*Quiet!* You will go." That was the end of it.

A week of torture passed. I dreamt of crosses and chants, of lonely bells ringing and echoing through drafty corridors. On a moonless night, suited to dark purpose, a rough hand shook me awake and foul breath assaulted my nostrils. When I opened my eyes a hooded wraith hovered above me.

"Come. We go now." It said.

Emerging from a deep sleep I had no idea this was a priest. In the dark it looked more like a formless demon, swimming in dark and evil veils. He shook me again, this time forcibly. I realized what was happening.

"You will come with me. We go to Italy tonight," the priest murmured.

Still not fully aware (this must be a dream) I packed my meager store of clothes, and was standing, ready to go. Yela had come up behind the priest. Running to her I circled my arms around her waist. She held me for a very brief moment then put her hands on my shoulders, pushing me away from her body.

When I looked up into her face she said, "Branko, you must go with the priests. They will teach you many things. You have a chance to be more than a farmer-just as you've always wanted. By the grace of God and our Holy Father in Rome you can become a priest and serve our Father in Heaven to His greater glory."

The priest stood to one side, waiting for the goodbyes to be over. I had never heard Yela speak so devoutly before this. Perhaps we were better Catholics than I had thought?

I asked the priest if I could say goodbye to Regina. The hood shook back and forth-a definitive no. I reached out to Yela. Scrunching my face into her nightshirt I held on for dear life. I didn't want to leave! Yela pushed me back again and without looking down thrust me into the grasp of the priest. He commanded my elbow, leading me away into the night. As he pulled me from the dark of the barracks I looked back at the sleeping forms of my family. Making our way through the blackness of Asten's slumber, thoughts of what was to come, and memories of things past, collided in a jumbled heap in my mind.

I was pitifully shy on information regarding my future. I knew I was going to Italy. The priests had given us meager information regarding our future while in class. I learned the town itself we were going to is called Grottammare, but we would be living in a monastery. They told us the monastery sat on top of a hill overlooking the Adriatic Sea. I knew from my lessons the Adriatic Sea is the northern offshoot of the Mediterranean Sea, that it is a body of water pushing its way into the belly of Eastern Europe, separating Italy from the Dalmatian coast. The name of the monastery is Santa Maria degli Angeli, or St. Mary of the Angels. On the western coast of the Adriatic Sea, Grottammare reposed approximately two-thirds of the way up the eastern coast of Italy. We were told our learning would be mainly in languages and church doctrine, and other things required in becoming a priest in the Holy Roman Catholic Church. The priests were from the Order of St. Francis. This was important to them and they spent quite a long time explaining it. The Catholic Church has numerous religious orders in its hierarchy. They told us the Franciscans owed their namesake to the son of a merchant from the Italian town of Assisi around 1200 A.D. Renouncing his wealth and social status, Francisco Bernadone made what many would consider a foolish decision. Stepping before the Bishop of Assisi and the church council he removed every stitch of clothing covering his body until he was completely naked. Claiming he had no requirements that could not be satisfied by God Himself, he renounced his wealthy *earthly* father, Pietro Bernadone, for another Father-*this* one in heaven. Not surprisingly, he was soon penniless. All of the Franciscans I had seen thus far wore robes, so I guess he decided God was, after all, in favor of *some* form of clothing. Undeterred, but fully covered, he began wandering the hills of Italy. Preaching the spiritual benefits of poverty and furthering God's message of love on earth, he eventually drew the attention of the Pope of the day, Innocent III. Not long after that a religious order was created with Francisco Bernadone as its Head of Order. The future St. Francis of Assisi was uneasy with this all of his life. Leading a religious order was in direct contravention to his basic beliefs. He message was the more simple in worship and bare of earthly trappings, the closer a person came to God. In spite of his unsought leadership the Franciscan order exists to this day, eight hundred years later. The ultimate goal of the Catholic Church was for us to become priests. Not all of us would, we were told. To become a priest one had to be intelligent. For those of us not making the cut academically the Franciscan brotherhood of monks awaited. The Monks were the workhorses of the order. Monks', or brothers', duties consisted of sweeping, raking and washing dishes, and a host of other menial but necessary tasks considered below the duties of priests. I vowed I would study as long as it took to *not* become a monk. Sweeping and cleaning for the rest of my life? No thanks!

    The priest that had rousted me from sleep let loose of my elbow only when I was safely grouped with the other sixty-two children selected. There were kids even younger than I, some barely seven years old. The oldest was thirteen. I was nine. Out of sixty-two children selected, fifty-two were boys and ten were girls. The girls had been chosen to become nuns. The Church needed nuns as much as it needs priests. Milling my way through the shuffling group, anxious whispers floated to me on all sides. Listening to snatches of conversation I realized most of the kids were just as scared as me. We were *all* leaving our families. Some families were better than others, but regardless of the quality of the relationship they're still the ones we are most familiar with. I was luckier than most-I had at least one person I could be with that was family, close or not.

    Ruska, the prettiest of my five sisters, had been chosen to go to the convent for studies. I searched every face for her as I wound my way in the dark. The light of a timid lantern illuminated her dress, a familiar pattern. I zoomed in on it, catching her eye just as she caught mine. We gave each other scared little smiles as we came together. She was getting ready to say something when the rumbling of a dilapidated truck interrupted as it clunked to a stop close by our group.

    The priest in charge was unfamiliar. When the truck came to a complete stop a few long strides took him to the running board of the truck which he deftly hopped upon. Rapping on the hood to get the driver's attention he leaned through the open window and spoke to him for a moment. When he was done he stepped off the running board and turned toward us, his charges.

    "You will be quiet now." He said this softly, but his voice was deep and carried well. "My name is Father Brkan. You will address me as Reverend Father Brkan. I have been assigned by Rome to escort you to Santa Maria degli Angeli. Once there, we will teach you what is required to become a priest or nun in the Roman Catholic Church. Helping me with this task is Father Kozo. You will address him as Reverend Father, the same as me. There will be other Fathers you will meet when we arrive."

    He paused to hand a thin packet of papers to Reverend Father Kozo. As he did I saw Reverend Father Brkan clearly in the light of the truck's headlamps. He was very tall. His robes draped an obviously healthy frame. He had removed the cowl shading his face. Thick black hair wreathed a bald crown. A fine, strong forehead topped his well-proportioned face. Ruddy cheeks splashed color on his tan. He boasted a nose that possessed the fullness, flair and slope a perfect nose should, and his lips (just the correct distance below) composed symmetry of curves. All in all, a vibrant, healthy man.

    Father Kozo removed his cowl as well. He was shorter and heavier, and his robes didn't so much flow about his frame as define it. His face followed the roundness of his body. Puffy cheeks formed mini-mountains, sloping in unison to the valley of his lips. A large rounded nose dominated and completed the portrait of heaviness. I couldn't tell if his eyes were kind or unkind. He was looking down at the papers-focused on the task. Father Brkan finished conferring with Father Kozo and turned toward us. He resumed his tutorial.

"I am going to call out your name. When you hear it respond that you are here then get in the back of the truck. We will be going to Linz. This will take about an hour. When we get there we will go to the rail station and board a train for Italy." He paused.

"All of you are blessed by God. It is a great honor to be chosen to serve our Father in heaven. As future Franciscans you must always be aware of Satan's temptations. We will be going into a big city. You will see many things you may want. *Remember!* Most of those things are evil! You *must* be aware of Satan. He is everywhere . . ." He stopped. Composing himself, he delivered the real substance.

"I am a protector of the faith. My duty lies with God-*always*. You can expect me to punish you should I find you committing sin."

When his speech concluded I looked at Ruska. Fear strolled freely among us.

"Ruska," I asked, "what will happen to us? This doesn't sound good. I want to stay *here*, even if Yela doesn't want me. I-I'm scared."

"Why are you complaining? Momma is right! You *are* never happy. You *have* to do what others say. You can't have your way all the time!" Disgusted, she turned her back on me. I never felt as alone as that moment.

Father Kozo began calling our names. When he said Berislav Dujlovich, I spoke out.

"*Ya-sam Ohv dyeah.*" I am here.

As Father Brkan instructed I went to the back of the truck, climbing up and onto the wooden bed. There were seating planks about one foot wide running down either side of the truck's bed, but they were filled hip to hip with kids having a last name before the letter D. Names after 'D' were relegated to the floor. Ruska found a spot near the front by the truck's cab. I sat near her, but not with her. At last roll call was completed, and the truck was filled to the brim with children. Fatty Father Kozo sat in the back with us while slim Father Brkan sat up front in the driver's cab. Considering the tight quarters I wish it could have been the other way around. The entire truck shuddered as it rumbled to a start. A loud belch of exhaust, and we were off. The truck ride to Linz was dark, unpleasant and uncomfortable. We were sixty-three people crammed in a space designed to hold thirty, but most of us were small so we made it work. At last, we arrived at the train station in Linz, Austria. As we pulled to a stop Father Kozo climbed down and spoke with Father Brkan, who had likewise gotten out of the truck's cab. They turned toward us, and Father Brkan motioned us to disembark. Since Ruska and I were sitting on the floor of the bed with our backs resting against the back wall of the cab we were almost the last ones to jump to the ground. Once again, we were told to stay very close together. In the crush of bodies Ruska and I had become separated. Father Brkan called out for the girls to form a separate group with two nuns that must have been waiting for our arrival. I had seen the nuns standing off to one side by a pillar when we pulled into the station. Both of them were small, but they possessed a serious air. Their black robes ascended from the floor to a constricted neckline. At that point, white abruptly took over. The starched stiffness of their habit followed the course of their heads, leaving only their faces visible. The habit left little or no space between itself and their skin. No wonder they didn't smile, I thought. I would go insane if I had to wear that thing all the time! Father Brkan told us the girls would go to a Convent in Italy called Grotta Ferrato. It was in the same region as Grottammare, but far enough away that I wouldn't get to see Ruska at all. I started looking for her, jumping up for a quick sweeping view before gravity returned me to a collage of shoulders and backs. Father Brkan saw me jumping, and with a few quick strides he towered above me.

"What are you doing child?" He asked me in an exasperated tone.

"My sister is Ruska Dujlovich. I am Berislav Dujlovich, Reverend Father Brkan. I thought we would be staying together, and now I find she is going to another place! I won't get to see her and I want to say goodbye to my sister! Can you help me please, Reverend Father Brkan?"

It was not to be.

"Your sister goes to Grottammare with us. All of us will go on to the Monastery. She will be leaving for Grotto Ferrato within days of our arrival. You may see her there, but I doubt it. They will be in another wing of the monastery. They are already boarding a car in front of us. Now stop jumping and wait with the rest of the boys."

With that he turned away to address other concerns. On my last jump I had seen the small group of girls and the two nuns walking away from us to board a car further down the line. Ruska's back grew smaller with the distance. I wanted to call out her name, but was sure that would land me in hot water with Reverend Father Brkan. I got the impression many things would land me in hot water with him. In spite of this I risked one more jump. The last nun was stepping upon a footstool to board. All of the girls were already on the train. Now I was truly alone.

With the girls gone the priests directed us to a passenger car for our trip to Grottammare. The railcar we stepped into was filled with seats running the length of it. A middle aisle stretched between them from front to back. Just like a church with pews, I thought. Windows ran the length of the wall above the benches, which had a two-foot open space beneath them. Fifty-two boys and two adults gulped up every square inch of floor and seating space in the car. The smarter (and older) ones wriggled beneath the seats where they could stretch out for some sleep. Crammed in the middle I was not so fortunate. Small guys didn't get a seat, or even a seat to lie under. Small guys sat in the middle aisle. I was a small guy. With a chug and a tug we were off. Mashed in on all sides I was consumed with self-pity when Father Brkan spoke loudly enough to overcome the clacking of the wheels on the steel rails.

"This journey will take two days. We will cross into Italy in the town of Trieste. That will be sometime late tonight. You must all behave. This is a long ride and may get uncomfortable."

*May* get? I thought.

"Father Kozo will be passing out black bread and water. Anyone caught fighting will be disciplined harshly" he added before turning to the front of the car.

With that said Father Kozo began passing out the bread. We scooped water into our cups from a large bucket. My cup was nothing more than a tin can with the top removed. It *did* hold water though. The bread was stale, crusty and not at all pleasant. Father Kozo joined Father Brkan in the front of the car after handing out our meal. They opened a door leading outside to a small platform. When the door closed behind them several of the older boys began snatching bread from the hands of the younger ones. I saw the smaller boys have their meal taken away and I knew the boys giving up their meal without a struggle would have to deal with the same problem at every meal. I was *not* going to give up my dinner. Jozo, one of the largest boys, came toward me to make a grab at my bread. I moved away and told him it was mine. This was a mistake. There is a sizeable weight difference between a thirteen year old and a nine year old.

"Give it to me or I'll beat the crap out of you." He reached out, smacking the back of my head. I hunched around my bread. He pulled my arms apart to get at it, so I did the only thing I could think of. I lashed out with my foot. When it connected with Jozo's leg I heard a "krunk" in his right knee. He dropped to the floor, screaming in pain. Father Brkan heard Jozo yelling through the door and stormed inside. The bully on the floor pointed at me, telling Father Brkan I had kicked him. He rolled up his pants leg to show him as way of proof. His knee was already swelling.

Father Brkan turned toward me. The fire in his eyes twisted my insides to knots. I tried to explain what happened but all that came out of my mouth was the stuttering of a fool. No one defended me. They didn't want to be involved. Father Brkan towered above me. Reaching down in a swoop he slapped my face so hard my head snapped to the left. My ears rang and my face grew red with anger and shame-anger at what he did, and shame that I could do nothing about it.

"*You!* I spoke to you earlier. I can see already you're a troublemaker. What was your name again? Bratislava something . . . . Well, boy? What is your name?"

Father Brkan leaned close to my face. His breath reeked of garlic and wine. His voice meshed with the ringing in my head so I couldn't make out every word, but I saw his lips form the word 'name'.

"B-Berislav D-D-Dujlovich," I stammered.

"I will not forget *you*, Berislav Dujlovich. I would advise you to spend more time in prayer and less thinking about your sister or starting fights."

He drew closer. His breath bathed my face in stale warmth. Very softly, for my ears only, he said, "We will have years together, you and I. *Years.* It could be very bad for you if you don't learn the right way to do things. I'll be watching you."

Dismissing me with a turn of his head he stood as tall as the ceiling allowed and made his way back up front and through the door leading to the platform outside. Father Kozo had seen to Jozo's knee, determining it was not broken, though it was badly sprained. When he was finished with Jozo he followed Father Brkan back outside. When the door closed behind them the bully turned toward me with a grunt and a grimace. While the two Reverend Fathers were inside the car I had taken the opportunity to move a safe distance from him. I wasn't too worried for the time being since he couldn't walk or even stand up. The one good thing to come out of it was that no one else made a grab for my breakfast. I guess they figured my scraggly piece of stale bread was not worth a knee.

A war ravaged countryside unfolded before us as we chased the sun southwest. At one point we came upon a town, or what used to be a town. On the edge of it the crumbled walls of a church rolled into view. Only the steeple thrust heavenward. The rest of the town was a nightmare of gray, twisted destruction. A rolling panorama of burned out tanks and shattered vehicles peppered the landscape. Destroyed villages and collapsed bridges presented themselves a windowpane at a time until we finally lost our race with the sun. Trieste lay south of Linz on the borders of Italy and Croatia. We had departed the Linz station at dawn finally arriving in Trieste very early the next morning. All of us were hungry and thirsty. For the last fourteen hours on the train I had received only two cups of water and the one piece of "breakfast" bread from the Reverend Father Kozo. Almost a day of my life had passed in the closeness of the rail car. According to Father Brkan I had another day to go.

When the train came to a complete stop two Italian border guards rapped on the door demanding papers with an air of impatience. Exhibiting the hurried gestures of very busy men they held out their hands, gesticulating and jabbering incessantly at the same time. I saw Reverend Father Brkan reach into a pocket of his robe and retrieve his crucifix. It signified his papal authority. When the Reverend Father Brkan opened the door and stepped out to meet the border guards their attitudes changed instantly. This was Italy, home to the Holy Roman Catholic Church. Father Brkan reached in his robe again even as he spoke with them. Unfolding a document, the scarlet and gold of the Vatican's colors produced even greater respect. By the time he was done speaking with them the two guards were ready to help our group any way they could. The best service they could render was to help us be on our way as soon as possible. We got off the railcar gathering near the pillar Father Kozo was standing next to. I noticed immediately the air was much warmer here, hundreds of miles south of Linz. This was a new place; new sights and sounds greeted me. The low moan of a ship's horn floated to my ears, rumbling from the port. Everywhere, Italians spoke rapidly to each other. I understood nothing beyond a few basic words.

To the east a sky in the grip of night grudgingly broke its bonds with the darkness, giving way to the blushing approach of a new dawn's sun. To the west the dark sheet of the Adriatic Sea spread into blackness. The ship's lanterns, coming and going, dotted the port like so many fireflies.

Father Kozo spoke, directing us to form a single line facing him. Sixty-two people shoulder to shoulder make for a long line, so when Father Kozo told us it was mealtime he had to speak up for all of us to hear him. Father Brkan had left our group to speak with two other priests who had been waiting for our arrival. They brought back the promised food and water. Virgin Mary be praised! At this point I had no problem with black bread and water. It was the best I had ever eaten. After wolfing down our sumptuous meal we were directed to board the train for the final leg of the journey. The border patrol was as good as their word and we were soon thumping our way into the Italian countryside. We were informed we would not be stopping until we reached Grottammare—except for two quick stops to take on replacement water and coal for the steam driven turbine on the locomotive. Father Brkan told us the engineer informed him we were making excellent time. This didn't surprise me. I was full of sour thoughts. They certainly didn't have the time consuming burden of *feeding* us more than once every twenty-four hours to impede our excellent progress.

Trieste was left behind as we headed west, skirting the shore of the Adriatic Sea. The priest had shown us where Grottammare was on a map. I remembered the shape of the Adriatic as it thrust up from the Mediterranean into southern Europe. Its waters lapped the northernmost shore merely fifty miles from the southern border of Austria. We rounded the top of the Adriatic Sea around mid-morning, then railed south. That was our final change of direction. Grottammare was *well* under a day's journey now. We stopped in Ravenna, Italy late that evening to take on food and water—for *us* this time, not the train. In rounding the top of Italy and heading south, the Adriatic Sea now lay to the east. Trieste lay somewhere across the water. While Trieste was part of Italy it was more Slavic than European. I could see the difference between Trieste and Ravenna immediately. In Ravenna clothes were looser and people seemed calmer. Smiles greeted smiles, and the furtive glances and air of fear had evaporated in the new climate.

My mind wandered back to Ivanjska, to simpler days. I was nine years old. I had endured three years of trains and trucks, woods and snow, smoky gymnasiums and frozen barracks, yelling and beatings and death. I was ready for a change. Grottammare sat on shore's edge. When the train finally came to a halt all of us were bustling with excitement. We were from an inland area of fields and mountains.

This place was paradise! The morning sun turned the water an electric blue. A cool September breeze gratefully made its way beneath buttoned shirts. The wind was sweet relief to the stifled air of the rail car. Father Kozo took charge of us immediately. He barked at us to stay close together. A few of the older boys were whispering in groups of two or three. I snuck a look at the sea with the rest of my group. It wasn't hard to figure out what they were discussing.

# CHAPTER VIII

## "Servants of Saint Francis"

"Your feet stand on cobblestone." An unfamiliar priest spoke loudly, with a voice iron in its authority.

All plans for the beach ceased in a breath.

"My name is Monsignor Mandich. I am in charge here at Santa Maria degli Angeli."

Thankfully, he spoke Croat.

"The beach some of you are looking at is a place of sinners. The people who go there indulge in pleasures of the flesh. These are the pleasures of Satan. The men and women wear clothes of little covering, exposing themselves for the gawking pleasure of others. That is a sin. *Wanting*, or coveting is a sin" Monsignor Mandich harshly intoned.

Father Brkan was studying the cobbles with great interest.

"You! **All** of you!" he continued, "have been chosen by the grace of God. Your thoughts and eyes must *not* be rooted in the flesh. Turn them towards heaven! I can assure you, my young seminarians, your new life here will be *far* more pleasant." He said this last bit with a menacing softness. "I will make this plain for you. A beach is composed of sand. Sand has a way of getting into every nook and cranny-your toes and shoes, your hair and your armpits. If you have been to the beach we will know it. Let me explain something to all of you. Santa Maria degli Angeli has been the home and school for hundreds of boys over the last fifty years. We have seen everything that can be tried. We know *all* the tricks. Enough on this subject. Please form two lines side by side. We will now go to Santa Maria degli Angeli."

When we had done as Monsignor Mandich instructed he led us on the cobblestones through the village to the monastery. As we began walking the cobbles did their best to trip us up. This cobblestone street was old, older than my father-older than my father's father, and his father before him. Uneven waves of rolling stones did their best to snag the toes of our shoes. A few boys stumbled, and when they sprawled to their hands and knees the older boys snickered at their clumsiness.

Reverend Father Brkan, Reverend Father Kozo and Reverend Father Stephen herded us up the narrow, deeply shadowed street. The buildings on both sides of us were two or three stories tall. They were constructed in a symphony of rectangles, each one of the large gray limestone blocks married to a slab of mortar stacked upon each other. Rectangle upon rectangle upon rectangle, building upon building, and so on up the street until a green field at the end broke the gray expanse of geometry. Chancing a look upward (they *did* say look heavenward) every roof was the same, composed of terra—cotta tiles forming an orange-red crown on every building. Rounded, like a pipe cut in half, they lay upon each other in succession from the top of the roof, sloping down to the edge and hanging over the street.

The stench of raw sewage was strong. Trash littered the gutters of the narrow streets. This had to be the poorest part of town I thought. As we left the village behind the cobbles gave way to dirt. Santa Maria degli Angeli perched at the crown of the hill before me. As we walked closer I noticed the top of the surrounding wall sparkled with flashes of light along its entire length. I thought how neat it looked until I got close enough to see the flashes of light were actually sunlight bouncing off chunks of broken glass embedded into the cement on top. Was it built to keep people in, or to keep people out? I was looking down in contemplation regarding that topic when I bumped into the boy in front of me. The line had come to a stop. We arrived at the front door I had seen while coming up the hill. Up close the door was massive. At least ten feet high and ten feet wide, it was as solid as a door could be-slabs of trees tamed into a door.

Father Brkan went up to it, grabbed hold of a huge knocker in the center of the door and pulled the knocker upward in an arc a foot away from the wood. The knocker was an iron ball the size of a small head of cabbage. The ball was welded to a steel bar, which in turn was welded to a hinge bolted to the thick planks. When he let loose of the iron ball it boomed into a well-worn depression in the wood. He did this three times. After an interval we heard a key turning in the old tumblers. With a creak the huge door swung inward. As we filed into the monastery of Santa Maria degli Angeli, I snuck a sidelong glance at the burly robed man who had opened the door for our group. His head was shaven just like the other Reverend Fathers. I didn't know why they did that. I only know every Franciscan friar and priest I saw had the same haircut. Once all sixty-two of us were through the door and inside the walls we came to a stop. We were in the middle of a large open area. The door swung shut behind us with an ominous thud. This was it—seminary life.

The Reverend Father Brkan turned toward another priest that had come out of a building at the far end of the open area. Monsignor Mandich walked toward the approaching priest. Long strides brought them together quickly. After exchanging a short greeting they talked softly and earnestly for a few minutes.

When they were done, the unknown Reverend Father supplied us with his name.
"You will address me as Reverend Father Vasilj."
He spoke with a thick Croat accent so his name sounded like "Vahsay." One hundred and twenty-four eyes scrutinized him. His thinness began with scrawny ankles peeping beneath his swaying robe as he stepped first this way, then that. One of Father Kozo's robes would have made two robes for him. His hands differed little from his ankles-just add fingers. Father Vasilj's cold face was a pinched nerve. Some are born with noble chins. The Reverend Father Vasilj was not one of those, and by genetic disposition he was in the opposite camp. His chin was a pointy affair of which nothing flattering can be said. The uninspiring strip of two lips formed a slash of a mouth that looked as if cracking a smile would be a bothersome annoyance. I had seen many of these people in the camps.

Tragedy is a beast walking silently among us. The horror of this beast is the affect it leaves upon those it touches. I had seen people for whom death would have been sweet release, yet they continued forward, helping and enriching those around them by their strength. Then there were those that lacked the will to live. Tragedy had visited, draining them to empty husks until their spirits departed for more fertile ground. Father Vasilj fell into the category of the living dead. The armies of weakness had overrun any emotion of positive substance. His eyes told me everything about him by virtue of the nothingness reflected in them.
"I am the priest in charge at Santa Maria degli Angeli. You've met Monsignor Mandich. He is the papal envoy for all Croats living in Italy. He will be visiting periodically for inspections of the monastery and to gauge your progress here. His decision will determine your future within the Church which is final and absolute. He is not here on a day-to-day basis to evaluate your progress so he relies heavily upon our recommendations, favorable or not. You are familiar with Reverend Father Brkan and Reverend Father Kozo. You will meet Reverend Father Lawrence and Reverend Father Kadirin quite soon. The six of us will be your teachers and we take our teaching seriously, which is only fair to tell you from the start. If you forget what I've said I have no doubts you will suffer a reminder at some point in the near future." He paused, then flung his arms forward and began expelling his next volley of thoughts. "So! You will receive two forms of training. We will teach you languages and theology. You will learn to read ancient classics in their original language and recite them in their original tongue. You will be educated seminarians when you are done here. The second aspect of your learning concerns your immortal soul. As future priests you must be far more vigilant than the average Catholic. You

are part of a higher order." He paused to deliver this very important information. "God will judge you when you die. We live in a world of sin. This is Satan's playground and we will teach you, by any means necessary, how to recognize him and turn away. In the Holy Scripture you will learn of the wrath God pours on the wicked. His punishments are severe. We *also* believe in punishment. Through suffering, as Jesus suffered, you will learn the path to goodness. Evil comes in many forms. As priests we recognize evil when it appears, and have been trained, as you will be, to defeat it. Beware of Satan! He wants your soul and he will *never* stop trying to get it. If you give in to sin you give Satan the hook he needs to possess your soul. An eternity of burning hell awaits you at that point. Do you misguided children understand me?"

Sixty-two heads nodded up and down. Not one voice stirred the air. Neither expecting nor receiving an answer he continued.

"A little history on your new home." He was addressing the boys only. "Santa Maria degli Angeli was founded many years ago. Built as a training ground for young seminarians like yourselves, if you make it through all four years here you will leave prepared to continue your studies. After completing advanced theological studies in Rome you will be ordained as a Franciscan priest in the Holy Roman Catholic Church. I see some of you looking around. I'm sure you're all curious about your new home so we will tour the grounds. Follow behind me. If you leave the line you will be punished. If you talk you will be punished. Father Stephen will see to that as he will be following behind."

With that, he turned to his right. He headed toward a strand of trees about a hundred yards away that was bordering the field we were on. When the boys closest to him followed the rest of us fell in like so many ducklings, off to see our new world. As we got closer to the trees I noticed they grew in organized rows. The leafy tops of the trees formed a canopy creating a shady avenue below until they disappeared over a small rise.

"This is our olive orchard. We grow olives and process them into oil, which we sell to help defray our expenses. All of you will become familiar with the orchard. You will be working here and in the pressroom. Food and clothes are not free and everyone must do their part."

As Father Vasilj seemed ready to lead us into the orchard proper he abruptly turned to his right. About two hundred yards ahead of us the main group of buildings bathed in the afternoon sun. I saw a wall built off the back of one of the buildings. It extended out about thirty feet, meeting another wall that disappeared into shadow. When we were almost upon it Father Vasilj resumed his duties as tour guide.

"This wall encloses the cemetery. It is strictly forbidden for any of you to *ever* go inside it, or even near it. If you are caught sneaking around here the punishment will be severe—*very severe*!" A short pause to let us think that through, followed by more information. "These are the main buildings of Santa Maria degli Angeli. The two-story building you see to your right is your new home. The dormitories are on the second floor. My quarters are there as well so don't even think about sneaking out at night. On the first floor are classrooms, the dining room and the kitchen. Most of your time will be spent in that building. There, and church." He pointed to the church as if we might have missed it. Beyond satisfying the criteria of what one would expect of *any* church there was nothing remarkable about it.

When Father Vasilj concluded the outdoor portion of our tour we filed behind him into the main building. I was curious where I would be spending the next four years of my life. The smooth stucco walls, painted a depressing gray, exuded drabness. The occasional picture of Jesus hung in plain wooden frames adorning the walls in varying degrees of likeness. Father Vasilj pointed toward a door with a large glass panel above it. This was a classroom. There were four of them. Apparently he felt a quick peek through the glass and his terse statement was enough for now. Moving on he led us upstairs to our quarters. There was nothing unusual or ancient about this building. I learned it was only fifty years old. The church was older but the main building had been added as the seminary grew. The boys directly behind Father Vasilj were the first ones inside and had claimed their bunk by the time the last of us were actually in the room. The dormitory had the same layout as any number of barracks I had lived in. The bunks were spaced two feet apart all the way down the room, the bathroom at the far end, the entrance door at the opposite end. These living quarters had showers though. The beds were the best of any place I had stayed, including my own in Ivanjska. The mattress was thin and when I laid on it the first night I had to get accustomed to the steel bands that ran every six inches from top to bottom of the bed frame. But! It was a real mattress and was soft by comparison to what I was accustomed to.

After an explanation of what was what and what was where we followed Father Vasilj downstairs into the cafeteria. He said it was time to eat. We filed in, sitting as quickly as we could. I was ravished. I *so* looked forward to this meal. I had been in enough refugee camps to learn the first meal was a good indication of what the rest of them would be like. My first meal at Santa Maria degli Angeli was spaghetti, a first for me. It tantalized my taste buds, giving me a new definition of enjoyment. It was thick; a tomato richness, swimming with chunks of green pepper and onion, sausage and mushrooms. And spicy—oh, was it spicy. I loved it. I was savoring the heaviness of the spaghetti swimming in my tummy and imagining settling into my bed when I was rudely jolted. I turned around to see who shoved me and there was Jozo's face a few inches from mine.

"Hi there, Berislav. How do you like it so far?"

He smiled with his mouth only. His eyes radiated hate and malice. He was a bully. My father had told me early on how to deal with them. Well, not me actually, but he had told Milan. I had listened and remembered.

"I'm fine Jozo," I answered evenly. "How is your knee?"

I turned away quickly skirting between two boys in front of me. Jozo didn't follow. Maybe he was thinking about my question, or perhaps evaluating his unspoken answer. No matter, I would have to deal with him eventually if he so chose.

We were being led to the side door of the church. I had seen the front door on the tour, but the one we were going through was on the cafeteria's east wall opening directly into the middle of the church. In spite of myself, I felt a rush of privilege. I didn't know it at the time but I was being led to my first of oh, so many prayer sessions. I didn't know what to expect as we followed Father Vasilj into the church. In Ivanjska the church my family went to was little more than a long room with a slightly taller ceiling than the average dwelling. A plain wooden altar squatted at the far end. Our seats were nothing more than rough planks nailed together, barely satisfying the basic requirements of a pew. The floors were wood, and the walls were painted white.

But *this* church! The sound of our footsteps bounced around the stone floor and walls. The air was still and the smallest sounds had a field day in their confinement. As Father Vasilj spoke in the professional hush of a career priest he led us up the center aisle between smooth, dark polished pews.

I decided it would be wise to listen to these people. Father Vasilj was explaining the many benefits to be found in obeying God's commandments, and conversely, the consequences of disobeying.

"The first thing you must learn is this, it is our job to mold you into a vessel pure enough to become a fortress of the faith. Sin must have no place in your hearts or your minds. There is much evil in the world. Not just the evil of the demon possessed rapist, or the Satan inspired actions of Tito. Evil is everywhere. Search your hearts. If you allow sin to flourish inside you over the course of years, your spirit will pull away from the light. The kernel of self-deception grows strong over the soul. But God always waits. He could smash the deceit that enslaves us in a blink, bringing us all into His light, but it is up to us to go to him." He paused. "I see you are listening now. Good. As I now have your attention I would feel remiss in not taking advantage of it." He brought his hands together as if in prayer, raising them just so. With pursed lips resting upon his fingertips he resumed his platform. "You are here to learn. As I have said, we Franciscans take our learning very seriously. You will be taught many things. We will teach you to read classical Greek, French and German, and to speak, read and write Latin. You would not be here if you were not somewhat intelligent. Your friends who idled the day away fishing in the river, instead of learning in class are still doing that—*in an Austrian refugee camp!* You are *here*, in the very seat of Christ's Church, on the verge of joining the brotherhood of St. Peter." An abrupt change in demeanor. "To the day's schedule."

With a flick of his wrist and flippant turn on his heels he drew us behind him, walking slowly down the wall to our left. He stopped to admire the first mosaic he came upon.

"The stations of the cross, seven on each side. They represent the sufferings of Christ, depicting his path to Golgotha. His suffering made him pure and unshakeable in his resolve to thwart the temptations of Satan. He *knew* there was a beyond. He had the certainty of real faith. *This is no playground you've come to!* This is a place of training. Christ accepted all that came to Him—e*veryone*, from the pure of heart to a murderer near death. But faith is not easy. Even his disciples swam in the sea of doubt. Peter denied him thrice in an evening only to hold on to this life and avoid the uncertainty of death—forgetting the next life Christ himself promised. Thomas did not believe He was the Son of God until he could touch His mortal wounds after returning from the grave. And Judas, oh Judas. A preordained hell of betrayal." He stared at the ground, his thoughts grabbing him. He whispered to himself, all of us forgotten.

"One could almost feel sorry for him . . . afforded no choice in his destiny . . ." Father Vasilj shook his head, his shoulders stiffened, and his eyes refocused.

"I expect all of you to listen to what I am about to say. The following is your daily schedule."

He began rattling off the events that would shape our days, and hence our lives—beginning with the rise of the sun, and ending well after its departure. As he droned I created a mental checklist of the day in my mind.

    5:30 AM-6:00 AM—Wake-up and dress
    6:00 AM-8:00 AM—Prayer (in church on our knees)
    8:00 AM-9:00 AM—Breakfast
    9:00 AM-12:00 PM—Schooling
    12:00 PM-1:00 PM—Prayer (in church on our knees)
    1:00 PM-2:00 PM—Lunch
    2:00 PM-3:00 PM—Schooling
    3:00 PM-4:00 PM—Study time—in the classroom
    4:00 PM-5:00 PM—**FREE TIME!!**
    5:00 PM-6:00 PM—Dinner
    6:00 PM-8:30 PM—Vespers (in church on our knees)
    8:30 PM-9:00 PM—**FREE TIME!!**
    9:05 PM-9:15 PM—Bedtime

He led us around past the Stations while reciting our schedule. The mosaic Stations of the Cross were very colorful and intricate. I listened with one ear to the Reverend Father as I stared at every mosaic.

The day had been so full. With a hazy direction to bed I chose an unoccupied bunk. Bedtime prayers were mercifully short that first evening and in scarcely any time at all I was drifting off to another land—a certain farm I was familiar with.

The first morning began just as Father Vasilj foretold. Awakened with the flip of a light switch I emerged from the sweet comfort of darkness to the blinding, harsh reality of my new life. After showering and donning our clothes Father Vasilj instructed us to go downstairs for breakfast. I wondered earlier if we would be given clothes when we arrived. We were not. We didn't have uniforms to keep us, well, uniform. Our clothes were a mish-mash collection of colors and fabrics. I was wearing a pair of pants given to me in Andorff. As we filed downstairs and into the dining room I was thinking of the spaghetti I had eaten last night. What do Italians eat for breakfast? I was hoping it would be some delicious morning equivalent of spaghetti. It was not. Porridge is considered a morning staple in Italy, I discovered. So be it-I had dinners to look forward to. When all of us were seated at the long tables Father Vasilj began the Morning Prayer. To start every meal with prayer was a given. I automatically lowered my head. When I ate alone in Ivanjska prayer took a backseat to the meal itself, but not here.

After breakfast we filed through the side door from the dining area and into the church for two hours of prayer. Oh, good! Another two hours of aching knees and numbing, repetitive Latin phrases. It was only eight o'clock in the morning. My God, my God, why hast thou forsaken me?

With the conclusion of morning service we were directed to the classrooms for our first academic step on the road to priesthood. The doors leading to the classrooms were in the hallway Father Vasilj had hustled us through the day before. Father Kozo commanded us to stop. He hadn't spoken much since the train, at least not in our company. It seemed he preferred to do the bidding of Father Brkan or Father Vasilj. He had no qualms about taking charge when it came to us though, his much younger and less formidable charges.

"All boys ten years old or younger go to the classrooms on the right, eleven years and older to the left. Do it now, we have much to learn."

We divided ourselves as instructed. Sitting on my slice of a long bench I waited for class to begin. The classroom was not large. A window on the far side of the room gave a view of the back wall of the cemetery. I wondered why Father Vasilj had been so firm in warning us to stay away from that area.

The desks were better than the ones at Asten. The top hinged on the far side, allowing me to lift it up and store my stuff (when I *got* stuff, I guess). When I peeked under the lid there were some small boxes and what looked like a big feather inside. I would have investigated further but I was scared one of the Fathers would walk in and catch me. There were two benches that sat six each. We all shared the benches but our desks belonged to each of us alone. There were eleven boys in my class. The other three classes held around the same number of boys.

The nuns had hustled the girls away, including my sister Ruska, while we were being given our tour of the grounds. I hadn't seen Ruska since the train station.

The door creaked open. With three long strides Father Brkan was in the middle of the room. Fit as ever, his brown robe flowed in soft eddies on his well-constructed frame. He strode to the middle of the room, coming to a stop with clipboard in hand. His eyes focused on a piece of paper on the clipboard. In a flat tone, he instructed us to call out our names, beginning with the boy sitting on the far right and closest to the hallway door. Names rolled forth in varying degrees of anxiety. I was seated on the far left; closest to the window (and the bathroom), yet not under the scrutiny that comes from front row seating. I had picked up a thing or two from Yela.

As the boy in front of me spoke out his name Father Brkan wrote it down in a ledger, doing the same up the row as they called out their names. Father Brkan had not looked up from writing until he heard the name Berislav Dujlovich. With a slow, measured rising of his head his eyes found mine. I squirmed in my seat, but held his gaze. He dismissed me in a moment-a fly to be dealt with only if it makes a nuisance of itself. When he had completed his class roster he spoke again.

"Inside your desk you will find two boxes and a quill. For those of you not familiar with the quill it is a writing instrument. You will become masters of the quill. It is nothing more than a wing feather from a large bird. The point of the quill is heated then sharpened to a tip. Many of the Church's greatest ecumenical papers were written with the quill. St. Augustine himself used a quill."

He went on to instruct us in its use and maintenance. Inside one of the boxes I found a bottle of ink. In the other was a small, slightly squishy chunk of something I could not identify. Father Brkan was explaining how to use the ink and quill while I inspected the quill and contents of the boxes. He told us what the squishy thing was. It came from a squid. The back of the squid was removed from the body of the squid itself then dried out. He explained the more a quill is used, the more gunked up it becomes. He showed us how to rub the quill against the rough surface of the squid back, and so remove the buildup of ink and at the same time sharpen the point. The hours meshed and before I knew it it was time for prayer again. I was sure I had conveyed the vast majority of my thoughts and wishes to God during the two-hour long Morning Prayer but perhaps I had more to pray on, and for. An hour on my knees and it was lunchtime, a light meal of fruit and bread. After the humdrum porridge of breakfast this was a pleasant surprise.

Afternoon classes lasted an hour. And after another hour was spent reviewing our lessons the best of the day came into being. Free time! On the first day only Father Brkan led us outside and we took another tour. Keeping up with his long legs was not easy. I was in the "eleven and under" class. At nine years old there were boys both older and younger in my group so I wasn't the only one having trouble keeping up. However, the Reverend Father was not concerned with our limitations, and strode forward in confidence we would run to keep up with him if we had to. A few of us did break into a light jog.

Don't go past the gate. Don't go beyond the gravel road. Don't go into the orchard unless you are scheduled to work there. After ten or twelve "don't goes," I tuned them out looking around the monastery grounds. We were approaching the cemetery when he stopped suddenly.

"This place is off limits. The cemetery is for the people of Grottammare. Punishment for going inside the cemetery is severe-unmentionable, really." His gaze chilled me. It did not, however, crush me. I had suffered as a student from the school of 'Dujlovich Discipline', enduring the wrath of Headmaster Joseph. When Father was done with me Yela took her turn. In spite of what I knew would happen to me if caught, I had *still* taken the bottle of *Sljivovica*. This cemetery was not beyond my curiosity.

Our tour concluded at that point. We were instructed to enter church through the dining room side door. Once we were inside on our knees it was time for evening vespers to commence. The incomprehensible Latin chants were made all the more chilling by candlelight wickedly dancing off the mosaic Stations of the Cross lining the walls. The glow and flicker brought sporadic life to the eyes of a dying Christ. The absence of light left pockets of black shadows where *anything* could happen.

The fear of this new life combined to overwhelm me, and in that moment I really *did* pray to God for help. A torturous one hundred and twenty minutes later it was time for bed. However, not before Father Vasilj told us much the same thing as Father Kozo had told us when going to our classrooms.

"Boys twelve and older go to the dormitory on the left. Boys eleven and under go to the right. I will be sleeping in that room." Our dormitories could be entered (and exited) by only one door. The hallway had two doors on the other side of the hall. He pointed at one of them. "That room is mine and I am a light sleeper. These will be your permanent sleeping arrangements. Once in a room that is your room until you leave here or you turn twelve years old. If there are any fights over beds *we* will arrange who sleeps where."

Done with the Reverend Fathers, my bed selected and the lights out my mind turned to memories of my old life. Already they were blurry on the edges. Was it ever there? Did I *really* know how many snakes lived in how many holes? Did frogs *even jump* in the pond? I was unsure of events, what *really* happened and what was simply the residue of dreams. Peaceful thoughts of happy times were increasingly hard to summon. My day began before the sun rose in greeting, and ended well after bidding us good evening. Five hours of every day were spent on my knees in prayer.

Sometimes I asked God questions as if He were an old friend sitting with me. A number of times I asked God if being on my knees was really what He wanted of me. And if so, why? Why would a God who wants his subjects to find joy in worship expect pain and discomfort to be part of this worship? It didn't add up.

Many days drifted together. My weeks did the same, and a year passed. Ruska had long since left. I received two letters from her, replying both times. Her life seemed to be a mirror of mine, at least in the number of hours spent in prayer. To judge by her letters it appeared Ruska was happy. *My* letters painted the picture that I was happy as well. So much for honesty. Neither of us could assume the letters were sent unmolested and God wouldn't help us if we were discovered writing anything negative.

# CHAPTER IX

## "Dark Secrets"

A thousand hours of prayer and equal number of hours in class had taught me much. I knew the devil was everywhere! He lurked in the shadows, always waiting to personally damn my soul to an eternity of flaming agony. My lessons over the last year had taught me Satan is hovering all around us, always eager for a slice of soul pie. Day in and day out the message was always the same. The devil was in a constant battle with God for our immortal souls. The devil, we learned, however, had leverage over God in this spiritual tug of war. Firstly, the devil had home team advantage. We lived and walked in his playground. Secondly, the devil actively sought to corrupt us whereas God left it up to the individual to come to Him. This made things very easy for Satan, the priests explained. Most people are like water, I was told. Water always seeks the easiest path. Satan smoothes the way.

Father Brkan was reinforcing the value of suffering. A boy sitting three seats down from me raised a timid hand. I leaned forward to see who was so bold. It was Ante. Oh no, I thought. He never seems to learn when it is okay to speak and when it is best to remain silent. The bruises under his left eye and most of his right cheek apparently did little to subdue his questioning nature, or prompt his sense of self-preservation.

"Reverend Father Brkan, you speak of suffering. Haven't I, haven't we, suffered enough? I have bruises all over my body. My hands have been whipped so many times I can hardly use my quill. Is this not enough suffering for Him?"

Reverend Father Brkan impaled him with his eyes, walking to him in measured steps and stopping only inches from the desk in the front row. Leaning down between the two boys separating them he pushed his face an inch from Ante's. I recalled Father Brkan's breath, feeling doubly sorry for Ante. It was part of his inevitable punishment, a negative bonus if you will.

"You will stay after class for 'special' instruction." He resumed his teaching as if nothing happened.

We all thought the same thing—we just hadn't spoken it aloud. The Reverend Father's forms of punishment were varied and inventive. I had experienced all of them. Over the last year I had become terrified of these monsters. We all were. They stopped just short of torture. Slapping and hitting was commonplace.

My fingers were still in pain due to my inability to correctly answer a question asked by Father Brkan in class not long ago. Upon hearing my mumbled answer he tersely instructed me to put my hands on my desk. They had to be face forward, palm side down. I did as he ordered. He turned back to his desk, picked up a hefty wooden ruler and returned to stand in front of me. Without fan fair he slammed down on my fingers using the narrow edge of the ruler. He whopped ten times on my outstretched fingers until they were bloody little things. I was not allowed to go to the washroom to wash off the blood. I had to continue with my lessons.

A large willow tree near the front of the church provided an endless number of disposable whips for the priests. It was Father Kadirin's weapon of choice. I knew this from personal experience. My first (of many) encounters with Father Kadirin resulted from my telling the truth during confession.

"Forgive me Father, for I have sinned. I stole a piece of bread from the kitchen. I was hungry and I know it was wrong."

This was one of the few times I really *did* have a sin to report. We went to confession every Friday without fail. To go into the confessional and have no sin to report was unthinkable. I could hear it now. "I see. You are without sin. Is this Christ himself sitting in my confessional?" I was sure the Fathers would not take my declaration of purity as a victory over Satan. I was relieved to hear Father Kadirin tell me, "God forgives you of your sin my son. Say twenty Hail Marys and do not steal again."

I was as relieved as I was naïve. I didn't as yet realize the depth of malice and willingness to inflict pain these priests possessed.

"I will do that right now. Thank you Reverend Father." I quickly and gratefully answered.

I made a hasty retreat from the confessional. It wasn't hasty enough. As I turned away from softly closing the confessional door a viscous tug on the collar of my shirt stopped me in my tracks. Father Kadirin had also come out of his side of the booth. Not saying a word he proceeded to drag me backward by my collar down the side aisle. As my heels bumped uselessly across the flagstones the Stations of the Cross unfolded one at a time before me in reverse order. If nothing else, I was chalking up another session of suffering for His greater glory.

Father Kadirin was a big man. A strong body, but without the form of Father Brkan, he possessed an un-chiseled largeness. A ring of thick black hair crowned a coarse peasant's face. His eyes held fury just beneath the surface on any given day, but at times like this he let his anger reign. Turning to his right after exiting the front of the church he dragged me to the willow tree. Half pushing, half dropping me to the ground he pulled on a long, narrow branch. Gently tugging it he bent it to ascertain the pliability. Satisfied, he had tested two or three until he found "the one". Such a connoisseur. Fifteen minutes later my entire back was a busy map of pain, a network of angry welts. Dismissed to contemplate my sin I made a hasty retreat. I had been under the impression if God forgave me I would be absolved of my sins. I guess I was wrong. At that point I wondered if stupidity is a sin. If so I might as well go back for another whipping. Never again would the truth come so thoughtlessly.

There were fun times also. I still had my slingshot from Asten. I found Italian birds were no faster than their Austrian cousins. I felt twinges of guilt in killing them but not to the extent a confession was required to ease my burden. Less destructive past-times included throwing marbles and playing telephone. To make our telephones we took two small tin cans punched a hole through the bottom of both and then strung a length of twine between them. The vibration of the voice spoken into one can was transmitted on the twine, magically heard and converted by the ear into a legible sound on the other end. It was one of our favorite things to do. Free time passed quickly when we possessed the items required to make them. My first summer during free time in Santa Maria degli Angeli was spent exploring the grounds, with the exception of playing games with other kids. Though curious about the cemetery I had neither explored, nor even seriously contemplated climbing the wall. Well over a year into a four-year curriculum I knew at some point I would see this oh so private cemetery for myself—regardless of the possible consequences.

Whispering to each other late in the evening when the lights were out, talk of the beach always surfaced within minutes. "What was it like? Was the water as cool as it looked?" In our mind's eye we swam and played with fish, reveling in the freedom of the waves. Reality was always a letdown. We were convinced the Fathers would *never* let us go to the beach. It was there Satan reigned. All of that exposed flesh . . . a sea of lust to swim in. Not all, but most of the Reverend Father's teachings and sermons invariably wound themselves around to the subject of sex. Anything of a sexual nature was categorically deemed a sin. According to them men are in a constant state of coveting the female body. Lust is Satan's most available tool. Women, while luring men into damnation, are themselves subject to damnation by virtue of their seductive activities.

At the evening meal Father Vasilj announced we would be going to the beach the next afternoon. I couldn't believe it! We were handed a set of swim trunks as we left the cafeteria that evening. They were all black, knee length and identical. No matter to me. The beach! I was going to the beach! Evening vespers went forward, as did the morning prayers, then class and more prayers until at last it was time to hit the waves! Father Kadirin told us to put our swim trunks on our towels, and then roll the towel up with the trunks inside them. We would be changing at the beach, he said.

We were a line of ants marching down the hill, tripping over ourselves in excitement. I was deliriously happy. Many nights had been spent dreaming of the water so close to where I lay my head every night. What yesterday was impossible had today become a reality with the uttering of a single sentence.

Soon enough we were standing in line at the changing rooms with the villagers. We had been instructed to have nothing to do with them. We were not to answer them if asked a question. We were not to initiate a conversation nor ask any anything of them. We were not even permitted to make eye contact. If a villager looked us in the eyes it was our responsibility to turn away. From their reaction it seemed they were familiar with these rare visits. Not one villager spoke to us while waiting in line. They did not stare at us at all. I felt like a leper. At some point they had learned the rules of these visits as well. My turn came to change into my suit. As I stepped inside the small room and reached for my trunks—horror! A realization of horror! I had *forgotten* my swim trunks! They were lying on my chair at the foot of my bed. I was so excited about coming to the beach I left the *only* item required to make it all happen. I looked around for the nearest Father. Spotting Reverend Father Vasilj, he stood still with his back to us as he gazed a short way up the beach. I followed his eyes and saw a group of young girls building a sand castle. They were between twelve and fifteen years old. One of the girls saw him staring. She looked directly at Father Vasilj. Her smile fled, quickly replaced by a look of discomfort and fear. Glancing quickly to the sand she turned her back on him. I went to him and told him what happened. I begged him to let me get my trunks. Not even looking down, he told me to go and hurry back.

Running as fast as my ten and half-year-old legs would carry me, I raced along the cobbled street, up the dusty road, through the gate, into the cafeteria, down the hallway, up the steps and into-my door was locked! In my anxiety to get my trunks and get back to the beach I gave it a few quick pounds in frustration. The door opened quickly but only halfway. Father Brkan's bulk filled most of the open space. Peeking around him as he opened the door, I saw Sister Anka, the prettiest of the three nuns, lying naked on the beds nearest the door. She was pulling her habit over her body, but not quickly enough. I saw her breasts right before she covered them. Her hair was messed and she was breathing hard. Part of her habit lay on a bed next to her and Father Brkan's robe was on the floor next to it. He had opened the door in a white t-shirt peeking around the opening with his lower half hidden.

"What do you want? You're supposed to be at the beach with everyone else!"

"Reverend Father Brkan, I'm sorry. I forgot my swimsuit," I stammered, remembering something that happened a while back.

Last winter a nun named Sister Theresa had come to live at Santa Maria degli Angeli. She was young and very pretty. Her nun's habit failed to camouflage the curves of her waist, the roundness of her rear end or thrusts of her breast. More than one boy fantasized about what she looked like without her habit on. Shortly after her arrival Father Stephen and Sister Theresa began spending many hours in prayer together. Not in church, but in his bedroom. In the middle of the night I awoke to the sound of a woman moaning. The sounds were low, then would rise in tempo and volume, then subside. At one point I heard a man groan and exhale loudly. I had lived in a three-room farmhouse with blanket walls-I knew *exactly* what was going on. As I lay in the dark listening the door at the far end of the room opened. Father Vasilj slipped inside and closed the door behind him. Walking soundlessly down the row he checked to see that we were sleeping soundly. As he approached my bed an irresistibly strong desire to close my eyes came over me.

Ante, God help him, sat up as Father Vasilj came upon his bed.

"Reverend Father Vasilj, what is that sound? It's scaring me."

The Reverend Father said nothing. He slammed his open hand across Ante's face so hard his body followed his head and he landed on the floor in a lump.

"Sister Theresa has been possessed by the Devil. Father Stephen is trying to draw the devil out of her. Pray for him to have strength, and for Sister Theresa to be free of Satan. These are weighty matters of the Church, beyond the scope of your limited knowledge. We will speak no more of this. You will *never* mention this to anyone. *Ever!* Now go to sleep."

Turning quickly he strode to the door. He turned around to face us just before closing it behind him. "Ever" he said softly. With a click of the doors closing darkness resumed command.

That was many months ago and I was very clear on what the correct response would have to be if I was interested in avoiding a beating.

"We were praying together, Dujlovich. Do you understand?" Father Brkan was bending down close to my face and the same sickly smell of wine and garlic wafted over me.

"Yes, Reverend Father Brkan. I understand," I timidly answered.

"Good. Now, what were Sister Anka and I doing in here just now?" he asked.

"You and Sister Anka were praying Reverend Father Brkan."

"That is correct. Now, get your trunks and go." He was through with me.

I did just that, and even as I was running back down the stairs I heard the door being closed and locked. More praying.

The beach was everything I had pictured in a hundred day dreams. The water was just as blue, the sand just as white, and the girls just as pretty as any of my most fantastic imaginings. Nothing in my life to that point had *ever* measured up in my dreams to the actual reality. But this *did*, and it was paradise. However, in paradise, an hour is a minute, and it ended all too soon. Evening vespers waited for me as I trudged back up the hill. I was exhausted from an afternoon being tossed by the waves and running up and down the beach. I spent vespers praying vespers would end so I could go to bed.

The seasons changed and my voice changed with them. Almost thirteen, I had grown four inches in height but still had a way to go before I could look the shortest Reverend Father eye to eye. The last three years, spent on my knees with the cold stone of the chapel floor for cushion, gave birth to calluses so thick I thought they would never fade. My mind retrieved the correct Latin response for every type of ecumenical service in the Catholic arsenal. I was a sponge, soaking up languages and concepts by the book full. Of the original fifty-two boys that traveled with me from Asten only twelve remained. Over the last three years families claimed many of them. Sturdy backs were needed to man the plow, lift the bales of hay, and in many cases, rebuild destroyed houses and shattered families. In some cases, a family simply ceased to exist-from grandma to wailing newborn. Their lands the spoils of war. In varying degrees this was the case with the eleven others still with me.

Rotation seems to be a recurring theme in the order of all things-from the changing of the guard in the smallest snake hole in a puddle of a farm-pond to the vastness of space itself. Our sun, so vital to human existence, is but a speck of gas enslaved by gravity to dance in a choreographed universal opera. Gods were born in the light of its heat. Civilizations rose and crumbled, fighting for or against the power of its magnificence. Earth, a bit-player in so fantastic a production, had encircled our God-spawning sun almost four times since my arrival on the shores of the Adriatic Sea.

Evil walks among us! As disciples of Christ, we are the chosen ones; those fortified in the eyes of God with the might of the Holy Father Himself lending hand in our bid to cast Satan asunder, freeing His children for a fair shot at salvation.

A young farm girl, living on the outskirts of Grottammare, was reportedly possessed-a captive in the grip of Satan's minions, or even *Satan himself!* Father Vasilj announced during dinner that four of us would accompany himself and Reverend Father Stephen to aid in the exorcism. The next morning they announced their selection. I was chosen as one of the four. Dread and anticipation, fighting siblings, sought equilibrium in my mind. They gave us white robes. Verisic and I were handed large crosses. Instructed to hold them high above us, they were beaten of silver, mounted on the end of a smooth six-foot long wooden pole. They were not ornate but they *were* well polished. I was certain of it. I had spent many hours coaxing forth the luster within. The priests mentioned more than once we all have our crosses to bear, so this was my chance to literally do just that. I was relieved to be assigned as a cross-bearer, as opposed to candle duty. Wind could never extinguish the light of the heavenly cross, but the slightest breath of Mother Nature will snuff a flame. A dying candle made for poor appearance, an omen of ill will to uneducated peasants. *This*, the Reverend Fathers, would not tolerate.

The time came to depart for the possessed one's dwelling. Fathers' Vasilj and Stephen were imposing with their gold embroidered cassocks and heavy gold crosses hanging around their necks as visible signs of power. Obviously, meeting the devil demanded formal wear.

At last we were on our way to save a soul. We were ready; a neat line of four white ducklings led by yet greater finery, gold plumage and all. Facing us, Father Vasilj spoke in as serious a voice as I had ever heard from him and I was around him all the time. I lived across the hall. I shared every meal with him, month in month out, year in year out.

"We fight for the soul of a young girl. Sometimes this can be required of us. Satan is strong-he is not mortal. Swords mean nothing to him-he laughs at bullets. A special soldier is required to fight this enemy-a soldier of *Christ! This* is the type of war you will fight as priests. The eternal battle for God against the evil of Lucifer." He paused a second, looking into the sky deep in contemplation. With a small nod it appeared he arrived at a decision. He continued. "I attended an exorcism as a young seminarian. I was around the same age as you. The possessed was an old widow. I went into the hut where she lived and saw her moaning on the bed. The Fathers sprinkled Holy Water on her. She screamed as if the water was liquid fire. Sitting upright and looking directly into the priest's eyes she spoke in a voice of distilled hatred. The voice was of a deepness no female could ever achieve. It moved about the room, invading every ear with it terribleness. Satan spoke through her, "I will keep mine, you keep yours." Every hair stood up on my body, the chill of the moment has never left me."

The Reverend Father Vasilj paused . . . A slow ten seconds passed. "Chills consumed me and I wanted to run away. But! I drew the strength of God around me. You must now do the same! We battle the Evil One! The farm where the girl lives is to the west, but we will go through the village so they see we fight Satan wherever and whenever it is required. We are there for *them* and they must know it. Follow behind me . . . I will be swinging the censer so it will be smoky. The pace will be slow. This is for the benefit of the faithful. Tomas and Macek, it is not our desire to punish you if the candles go out, but we will. Now we go."

With that we began the longest trek of my life. We couldn't simply walk. We had to *plod*, a measured step at a time, all the way down the hill, through the village, and on the road leading to the farmhouse of the unfortunate. At last reaching the front door, the girl's Mother and Father bid us enter as they pointed to their daughter. She looked the same as any other girl I had seen. She was around twelve years old. When we first came into the room she was sitting by the kitchen table. When she saw Father Vasilj enter the room with censer swinging she gave a cry and ran to her bed in the corner of her curtained area. Surly this was Satan's quite natural fear of God's emissary.

With a grimace, Father Vasilj's eyes assessed the extent of Satan's damage. Taking command of the situation he briskly stated the first order of business.

"First we must bless this house so Satan has no berth when we drive him from the child's body." Looking to the helpless father he spoke gently,

"Now, please, my son, take your wife and go to your daughter."

Father Vasilj began chanting in Latin. I understood every word after years of lessons. Every single word. More than one boy suffered broken bones due to Father Brkan's penchant for the ruler as an incentive tool.

Father Vasilj was blessing the house, asking God to place His favor upon the dwelling. After we blessed all three rooms, the foot of the bed where the girl huddled was our logical destination. With her covers drawn around her neck only her scared face appeared, shimmering in the glow of two timid candles.

The Fathers got right to business. Extracting bottles of Holy Water from their robes they began sprinkling it over her while chanting in Latin for the devil to leave this spirit in peace. Our candles were the only light in the room. The censers smoke created hazy clouds, contributing to an atmosphere of darkness and fear. The girl screamed as they splashed the water on her. She was only twelve and didn't know any Latin beyond the few words picked up in church. Unevenness sought level ground in the cottage. Flailing smoke twirled, candles sputtered, and the eerie chanting drove the girl to the brink of madness. The priests ignored the hysteria building in her. They enforced the will of God over Satan's pawn praying for her soul all the more fervently. After an hour of alternating between splashing Holy water on her entire body and praying over her shivering form the girl settled down and thankfully drifted off to sleep.

Father Vasilj pulled the parents to the other side of the room. He asked them exactly *why* they believed Satan possessed their daughter. They replied their daughter heard scraping and movement in the ceiling. It was only at night and came from directly above her bed.

"Surely this is Satan come to steal her soul!" the mother exclaimed.

The two priests looked at each other. Father Stephen took a candle out of Macek's hand and walked across the room stopping beneath an opening leading to the attic. He climbed the ladder. We waited. He climbed back down with a disgusted look on his face. With an angry glance at the parents he asked Father Vasilj to step outside with him. They were gone for a short time when they reappeared. Father Vasilj now had the same look of disgust on his face as Father Stephen. He went to the parents and leaned into them.

"Why do you store your grain in your attic? Don't you know that mice and bats get in there to eat it? *That* is the scraping and shuffling your daughter is hearing . . . Fools!"

He drew back from them. They were frightened out of their wits. It took Father Vasilj a full minute to compose himself. I imagine he was placing his anger in a compartment that would no doubt be opened by one of us seminarians. I knew him better than I knew anyone in my family.

He turned back to them with another question. "Are there any other reasons why you think your daughter might be possessed by Satan?"

The fear in their eyes was palpable. The husband answered in a hushed tone of voice.

"Sometimes, Satan takes over her spirit when my wife and I are being intimate. It is always then, as if he knows *that* is the time to take our daughters soul. When we are done the Devil leaves her. This has happened for the last year."

He finished. With bowed head he and his wife waited for God's representative to solve this problem. Father Vasilj exploded.

"You are ignorant fools! Your bed is there-behind that wall, yes? Your daughter's bed is here, on the other side of it, is it not? Is there a door? NO!" He stepped back abruptly pursing his fingers to his lips as he did. It was a composing moment. I wish he possessed such control with me. "Don't you make sounds when you make love? Do you think she cannot hear them? Have you explained to her the source of those sounds? *You*-you foolish woman! You moan in pleasure as your husband enters you yet you think *nothing* of your daughter. She is coming of an age when she thinks of things involving the other sex. Nature's forces are beginning to tell her to take a man into her. When she hears these sounds she does not know what to think! You are both ignorant fools and we are leaving. Get the grain out of your attic and store it elsewhere like any right-thinking person. And stop your moaning and groaning when you make love! If you cannot control it then build a wall to muffle your sounds. I will be looking for you on Sunday. I expect to see you on Friday in confession as well. Now, good night."

With that he gestured for us to exit the farmhouse. We promptly headed back to the monastery. This time, there was no swinging censer or measured steps. Father Vasilj walked ahead of us, fueled with anger, propelling him quickly out of sight. Father Stephen adopted our slower pace.

My mind was an angry sea, crashing upon the rocky shores of itself. I was no longer a little boy hugging Yela's skirt. I was almost thirteen! So *this* was our fight against evil? Exactly what *was* the evil we fought? From my point of view, it was the ignorance and fear bred into the rank and file catholic. From their earliest memories they were brainwashed by the Catholic Church into believing God and Satan battled on earth for our souls and *the Church was their only defense*. Natural occurrences took on mystical proportion to the uninformed, illiterate mind. Satan wants your soul. Sin will put you in hell for all eternity. God will let you burn if you sin. To think of sin is the same as committing sin. Pitching the same theme, only the clothing covering the body of their message changed. They heard the same rhetoric, Sunday after Sunday, month after month after year after decade, until death shut out all sounds.

Is the suppression of knowledge a sin? Is the organized effort to keep an entire village in ignorance a sin? A continent? An empire? My answer? Yes. I came to a conclusion-the Catholic Church exercised a program designed to promote illiteracy, *actively* keeping their flock ignorant and uneducated. This, it seemed to me, was a mighty sin indeed.

Morning found me in the blackest of moods. The exorcism had made me ill. The girl clearly wasn't under the influence of Satan. She was simply a scared little girl hearing the midnight foraging of mice. Satan does not come in the form of mice or bats, and sex is not a product of evil. I heard my own parents making unusual noises in the deep of night. Three years of academic study at Santa Maria degli Angeli had given me the ability to understand far more than I would have learned on the farm. I now had perspective. I was learning to read the Iliad in Greek. I was improving in Latin, French and German. I knew many Gregorian chants word for word, note for note. I was versed in the teachings of the greatest theologians in Catholicism.

The people I had seen last night were illiterate peasants. They expected the priests in Grottammare to have answers to *all* of their questions regarding anything they could not see, touch or taste. They didn't simply hope the church had answers. They *expected* it! I learned in my readings it was a system of educational suppression well established at least twenty generations ago. The village girl I had seen last night had no affliction; if anything she possessed exceptional hearing. The modern day priests were victims of their forebear's teachings. The whole subject sickened me.

# CHAPTER X

## "Viva il Papa"

Monsignor Mandich favored us with one of his infrequent visits. He had a dour look about him-the imparting of good news apparently not one of his strong suits. Sitting at the head of the table he spoke softly but we heard every word. The dining room was positively cavernous with only twelve boys' left to fill a space generously seating well over eighty.

"Tomorrow we leave for Rome. Pope Pius XII himself has scheduled a time to receive us. You will see many splendors inspired by God. Among them, we will visit the Sistine Chapel and the Cathedral of St. Paul from outside the wall. You will be walking inside St. Peter's Basilica within two days." He paused. Upon resuming, he looked at each of us, finding our eyes. "I will speak frankly with you, the final twelve." He smiled, the maker of a fine jest. "We will be with you at all times. There will be no wandering off. There will be no unauthorized excursions. You will be in Rome to do two things. The first is to appreciate the beauty and majesty of the church's trappings. The second is to work. You will be serving mass several hours a day every day we are there, which will be one week. You will see and learn much, but this is no holiday . . . There are no holidays for us."

Almost finished he raised his glass of wine in toast.

"To Pius XII! *Viva il Papa*!" Long live the Pope! He stated firmly and loudly.

"*Viva il Papa*!" we replied as we held our glasses of wine aloft. It was customary to drink a glass of wine every night with dinner. It was medicinal in nature, the Fathers had informed us.

We were off to Rome!

A train ride is a train ride is a train ride. There weren't any fingernails embedded in these walls and no blood or feces stained the floor. However, the never-ending click clack of wheel on steel was enormously redundant until the Seven Hills of Rome broke the rhythm.

Rome was a whirlwind of color and sound, unlike anything I had imagined. Its grandeur humbled me. Chills took my back, enjoying a field day in their rippling. Goose bumps grew in flocks on my arms and neck. The first place we visited was the Cathedral of St. Paul from outside the wall. The marble columns fronting the entrance were massive, sculpted twisting affairs. I was confounded at the amount of energy that must have gone into their creation.

That same afternoon, Father Vasilj took us on a tour of the famous statues sprinkled throughout Vatican City. One marble relief reached through the centuries, grabbing first my eyes, then my mind, releasing me only after a full-scale live battle fought itself to conclusion in my imagination. It depicted a battle twenty centuries gone. Hewn from white marble, gold was beaten and woven throughout the entire relief. Death and victory were pounded into the marble with the same ferocity as the Romans dispatched their victims. The cold, pale marble breathed life, a testament to the magnificent skills of the sculptor. His chisel and hammer infused agony into falling soldiers. Rulers were defeated, offering their swords to the Generals of Rome. Forever frozen in victory and defeat these two thousand years legionnaires fought, and battalions fell. I stared and stared and stared some more. The sun was generous that afternoon, illuminating the tears of a dying warrior, flowing in liquid golden light.

The Fathers hustled us along to the next work of art. I had never seen anything as beautiful in my entire life. Rome was worth the visit after all, in spite of the work. Next, we went to the Sistine Chapel. It was a dark, cavernous place. The ceiling was pointed out to me but didn't affect me to the same degree as the battle scene.

My second morning was spent in the church of St. John the Lateran Cathedral, one of many Churches throughout Rome. We shuffled in at five a.m. to prepare for early mass. The trappings of Christ's servants must of course be laid out. It was the same with the wine, the candles, the missals and twenty other things. I was bone tired when the last of the faithful departed. Only five more days in a row of this. I was not swimming in gratitude to the Monsignor for this 'vacation.' Father Brkan informed us we would tour the catacombs after completing our duties. They were close by and in no time we were descending into the tunnels hiding early Christians from persecution by the Roman Empire. The catacombs of Rome are a dark, dank, dismal place. Bones reposed in cavities hewn into dirt and rock. Miles of corridors-miles of corpses.

Several days followed serving mass, then another mass and yet another. The last one took place in St. Peter's Basilica. It is a huge place-I was nothing more than an ant scurrying to my task. Around me five hundred ants did the same. There was a multitude of reasons for how these silent servers came to be here. Some were here to serve and some to receive. Some came to grieve, some to rejoice. For some it was a job-for others, a calling. For many it was a way out of poverty-for a few an escape from the guilt of wealth. With numerous altars serving mass at the same time the vastness of St. Peter's swallowed servers and worshipers without prejudice.

On the seventh and final day I kissed the ring of the Holy Father, Pope Pius XII. I'm not sure if it was the man or the office he held but I felt as puny as one possibly could when I stepped before him and knelt. With a soft version of indifference he accepted my kiss upon the fisherman's ring. One more set of lips in a day with a hundred more waiting in line to do the same. He didn't smile or offer a blessing. He was dressed entirely in white, from silk slippers to silk skullcap. He possessed the eyes of a powerful and serious man. Wire rimmed eyeglasses did little to soften his severe countenance. However, none of this kept me from thinking I was in a holy presence.

This man talks *directly* to God! I was sure this was the closest I ever came to the One that sits in Heaven.

Our return to Santa Maria degli Angeli was as uneventful as our trip away from it. I was a veteran of train rides. Once back we quickly settled into our routine. Mass still began promptly at six a.m. Classes still consumed the day. Free time was still from four to five p.m. Vespers resumed with numbing regularity, and months became a flowing waterfall of time.

# CHAPTER XI

## "Secrets and Bad Habits"

Three and a half years now I slept behind these walls. The priests had taught me many things in the classroom, and many *more* things outside of it. In addition to my proscribed academic curriculum their actions showed me first hand these evils they spoke of in the light of day. In some of the priests I saw a working model of functional hypocrisy. I wondered if Father Brkan considered his teachings regarding the consequences of lust while plunging into Sister Anka. I knew the answer before I asked it. I was quite sure his focus was directed elsewhere.

Despair clung to me with chains that shuffled my steps and shackled my mind. I was sickened at the scope of the Church's manipulations. Their God was not the one I had come to believe in. *My* God, the one I came to know was not a God that approved of exquisitely woven robes, golden chalices and jewel encrusted crosses. My God came from the desert to save our souls. He spoke on a hill and fed the hungry. He helped people believe this world can be a good place to live in. Jesus taught me through the pages of the Holy Scripture that living a life of goodness would generate its own rewards. He is not a God of pomp and ceremony. Nowhere did I read that Jesus wore flowing exotic robes, walked in silken slippers or offered jeweled rings for kisses of obeisance. I was taught that the material trappings of an earthly existence are nothing more than obstacles keeping one from the presence of God. What was true? I saw so much artwork and so many priceless artifacts in Vatican City. I grew bored with them. Scarlet robed Cardinals, bathed and perfumed, strolled the marble corridors of the Vatican. I decided their manicured nails would lend them not an ounce of help in climbing the walls of hell.

Glory! Glory! Glory! I was going to America! Shortly after getting back from Rome at dinner on a night that was a duplicate of the night before and the one before that Monsignor Mandich spoke the words that changed my life.

"It seems the meek do indeed inherit the earth. Your brethren who have gone home to Croatia will remain in Croatia, probably for the rest of their lives. Providence has granted you an opportunity not one in ten thousand people have been afforded."

He raised his glass of wine well beyond the normal height. I was amazed when all of the Reverend Fathers, including that sour puss Vasilj, did the same. "In three months we leave for America!"

The room was silent. My heart was pounding. True joy never comes alone- disbelief is the doubting cousin that tags along. Twelve hands shot up. Twelve questions posed themselves wildly in twelve young minds. My hand was up first. Not waiting to be selected I blurted, "Will we be staying there permanently Monsignor Mandich, or is this a trip from which we will return?"

Father Vasilj glared at me, his pinched eyes hardening to little points of mean. I would pay for this transgression later.

Monsignor Mandich, however, was in an exceptionally good mood, brushing my breach of protocol aside.

"Yes Bernard, it is a permanent move. We leave for Bremerhaven, Germany in eleven weeks. We will board a ship for America and go to New York City. From there we go to Chicago. That is a city in the state of Illinois in America. It is located in the middle of their country. There is a Croatian Commissariat in Chicago. I will supply all of you with details as they are given to me. You see, I will be going to America with you." That explained his good mood. "The Reverend Fathers; Vasilj, Brkan, Kozo and Stephen will be going as well." He added this last bit with less enthusiasm.

I had written several letters to Yela over the years. I did so again with this miraculous news. I never received a reply. I wasn't sure if the letters ever reached her. I was curious that if they did, did she get an opportunity to have them read to her? This was but one unanswered question keeping me awake deep into the night.

Another unanswered question lay beyond the walls of the cemetery. For almost four years I had pondered the wall enclosing it but had never climbed it. Sometime in my second year two boys had climbed the wall and been caught. We never saw them again. Reverend Father Kozo came to the dormitory within an hour of their being discovered. Silently he gathered their belongings and marched out of the room. We whispered into the night. We all knew they were going to try it, but when they got caught our minds ran wild with the possibilities of their fate.

"Has Father Vasilj killed them? Are they even now floating in the Adriatic?"

Exhaustive examination wound us down to sleep. Morning came as we expected it would. As we sat to breakfast Father Vasilj looked slowly about the room. The evening prior we were twenty-eight strong. As of *that morning*, we were twenty-six. Two empty chairs waited in vain for their usual occupants.

Father Stephen looked over to Father Vasilj for the nod to speak. Receiving it, he spoke.

"Dominic and Jozo are no longer here. They are on a train back to Austria. Their inability to follow the rules we have laid down caused their departure. They were discovered inside the cemetery at night. Dominic and Jozo decided to ignore our warnings. That was their mistake. You are aware the souls of the dead can claim your body if you trespass over their grave? It is quite possible even now Jozo's and Dominic's souls are in grave jeopardy." Picking up his fork he let the chill linger on our necks, his eggs more worthy of attention. The morning left me with a deeply embedded fear. Where would I go if I were caught and expelled? Yela didn't want me. My father was dead. My brother might as well be dead. There was no one else. No one!

That was almost two years ago. This morning I argued back and forth with myself. If I were caught I wouldn't be going to America-that was a certainty. But, I asked myself, what would I have done if I had been caught drinking the *Sljivovica*? A severe beating at the *very* least.

In the end, I won against myself. Risk taking seemed to be in my blood. With less than two months to go before I left for America I just couldn't leave it alone. There is no wall that can keep Branko Dujlovich out if he decides he wants in! It was settled. I decided it would be prudent to have at least two other boys with me. One could serve as lookout and the other would come with me. I was not going in there alone. It *is* a cemetery and I *was* going at night. I corralled two friends my own age.

The Church had assigned us a Catholic name resembling most closely our original one. Mirko was now Mark, Berislav was now Bernard, and Livkic now Luke. Alone, with no Reverend Fathers around, Livkic was still Livkic and I was still Branko.

The night cooperated. As if on cue a wind picked up from the sea whipping the branches of the many trees surrounding the building into a frenzy. Tapping the roof and windows with blessed frequency the branches hid our sounds as we crept down the steps, out the side door and around to the waiting supplies. The moon had graciously crept beyond the horizon. Luke stayed on lookout. Earlier I had placed several candles and a length of rope at the base of the west wall of the cemetery. The wall did double duty as the east wall of the main building. The Reverend Fathers could see us from the windows upstairs if we used the north or south walls. I wondered if that was where Jozo and Dominic had erred.

Luke was to whistle like an owl if there was trouble. In no time Mirko and I scaled the wall dropping softly to the ground on the other side. We were in! It was a graveyard. That was all. We looked on the tombstones. No one had lain here longer than a hundred years. Grottammare is not a town the size of Rome. There were no more than a hundred headstones jutting from the ground. What was the secret, I wondered? I looked over at Mirko. He had the same puzzled expression I probably wore. What was the big deal? We decided to look around a little longer. I was investigating on the side away from the building when I heard Mirko whistle softly. Not like an owl-thankfully. I wound my way through the headstones, being careful not to step where Grottammarians lay buried. That *had* to be bad luck. Reaching his side I followed his finger spying a door built into the wall about ten feet above the ground. The door fit into the wall without any means of reaching it. There were no steps leading up, no rungs to climb and no ladder to ascend. We decided to investigate. Retrieving the rope we swung it over a nearby branch, accomplishing nothing. We fiddled about, thinking of a way to get up there. As I strolled through grass deep in "problem resolution" mode I wandered around the side of the small building jutting from the back wall. I tripped on something. Getting up and brushing myself off I felt in the dark for the offending object. To my surprise, I tripped over a ladder. I whistled for Mirko to come help me. We wrestled the ladder from the grass, laying it against the wall to the right of the door. It was quickly decided. I would go first. Mirko didn't look too thrilled about going up the ladder before me. This whole thing *was* my idea, he pointed out.

    I turned the knob of the door after climbing the ladder high enough to reach it. To my surprise it turned, and with a gentle push on the door it swung inward. I was relieved it opened. If it was locked that would have been the end of this adventure. Mirko was getting nervous and wouldn't stay with me much longer. I swung my leg up and onto solid flooring. I was a little nervous at first. The rest of my body followed my leg. I stood up inside the dark room, tip-toeing a few steps. I was afraid it might open into empty space just like outside. Once completely inside the room and no alarms had issued forth Mirko quickly joined me. We decided to light the candles. They performed with predicted success and in no time a soft glow bathed the walls of a small, lusterless chamber. Our first impression was that of a perfectly ordinary room. A little weird that there was only one door for both entrance and exit that opened to thin air but nothing else tweaked our investigative noses. We were about to climb back down the ladder, wrapping up our midnight foray when Mirko tripped in the middle of the floor. His candle spluttered into dark. I hadn't seen anything big enough to trip over when I walked around. I went to him, my lone candle lighting the way. He was pulling on a metal ring set into the floor. With my candle in one hand I offered him the other to help pull on the metal rung. With both of us tugging, the door succumbed to our superior strength. We wrestled it up and swung it gently behind the opening until the bottom side of the trapdoor now lay face up. A smell of decay assaulted our nostrils. We both stepped back. Covering our noses we quickly crossed the floor to the fresh air coming in through the entrance.

    "What is that smell Branko?" Mirko softly asked.

    "I don't know Mirko, but we are going to find out. I will go down first but I want you right behind me! Are you going to do this with me?"

    He nodded, so I quickly went to the trapdoor and lay on my stomach. I lowered my candle into the opening. A ladder shimmered into view. The top of the ladder rested against a dirt wall two feet below the opening. I showed Mirko then took a deep breath. I stepped down to the top rung, gingerly placing foot below foot until I stood on a packed dirt floor ten to twelve feet below. Mirko was true to his word and in a moment stood beside me. I leaned my candle to its side so Mirko could relight his. With both flames lending strength to each other the room glowed in the combined light.

I knew where I was in a second. It was the catacombs of Rome all over. The smell of death was cloying. However, unlike its Roman counterpart, these bodies were not ancient, nor were they adults. Every scattered lump in the hole was a newborn baby. There were around ten or twelve. Some of the corpses must have been here many years. None of them was wrapped in anything. Bones shimmered in the light.

Mirko looked at me in the light of the candles. His face was a silent scream. There was only one explanation. It hit him in the brain and spread numbness through his limbs. He sagged against me-I sagged against him. We were two flies caught in a web of terror.

The stench came from the body of a baby girl. She could not have been down here long. I remembered seeing dead animals on the farm in Ivanjska. Some of them rotted in the woods for months. I saw them decay until nothing remained but their scattered bones. This baby had not been here long.

The base of my neck gave birth to a chill. Growing in strength it rippled down my spine; a master of the vertebraic scale. Sister Theresa had left Santa Maria degli Angeli about two months ago. I remember thinking how sick she looked. Then one day she was gone. I didn't think much of it at the time. Over the years the priests had unfortunately remained the same but I had seen a number of nuns come and go. Now I knew why.

The babies had not been gently laid to rest. It was obvious from how and where they lay that their corpses had been tossed into this room from above.

"We must go!" I choked a whisper in Mirko's ear. We climbed the ladder as quickly as we could while still mindful of making noise. If caught at this point I was sure we would be killed. They murdered their own children so how much mercy could *we* expect? I was in the care of child killers. Mirko and I quickly climbed down the ladder still propped against the outside wall not uttering a sound the entire time. Back on firm ground we put the ladder *exactly* where I had found it.

We both leaned over vomiting. Liquefied dinner dribbled from my chin. My eyes flowed tears and my nose suddenly produced huge quantities of clear goop. I wished the moment away. Never in all the horrors I had witnessed did anything frighten me as badly as this. The dead babies I had seen were not the products of a miscarriage-they were full term infants killed for the misfortune of having a priest for a father and a nun for a mother. I told myself over and over what the priests themselves had drilled into me over the years-hell has plenty of room.

Time became the master of my day. I ticked along minute by minute with the clock in my countdown to leave this place. Any lingering thoughts I had of becoming a priest were as dead as the babies Mirko and I discovered. I thought of little else. What hit me hardest was that *all* of the priests must be in on it. They *had* to be. Why else would *all* of them warn us so repeatedly to stay out of *that* particular area? I had drawn obvious conclusions, and while they consumed my thoughts well beyond their fair share they didn't consume me *utterly*.

I was going to the land of the smiling soldiers and nothing, and I mean *nothing*, could dampen my enthusiasm for what was to come.

# Part II

# AMERICA
## 1951-PRESENT

# Any Part of the World

A strange country greeted me.
Strangers filed past,
Not seeing me.
An ocean of years,
Half fresh laughter—
Half salted tears
Have borne me to this day.

Skirted streets and
Smiles directed elsewhere—
Skittering leaves and
A thousand thoughts
Of nowhere.
Such a crowded room
My minds become—
Alone, yet filled with everyone.

Gypsies danced—
At least I think.
Fires pranced and jingles clinked,
Babies lay in sealed rooms,
Murdered secrets, darkest gloom.
The heart of hearts remains the same,
The core of man remains the same.
The day is just as long
In any part of the world.

Michael W. Goodreau

# CHAPTER XII

## "An Ocean of Change"

The day came at last. With a few quick peeks behind me the twelve of us and the four Reverend Fathers walked through the gates of Santa Maria degli Angeli for the last time. Mile upon mile of rail stretched behind us for three days. Upon leaving the train station in Bremerhaven we found quarters for the night. The Fathers immediately fell upon the task of filling out the mountain of paperwork required for us to leave the country. That didn't keep them from having at least one of them with us at all times. Another day passed as they took care of the details involved in our leaving for America. We went to sleep that night expecting a big day on the morrow.

A cold, windswept morning found me on the edge of an angry North Sea. It thrashed the pier with mindless intensity.

Tug, tug on my sleeve. "Branko, what will we find in America?"

I was silent, conjuring a suitable answer.

"We will find bread Mirko, more bread than we can eat-with jars full of fresh honey, and more milk than your tummy can hold."

My younger friend looked up at me, silently holding my eyes for a moment, then asked,

"Our mothers and fathers Branko, will we see them again?"

My throat closed and my eyes hurt. I felt an unceasingly dull ache of pain, almost as much for Mirko as myself. But I had been through a lot and seen so much, that while answering him with compassion I still provided the unvarnished truth.

"No Mirko, we may never see our parents again."

A tear, sprung from a pool of thousands, grew in size at the corner of his left eye until gravity took command, slipping down Mirko's cheek. A hand swooped up from below erasing its existence.

"Then why are we going to America Branko?"

Replying softly, "There is nothing left for us here." Continuing, I assumed an upbeat note, as much for his benefit as mine. "Everywhere, people talk of America. All of the talk is good. *This* is why we will go. They call America the land of the free. You remember the soldiers, how they smiled?" I asked him.

Mirko smiled at the memory. The two of us stood on the concrete dock facing the water as it smacked in angry rolls against the mammoth gray steel flanks of tied off ships, swaying on thick ropes. At last, we were going to America! The land of baseball and laughing soldiers, the place where *anyone* could become whatever they wanted.

A man gripped the deck railing of the transport ship U.S.S. Blatchford. He wrapped himself around the deck post as if his life depended on it. It did-but it didn't help him. The next wall of water had its way; he was swept into the motion and carried over board. Mirko and I saw four more people follow him. We were three days deep in the North Atlantic Ocean when the storm hit us. Mirko and I were on deck. As we talked the skies were clear, the sea was calm and we swayed with the peaceful roll of the ship. With water diving in protest against the prow's intrusion we leaned over the railing, watching bubbles slap down the length of the ship's flanks as it tore a path through the ocean.

My friend Mirko and I had been through a lot together. We were the only two (other than the priests) that knew about the secret death room. We shared a bond in our forbidden knowledge. He *was* younger, so he did most of the asking and I did all of the answering. We were discussing a game we saw American soldiers playing in Bremerhaven, Germany while waiting to board the U.S.S. Blatchford.

The game had two teams playing on a grass field. There were six or seven GIs to team. The game was played on an open grassy area shaped like a wedge of pie. One player from a team swung a big piece of smooth, heavy looking round wood. A player from the other team threw a ball at him and he had to hit it with the piece of wood. If one of the soldiers from the other team caught the ball before it landed on the grass the guy swinging the stick had to leave the field and another team member got a chance to swing at the ball. They had three chances to score. They scored a point by hitting the ball so far out in the filed that it left the catching area. When that happened everyone whooped and cheered. Usually the hitter would send the ball to an area where one of the GIs in the field could get to it and get the guy running to the safe area. It was the neatest game I had ever seen. There were so many rules I couldn't keep track of them all. I tried, and since I was a little older than Mirko (and smarter, I think) I understood more than he did, so it fell to me to explain the basics of the game-at least as much as I could remember. Mirko was tugging on my sleeve.

"Explain baseball to me again Branko. Why do the men swinging the piece of wood have to quit after three tries? They swing and hit the ball, yet still cannot go around the playing field! It doesn't seem fair!"

I barely heard him. My attention was on a wall of black clouds building on the horizon. The prow of the Blatchford was slicing its way toward the center of it, so the closer we got to the wall the livelier the ship rolled in response to the growing waves. As the Blatchford penetrated the darkness of the clouds lightening strobes punctured the blackness. Mirko and I ran from the deck railing to an open hatchway leading below. We stayed inside the metal walls looking out on the tempest. Hunkering down on the steps we gripped the railing to white fingered bones. A few hearty (or foolish) men decided to ride out the gale on deck.

    I watched the man gripping the deck railing disappear in a wall of liquid anger. Nature breathed into him and granted life; then nature took him and now he was dead. All of his experiences, all of his memories-of loves and children, of sadness and heartache, of death and birth and the million breaths he had breathed were now so much nothing. I realized *I* was nothing in the destruction of this squall in the middle of the North Atlantic Ocean. The four thousand refugees, the entire crew and the ship we traveled in were inconsequential. The Blatchford was a whimsical cork. At length the fury swept over and beyond us, a violence excelled only by its apathy.

    Mirko posed the same question about baseball the next morning.

    "Did you see the white lines of the diamond?" I asked him. "Yes, but you aren't answering my question, Branko! If they get to swing-"

    I interrupted. He is so *impatient*! "Mirko! Stop talking and listen. The ball must stay inside the white lines on the edge of the field. If it goes outside the lines it is a penalty." My well of baseball knowledge was quickly running dry. "Anyway, we will see more baseball when we get to America," I answered with finality.

    I was suddenly very interested in what was for breakfast and leaned forward to get a better idea how long the wait would be. I was standing in a line hundreds of people long. I shuffled a few steps. I stopped. I shuffled a few steps. I stopped. This went on for an hour. I didn't mind at all though. This was paradise! I ate three hot meals a day! Never in my life had this happened. This was our fourth day on the water and most of the meals I ate were different every time.

    As the waiting time drew long tempers grew short. Mini-fights erupted. More shoving matches peppered with nasty comments than anything else, they extinguished themselves quickly. A few selfish pigs grunted their way to the front of the line only to be prodded by American sailors to the end of the very line they were butting in on. I didn't see any of them try twice.

    My turn at last! Holding up my metal plate a sailor plopped a big spoonful of oatmeal in the middle of it. Next, a slice of bread that was, incredibly, white! *White* bread. Not *black* bread.

    I found a seat with the others in my group and immediately began shoveling oatmeal into my mouth as if it were my last meal. It *could be* I thought, remembering that for seven people last night's dinner *had* been their last meal.

    When a clumpy wet spot was all that remained of my oatmeal, I held up the piece of bread for inspection. Tearing a chunk off one corner I looked in the middle. It was definitely white on the inside, but looked a little burnt on the outside. Not much at all though, and not black. I took a tentative bite. It was crunchy with the first bite, but soft when I started chewing it. Delicious! My taste buds would run from black bread after this! When the sailor dropped it on my plate he said, "toast." My piece of "toast" joined my oatmeal in three chomps.

While my fellow seminarians were finishing their breakfasts I took the opportunity to look at the sailors again. I watched them every chance I could. They're Americans after all. These sailors didn't laugh as much as the soldiers I saw in Asten. Some sailors treated us with undisguised contempt. In their eyes we were Europe's trash, and *they* had to take the garbage to their very own country.

They sneered at our ignorance. I saw a sailor pointing at a man three tables down from me. He was nibbling the edge of his piece of toast, not sure of this bread that was not black. I looked back at the sailors. Two of them were aping the man and two more were laughing at their antics. My face grew hot, part in anger and part in shame. It was mean laughter based on a mean act. However, I was no stranger to cruelty and quickly set it aside. I was in a dreamland-I was going to America to actually *live there*! Nothing so petty could dim my spirits.

After breakfast I headed back into the belly of the ship. A small man with a *yarmulke* perched atop his hair-starved crown shuffled in front of me. As I inched around him I looked over. He was very old, his face a map of wrinkles. Thick brows of bushy white hairs sprang out above his eyes. Some of them were rodeo clowns, bouncing this way and that. The folds of his eyelids descended to tear dropped almonds. Threads of white hair sallied forth alone fighting for the privilege of reaching his ears. My gaze drifted to a scar on his earlobe. It was straight and deliberately inflicted. The scar didn't shock me. I didn't know why they did it, but I had seen them before on Orthodox Jews in Andorff.

Our sleeping area was nothing more than a cramped metal room stuffed to the ceiling with beds. It reminded me of Zagreb except this tiny windowless room was a toy box next to the openness of the gymnasium, and here there was no natural light at all. Smoke still curled and created a haze though. I spent more hours than I cared to in the belly of the Blatchford, forty feet below the waterline. We all sweated, the men cursed, and some of the old, especially the tired ones died. They were discovered in hallways, on deck and in their bunks. A few quick words over a sheet wrapped corpse, and with a heave-ho the sea accepted them. This was no different from the trains I thought. At least here we were rid of the bodies.

The sunsets took me beyond the ship, beyond the colors, beyond the water meeting sky and beyond my expectations. The sunsets took me to my imaginings.

Ten days later landfall beckoned! I was on deck at the time. I saw a man pointing south west. He was jumping up and down, yelling repeatedly in a language I didn't understand. I ran to him and tugged on his sleeve. When I had his attention I asked him in Latin if the distant land I saw on the horizon was America. Luckily, he understood me. Halifax, Nova Scotia shimmered in the distance. Upon sighting land sailors swarmed the decks and set about directing any refugees to go below decks to their sleeping berths—"Immediately!"

They didn't have to tell me twice. I ran as fast as the narrow hallways allowed, sliding down the rails of the steps as they lead ever lower. Out of breath I entered right behind two other boys in my group. I climbed up to my bunk and waited to see what was happening. Father Vasilj appeared unconcerned but I wanted to know what was happening, so I climbed back down and with three short steps crossed our area and asked him why the sailors told all of us to come below.

"Bernard Dujlovich, why is it so often *you* who comes to me with questions? Are you never satisfied with waiting for the course of events to unfold, or must you always question what's next, what's next, Hmmm?"

I had no answer for him. I had asked my question. I was due an answer, so I said nothing. I stared at him, and after an uncommonly long thirty seconds he shook his head and answered.

"Bernard . . . the Blatchford is carrying approximately four thousand refugees. About half of them, mostly Jews, will be getting off here in Halifax. Halifax is the capital of Nova Scotia, Canada." Forgetting his irritation the teacher in him took over. "Nova Scotia is a province of Canada, but not always was it so. This place has an interesting history. The first Europeans to land here were Vikings around 1000 AD. The Vikings traveled west, deep into North America, at length returning here and abandoning Nova Scotia in favor of returning to Norway. In fact, the Vikings went further west than Chicago, Illinois, our destination. Five hundred years passed. An Englishman named John Cabot arrived. John Cabot planted the flag of England in the soil of Nova Scotia and sailed back to England. He naively thought his claim would remain unmolested. It *was* the British flag after all-another century passed," Father Vasilj could get windy at times, "when the French shored the beaches a mile from this ship. They named the place Acadia from the Micmac Indians living here prior to the arrival of Cabot and the cursed British a hundred years before." We all remembered Blieburg. Continuing his lesson, "The British showed up shortly after the French to defend their claim. After almost a hundred years of conflict a joint resolution granted Nova Scotia to England. Not long afterward the British expelled all French living in Nova Scotia. They became as many of *you* have been for years-displaced people without a country. The French descendents sailed south, circling Florida in the United States. Florida is a state, like Illinois our destination. Leaving the Atlantic they followed the coastline of a body of water called the Gulf of Mexico. Eventually they came to the mouth of a very large river called the Mississippi. It means "muddy waters" in the tongue of the American natives that used to live along its banks. They are all but gone now, killed off or relocated from what I've read . . . the point where the river empties into the Gulf of Mexico is a swampland, and it is there they stopped. A swamp is a place where the river, land and ocean mix. It is full of fierce man-eating lizards that grow to twelve feet long. Their mouths are so big they can swallow a child whole. The descendents of the original French settlers live in the swamp to this very day. They are called Cajuns, short for Acadians."

He was out of breath, and I was out of breath listening to him. As much as I despised him (he *was* an accomplice to the murder of babies) Father Vasilj had the power of knowledge in the face of my ignorance. My original question was forgotten.

"In answer to your question Bernard, most of the Jews on board will be getting off here in Halifax. A number of our fellow Croats will also be leaving. We will be in New York within two days. Now, question time is over." He turned from me to speak with Father Kozo.

*What?* Question time is over? One question and question time is over? None of it really mattered though. I would be in New York in *two days!* My dream was coming true. I had vowed to myself in St. Martin five years ago that I would get to America, *and it was happening!* The next forty-eight hours could not pass fast enough.

I was leaning on a railing on the deck of the Blatchford, recalling Monsignor Mandich describe the surest way to know we had at last arrived in America.

"You will know you have arrived in America when you see an enormous statue of a woman holding a torch above her head. The Americans call this The Statue of Liberty."

The lazy roll of the Blatchford and a hot, windless summer morning contributed not only to the sweat stains under my arms, but also to my souring opinion of this whole affair. I was sick of being on this ship and impatient to get to America. This was going to go on fore—*there it is!* My complaints evaporated as I spotted the Statue of Liberty. Cheers erupted from every refugee's throat on deck that was not too young to understand, and not to old to not care. I fell safely in the middle and hurrahed with the best of them. Happiness traveled smile to smile, jumping eye to eye. Strangers became friends in the joy of the moment.

When the U.S.S. Blatchford positioned itself alongside Ellis Islands' dock sailors on board threw monstrously thick ropes to other sailors waiting below. The deck of the Blatchford swarmed with refugees; eager people smelling freedom-people just like me. We were being offered a chance to live in a new land with a new lease on life-in the greatest, strongest country *on earth!* At long last, America was a mere thirty feet away.

I was half way down the Blatchford's gangplank, gawking at the scene as I descended. Brick and limestone buildings took up most of the ground and concrete covered the rest. I had walked through the center of downtown Zagreb where greenery was scarce, but here on Ellis Island the earth was almost *completely* covered in concrete. The island itself, and the buildings, had looked insignificant from the ship as we came into New York harbor, so I paid them scant attention during our approach. I had no idea this was to be our destination. However, up close and on ground level, the buildings were large and intimidating. Larger and taller than any other, the Main Registration building was our destination.

After disembarking the ship, men in uniforms moved up and down the line of new refugees. They were busy pinning numbered tags on every immigrant's chest. Father Kozo got the attention of an immigration official when he pointed toward our band of twelve. A mixed lot, Mirko held the young end with the lanky Bartholomew topping out the group. After consulting his papers the official pinned a tag on Father Jozo's ample chest. Handing him the correct number of tags and an equal number of pins, he tugged the tag he had just pinned on Father Kozo and then pointed to us. With a quick nod, the man turned to another chest and pinned another tag on. My eyes followed him. He stopped in front of an orthodox Jew, performed his task, then moved down the line to a Serb and did the same, and so on with a Croat, completing his task with utter disregard to our ethnic origins.

"It's true!" I whispered to Mirko. "Look at that man pinning tags on people. See that, he doesn't care if it's a Jew or a Serb or Croat. It's because he sees us as *Americans!*"

"That's neat Branko, but look at those huge buildings!" He pointed toward the New York City skyline. I had stared at the huge buildings the whole way into the harbor. I couldn't imagine people could build anything so tall.

"Surely they will fall in the first good storm Branko," Mirko noted. Concern clouded his face. He softly said to me, "I'm not sure I want to go into the city."

"Mirko my friend, those buildings will not fall over in a storm. I'm sure they were built by people who know what they are doing, don't you think?"

"Yes, I guess so Branko, but still-"

"Everything will be fine." Changing the subject I pointed toward the Main Registration building.

"That is where we are going Mirko. When we are done inside, and come back out, I think we will be much closer to becoming Americans."

"I'm worried Branko. This is a whole other continent. We are *so* far from home that now we can never go back. I don't know where my family is, if they are okay or *anything*! I don't even know the language here. I don't know-"

Sometimes my friend needed cutting off or he would wind himself into a knot. "Mirko, I feel the same way. So do John, Bartholomew, and probably even Father Vasilj. Be brave! There is a plan, and this is just one part of it. Everything is going to work out."

The line drew close enough to the building's entrance that I could glimpse what was going on inside. It appeared the first order of business was inspecting our luggage. When my turn came the uniformed inspector didn't actually handle the contents, but used a small rod, or stick to move things around. Along with my sad little bulk of a few shirts and one pair of pants my suitcase contained a slingshot, a missal, and a couple of fountain pens with a bottle of ink-that was it. He raised his eyebrows a notch when he discovered the slingshot but must have been confident

America was in no danger from my slingshot, or me, and motioned me down the line. Snaking down a hallway that wound left then up a set of stairs that opened into a very large hall. At that point the thick line broke into a number of tributaries. On the far end of the monstrous hall doctors were prodding and poking every immigrant in a quick physical appraisal. Soon enough it was *my* turn to be inspected and detected. They left almost no part of me untouched. Prodding my chest, the white-coated man worked his hands down my body, a poke and push at a time. Rapping my knees with bony knuckles and swiveling my wrist in every direction, at length he determined I was limber enough to become an American. Motioning me to open my mouth and stick out my tongue I did as he instructed. Pushing my tongue down with a small, flat piece of wood he perused the inside of my mouth. Satisfied, he motioned me to proceed to the next station. The next doctor in line held a wicked looking syringe with a long, glistening needle. Pointed upright, a tiny spurt of clear liquid shot out the end as I stepped up. I kept an eye on the line ahead of me so I knew what the doctor was going to do. Lowering the syringe he slid the shiny silver point into the meaty part of my upper left arm. As he pushed down on the plunger my skin burned on the inside. Blessedly quick he withdrew the needle and handed me a soft white ball of fluffy stuff. I had seen those ahead of me place it on their arms where they received their shot, so before the doctor began to pantomime what to do my fluffy white ball was firmly in place. The last stop in line was the worst. Ahead of me, men and boys alike suffered the same powdery fate. My line passed in front of a man waiting with a scoop of white powder in his left hand. If the person stepping in front of him didn't move fast enough he reached out with his right hand, pulling the front of the persons' britches towards him (none to gently) and dumped the scoop of powder into his private area. My hand was poised to beat him to the punch, so when my turn came there was a generous open area for him to dump his scoop of mystery powder. I had no idea what this was for, but I knew instinctively that *not* going through with it could lead to serious consequences. My instincts also told me this place would not tolerate tantrums and disturbances. They were taking *us* in, not the other way around.

At the first moment I could do so I asked Father Jozo what the powder was. He was as fat as ever. It seemed American food agreed with him. Never one to give a free smile he answered in typical Grottammare fashion.

"The powder is to kill lice, but those in the care of the Holy Church need not fear lice. Those who lead evil lives contract the bugs through lust and sloth. I have answered your question Bernard. Now be silent."

His attention shifted, but I was not unsatisfied with his curt answer. Lust and sloth aside I did get the information I was looking for. It was delousing powder. Okay, that I can accept.

Hours of further processing led us out of one building and into another. We needed this paper filled out, and that form to be signed. With all the bureaucratic requirements satisfied we boarded a ferry to take us to New York City in the United

States of America. The U.S.S. Blatchford had punched my lifetime ticket for boat rides, so the ferry itself offered nothing of interest.

The view, however, was a different story. Mirko *was* right. The buildings of New York City were impossibly tall. One building in particular dwarfed the others hovering in its shadow. It was so tall it seemed to scrape the belly of the sky. A forest of buildings competed for attention, and all but one fell pitifully short. From Mirko to Monsignor Mandich, the sheer immensity of the New York City skyline captivated us.

The Reverend Fathers had not worn their Franciscan robes since leaving Germany. The Blatchford's crew was non-discriminatory in their treatment of refugees, hence the Fathers had nothing to gain by proclaiming their piety. However, before leaving the ship Fathers Kozo, Vasilj and Kadirin followed the lead of Monsignor Mandich and changed into their brown robes.

Monsignor Mandich had faded into the background the duration of the overseas trip. It appeared Monsignors in the Holy Roman Catholic Church did not travel in the belly of transport ships, but held quarters elsewhere. With the exception of a few meals we rarely saw him. Day-to-day supervision of the eleven other seminarians and myself varied little from Grottammare. Father Kozo remained the same rude, unkind fat man I had first seen in the headlights of the transport truck in Asten five years ago. Father Vasilj retained the smallness of an insecure man, ever the vitriolic spirit. Father Kadirin had not factored strongly into my daily schedule (hence, my life) in the early years at Grottammare. His supervision of the older group occupied all of his attention, but as my fellow seminarians returned home to plow the fields of Croatia I began to see more of him. He was a quiet man, but I still remembered the whippings he had inflicted so enthusiastically. My heart held no place for him. Father Brkan had fallen in love with a married woman. But Sister Anka, married to Jesus, loved Father Brkan in return. They departed for Argentina around the same time we left for Bremerhaven.

# CHAPTER XIII

## "Dreamland"

My feet now stood on the soil of America! I was not on an island, but in New York City, America! Elation and fear strolled hand in hand within me. Looking around I saw I was not alone in my feelings. I looked at Mirko, and of course *he* was scared, his face a roadmap to Fearsville. Even Monsignor Mandich, trying to act as if he hit New York on the weekends, gave himself away, craning his neck in awe the same as any 'old country' bumpkin among us.

"Welcome to America!" a voice proclaimed in Croat. Turning to the source of this greeting I fixed my eyes on a well-groomed man dressed from head to toe in black. A rectangular white collar was the only color deviation. It was the first time I had seen such clothing, so I wasn't sure what his business with us was. I looked into his eyes, finding kindness. He was of medium height with light brown hair. His lips turned to a smile and the ready lines his smile gave birth to showed they had formed the same pattern many times before. His brown eyes sparkled with amusement. Examining our group, it was an inquisitive perusal, quite opposite the cruel looks of the sailors or the contemptuous glances of the Reverend Fathers.

He inspected us-we inspected him. America sees Europe; Europe sees America. We both liked what we saw. He spoke first, the quicker draw against sixteen.

"My name is Father Cuvalo. Again, welcome to America on behalf of the Croatian Commissariat in Chicago, Illinois, and the National Catholic Welfare Committee. Both have worked hard to bring you here. These things are not without monetary cost, however, we will discuss this later. So! This is your first day in the United States of America! I think we should get you cleaned up and into a set of new clothes. A warning! The cars here travel very fast and there are more on *one* street than all of the cars you have ever seen in your entire lives. It only takes one to kill you. Stay behind me and walk when I walk, stop when I stop."

Turning to Monsignor Mandich, Father Cuvalo addressed him with the respect due his ecclesiastical seniority, while at the same time maintaining authority over the entire group. This was no small feat where it concerned Monsignor Mandich. I knew him to be a cold, ruthless administrator-a man who must *always* be in control.

My family's sheep in Ivanjska received more unsolicited care than he ever displayed for me. It was his job to educate us, his job to see we did not starve. I wasn't sure if he had knowledge of the death room, but logic dictated he did.

"Monsignor, please have two Fathers follow the boys."

Monsignor Mandich did as Father Cuvalo requested with 'nary a feather ruffling in protest. The good Father Cuvalo had not lied about the number of automobiles we would see. They were everywhere! An army of them careened the wide streets. Horns blared and people leaned out of their windows, yelling back and forth. I didn't have to understand English to know they weren't exchanging pleasantries. We approached a point where two of these car-filled streets came together.

Father Cuvalo's voice, "This is an intersection!" reached my ears over the din of revving motors, people talking, people yelling, car horns blaring and sirens wailing. He also said that while New York City was indeed New York City, it actually had something called 'boroughs' within it. Boroughs, he explained, were 'municipalities' within New York City. A street divided some boroughs while others shared a river as their border. Brooklyn, he told us, was the name of the borough we were currently in. We waited for the 'traffic light' to turn from red or 'stop' to green, or 'go.' Father Cuvalo is a teaching machine.

Two American girls around my age giggled to a stop, standing beside me while waiting for the light to change. They wore bright, crisp looking clothes. There were no holes or frays in them. No imperfections marred their shoes, stockings, blouses, hair, faces or smiles. They were the most beautiful girls I had ever seen. One of them looked me in the eyes asking, "*Ddhw'eudn, skdk'spjfkm sdffcid sfewqr?*"

"Huh?" was all I managed. My tongue grew thicker than speech allowed, and my throat constricted, determined to keep sound in and air out. My command of the English language began and ended with 'okay'. I remembered the one word I knew and garbled it out "Oh-kay."

They giggled. It was not mean laughter, but it wasn't comfortable either. Father Cuvalo must have heard the short exchange. He touched my shoulder, telling me the girl asked if I had just gotten off the boat. He told me by answering okay, I had essentially said yes. This was my first encounter with an American girl. They were so beautiful I couldn't breathe. Their clothes were so colorful and clean, I felt ashamed in my threadbare shirt. Worse, my frayed pant cuffs didn't cover up my clunky shoes. Their smiles brightened the world around them. Their eyes were pools of joy, security and peace. Both girls' perfect, sparkling white teeth completed the vision of dreamland beauty. The traffic light turned to green, and in a mishmash of heads and backs the crowd swallowed them and they were gone.

Father Cuvalo had firm control of our sixteen strong group. Leading us across the intersection I craned my neck, twisting around interfering bodies to see where the girls had vanished. One more look was all I wanted! Alas, it was not to be.

I vowed I would meet an American girl and marry her. This was the land I wanted to be a citizen of, the land I wanted to make a living in, and it seemed logical I should have one of these beautiful American girls to share it with. I had no idea what her name was, what she looked like, or the kind of person she was, but I knew she was out there somewhere and I would find her.

However, as Father Cuvalo had kindly pointed out to us, our clothing was less than acceptable attire in our new country, likewise our hair. We sported immigrant mops-hair grown wild; reveling in the absence of discipline only a pair of scissors can instill. As such, he proclaimed our first and second destinations would be the barbershop followed by the clothing store.

The sidewalk swallowed seventeen Franciscans with ease, along with ten thousand other people. Storefront after storefront slid past my view. Some I could see inside of, and some I couldn't. I came upon a solid wall of glass at least ten feet tall and twenty feet long. It must take a whole bolt of cloth to cover these windows I thought in passing. I really wanted to see what was going on inside, so I risked a quick stop. I put my face very close to the window. Reflections vanished between my cupped hands and I immediately pulled back in terror, bumping into the substantial bulk of Father Kozo.

"What *are* those creatures?" I stammered, moving back from the window. Father Kozo grabbed my shirt collar, yanking me around to face him. Our entire group stopped at this point. Father Cuvalo turned to see what halted our progress.

Here we go again, I thought to myself.

"You! Why am I not surprised? What are you doing Bernard? We are on a schedule here, and Father Cuvalo is in no mood to be delayed due to your foolishness. When we get to the rooms I-"

"Please, Father Kozo, thank you for your concern for my schedule." Father Cuvalo had walked back to the two of us just as Father Kozo warmed to his roasting. He placed his hand upon Father Kozo's, gently lifting it from my collar. Leaning down to my level he pointed toward the windows asking me what I had seen.

"Reverend Father Cuvalo, there are monsters in that building! They sit in strange chairs with huge cylinders covering their heads. They're probably there to feed their brains or something. Each cylinder has a tube running from their heads into the wall. We must leave! This place is full of creat-"

"Your name is Bernard, yes?" Father Cuvalo placed a strong hand on my shoulder, squeezing it so gently it did not hurt but firmly enough to let me know it could.

"Yes, Reverend Father Cuvalo," I stammered. The old fear came back.

I knew what I was talking about though! Space aliens could be out there! They could be *here*! I remembered many of the things I was taught. The universe is a very large place. Father Vasilj's words came bouncing through the years off the walls of my classroom at Grottammare. "Copernicus, born Mikolaj Kopernik in fourteen seventy-three, was a genius. He was ordained a Canon, an interpreter of Catholic law, at *twenty-five years old!* Focusing his attention on the celestial heavens, after his personal wealth was assured, he proved to the scientific community, as well as the Holy Roman Catholic Church's satisfaction, that all of the planets are in a massive rotation around the sun. One more example of the wisdom and laurels God grants those who follow Him." Father Vasilj's granite voice vanished in the gentle admonition of Father Cuvalo, bringing me back to New York City in the blink of a thought.

"You needn't fear the 'creatures' inside this store young Bernard." He said. "They are only women getting their hair styled." He stepped back, glancing at a sign above the top of the glass wall.

"This place is called 'Lee's Beauty Parlor.' The cylinders you saw on their heads are called hair dryers. The women have small tubes, or 'curlers,' wrapped in their hair then they heat their hair quickly under the dryers. When their hair is dry the curlers are removed. The quick drying process allows the hair to retain the intended curl. As for the tubes you saw, those are the electric cords that power the heater to warm the air and the blower motor to push the warm air around their hair. So you see, my inquisitive young seminarian, there is a logical answer, yes?"

"Yes, Father Cuvalo. Thank you, Father Cuvalo." His hand still gripped my shoulder. He leaned down again, this time very close. With his lips brushing my ear he whispered,

"There is nothing wrong with being curious Bernard. Those without curiosity learn nothing of interest, only what life requires of them to continue living." A firm squeeze on my shoulder and he was back to the front of the group. Turning to face us he spoke loudly. "If young Bernard will allow us," a fleeting smile directed to me, "we will go to a barber shop for your haircuts. In America, men go to barber shops and women go to beauty parlors. What Bernard saw through the window was a beauty parlor for women. I have been in America for twenty-two years. I have learned this country, new as it is, has many traditions and cultural distinctions. Beauty parlors are only for women, and barbershops only for men-one excellent example. It would be unthinkable for a man to get his hair cut at a beauty parlor, and even more so for a woman to sit in a barber's chair." He paused as if unsure whether to continue. He did. "This country is so unlike any place you have ever been, it will take *years* to feel as if you fit in. There are so many choices to make that your mind will become numb from the options. I went into a drugstore last week to purchase a razor. I counted eleven styles within several 'brands'. A 'brand' is a product produced by a particular company. The brand of razor I purchased was a Gillette." He paused, "Choices, so many choices." He glanced across the street.

"See there! Look at the yellow and red sign." He was pointing directly across the street to a sign above another glass-fronted store. "The sign says 'Lisa's Hair Salon.' This is what I'm talking about. A 'salon' is another name for a beauty parlor. On this side of the street is Lee's Beauty Parlor, on the other side, Lisa's Hair Salon. They both style and cut women's hair, yet they compete less than fifty feet from each other and both survive as a business. *Now* do you understand the enormity of choices in this country?"

Apparently enough heads nodded in the affirmative to satisfy him.

"To the barber then!" He turned, setting a brisk pace. We followed as best we could, dodging people walking the opposite direction. At length he stopped in front of yet another set of glass walls. A red and white striped pole twisted in a never-ending downward spiral inside a clear, round glass tube. I had never seen anything like it. It tricked my eyes. I wanted to look above it to see if more tube was coming from somewhere, and below to see where it all went. Logic quickly kicked in. I realized the spirals were simply painted stripes on the spinning tube, but nonetheless, it still sought to trick me. It confounded Father Kozo as well, judging by his puzzled expression. Father Vasilj had to nudge him along. He went through the barbershop door with one last look at the neat spinning thing.

In Croatia barbers are respected members of their community. Dropping tidbits of wisdom as they worked they supplied not only a haircut but often helped their customers with completely unrelated issues. I was expecting the same in America, but it was not to be. We were sheep waiting to be sheared. The seat was never warm from one butt, so fast did we move on and off the barber chair. *ZZZZzzzzZZzzz* . . . clumps of my hair floated to the floor. Like Mirko, Bartholomew and Jacob, my haircut lasted under two minutes and then I joined my close-cut brethren in the 'finished' line. Due to the efficiency of the barbers in twenty minutes all of us were done and on our way out the door. We sported the same style of haircut from Father Vasilj to Mirko. We are not so different, eh? I wanted to ask Father Vasilj. Oh, to have the courage to say that to his face. I recalled a Latin expression from class. "Discretion is the better part of valor." I understood the relevance, holding my tongue. Father Cuvalo opted to avoid the barber's chair for a gentler set of shears, so now we looked even sillier next to him as if the tattered clothes were not enough.

Impossibly large! Impossibly tall! Too many people! Too many cars! How can this place be? So much wealth! Everywhere I looked, jewels sparkled on the thin wrists and slender necks of beautiful women. A woman in a flowing white dress strolled to a waiting limousine. Turning around, I watched her look around. She saw me, but didn't see me. Quicker than a blink her mind dismissed me so her eyes never had time to register disdain, pity or interest. Newly arrived from Europe our clothes and hair, our gawking and craning necks marked us for what we were-immigrants.

Father Cuvalo was ever the teacher. "America is a place with narrowly defined windows of what is *perceived* as success. Particular hairstyles, certain fashions in clothing, 'correct' ways of speaking, these are the benchmarks upon which Americans judge each other. Speaking of clothing, this brings us to our next destination."

Father Cuvalo was leading us down the bustling sidewalk. It seemed he never tired of teaching.

"We are going to a department store. A department store is a place where they sell *everything*. It will be necessary to take a 'cab'. A cab is a car for hire to take you wherever you want to go—*if* you have the money. In New York, there are more cabs than privately owned vehicles." He pointed at a car painted bright yellow. I had seen a bunch of them on our short walk. I didn't know only cabs were that particular shade of yellow—I just assumed it was a popular color for cars. The whole concept of being able to hire a car to take me wherever I wanted to go boggled my mind. What a country!

Father Cuvalo raised his hand toward the street, waving at the yellow cars passing by. He whistled loudly. A 'cabby' pulled over with a sharp turn stopping directly in front of us, then hopped out and opened the doors for us. Father Cuvalo told us a cabby was a man who drove a cab. Makes sense I thought as we piled in. Seventeen people required two cabs. We sat atop each other even so. I was squished somewhere in the middle, the meat in a seminarian sandwich. Father Kozo, thankfully, was in the other cab. God *does* love me I thought.

The cabby, glancing at us in the rear view mirror shook his head at the solid wall of heads, arms and necks. With all the doors shut he accelerated violently into traffic. The other cabby followed as best he could. After crossing a wide bridge over a river called the East River we hit serious traffic. I assumed Father Cuvalo had enough sense to inform both cabbies of our destination prior to our departure. The trip from Brooklyn to Manhattan frayed my nerves. The cabby, obviously Italian, was not so different from his native countrymen. He swore at other drivers, cussing them out in staccato Italian for cutting him off or driving to slow. He smoked like a chimney, puffing nasty clouds throughout the cab. Stopping and going for next to forever, at last we pulled up in front of a massive building. I counted at least ten or eleven rows of windows stretching straight up. Once we disgorged from our yellow caravan we gathered on the sidewalk in front.

Father Cuvalo quickly hustled us around him. Concern clouded his features until he had a complete head count of sixteen. Relieved he looked up, pointing to a huge sign. He told us Macys is the name of the store.

"Macy & Co. is an excellent example of American success. The founder of this store, Rowland Macy, was an immigrant like yourselves." He pointed straight up. The facade of the building stretched up to where the roof was not even visible. "Eleven floors of goods for purchase-everything from camping gear to drills to gloves. Rowland Macy began this business in Eighteen fifty-eight. The red star on the front of the building is the company trademark. It is the likeness of a tattoo Rowland Macy had on his own body. For many years Macy's was the largest retail store in the entire country and he retired a very, very rich man. When we go inside you must stay with me. Even people who shop here often have gotten lost so large is this store. We will be going to the boy and men's clothing section. It is upstairs. Now remember, stay *with* me." Turning to the store he walked to the entrance.

I looked around at the rest of the group. Father Kozo registered the same blank look I'm sure I wore on my face. The opening Father Cuvalo was entering was a large spinning thing that had sections of glass panels fanning out from a round column in the center. The glass panels created a triangular space between each of them. As a person entered the slowly spinning opening on the right, another person came out on the left. It was incredible! Father Cuvalo had taken position to enter as an opening presented itself. He entered, and was gone. All sixteen of us stood outside. No one made the first move to enter the building. Twenty seconds became thirty. As we watched the rotating doors accept and disgorge people in a continuous circular motion Father Cuvalo re-emerged. With a slightly exasperated look on his face he walked over to our group and explained the process of entering the building. We must have looked like dolts with our newly trimmed hair and ragged clothes staring in fear at a doorway.

"My fellow Croats, please pay attention to me. This," he pointed at the spinning glass opening, "is called a revolving door. There is nothing mysterious here. Simply wait for an opening to appear and enter at the correct time. Push on the bar in front of you, and in two seconds you will be inside! You must push the bar. This door is people powered—not electric. Do all of you understand?" It was not a rhetorical question. I mumbled a yes with the rest of my group. Father Cuvalo again went through the revolving door and this time Father Vasilj followed him, disappearing inside as well. The mystery cleared up, we pushed and maneuvered our way inside.

Once inside the store Father Cuvalo grouped us yet again under his vision.

"We will be going upstairs now. Just follow me and everything will be fine. He was beginning to realize the extent of our fear and uncertainty. He led us to a set of stairs leading up. My eyes were not tricking me! These stairs moved! He hopped on a step as it appeared beneath his feet, standing on it as it carried him to the top. Now what? I was unsure of this new contraption along with everyone else. Monsignor Mandich, however, was through feeling like a clown, bravely stepping on the moving stairs only to be carried up and away. The rest of us, however, were not so confident. We huddled at the bottom as people stepped around us to go up. I saw Father Cuvalo at the top looking down at us. Frustration painted his face an angry red. He hopped on an opposite set of stairs to bring him back down. He yelled at us as he approached- his temper gaining ground on his patience.

"Fools! This is called an escalator. It is not magic, just basic engineering. Escalators are everywhere in America. Lose your fear and follow me! We still have much to do, and if we have to stop every time we come to something 'scary' then we will never get it all done!" Regaining his composure he continued. "Listen to me. I told you America is like nothing you have ever seen. I did not lie. You must trust me in this. You have been trained to use your minds. I ask you, is it logical to be afraid of something that is obviously used by many people? Would they not be afraid also? Think about it as you *go upstairs.*"

He stood at the entrance to the escalator, waiting for us to conquer our fears, and only got on after the last member of our group had done so. I was as unsure as the rest of my group. Gingerly sticking out a foot, when it caught a step I reached for the handrail (that also moved!) and held on until I felt sure this 'escalator' would not harm me. It was just starting to become fun when the steps disappeared into the floor and the ride was over.

The new clothes were crisp and uncomfortable. I was accustomed to materials that, if not soft, were not crunchy in their newness. My white shirt (the whitest white I had ever worn) tucked neatly into a set of creased blue trousers. Black shoes and socks completed my outfit. I was dressed the same as my eleven fellow students. The new clothes thrilled me and I vowed to take good care of them. It took an hour to get us all outfitted. When we left Macys the escalator was nothing to fear and I hopped on it like a veteran American.

"Okay, you have haircuts and new clothes. Now we need to get cleaned up for dinner." Father Cuvalo glanced at a timepiece on his wrist. "It's almost five o' clock. We will now go to the hotel for the evening. You will be able to take showers and relax. I'm sure this has been a big day for all of you." He led us down the sidewalk. "No more cabs today! We will have to walk twenty blocks to our destination. Please remember to stay with the group."

Twenty city blocks is a lot of walking. By the time we arrived at our lodgings my feet were as worn out as my mind. Father Cuvalo spoke with the front desk clerk. It was obvious we were expected. The attendant handed Father Cuvalo three gold keys after a very quick talk. Up the stairs and down a hall we went. Doors, identical except for different numbers painted in the middle of them, stretched before us, then behind us. Father Cuvalo looked at his keys, then at the numbers on the doors. When he found a match he handed Father Vasilj one key and Monsignor Mandich another. Keeping the third for himself we quickly divided into three groups and entered our respective rooms. An hour passed before it was my turn to take a shower. When all of us were clean and settled Father Cuvalo (I was lucky enough to be in his group) turned on the 'television.'

I had glimpsed televisions in some of the store windows during our walk to the hotel, and had seen them a few times before coming to America, but they were still fascinating to me. As Father Cuvalo changed the 'channels', as he called them, he stopped turning the knob when a baseball game appeared on the screen.

"Look Branko! Baseball!" Mirko nudged me in the side, leaning into the television. It was the same game we watched in Germany. Except here it was on television! The man swinging the bat hit the ball with a solid smack. The ball traveled to the edge of the field disappearing over the back wall. He ran the bases at a leisurely pace, crossing the home plate to the roar of the crowd.

Father Cuvalo noted the player. "You see the man who just hit a home run? His name is Jackie Robinson. He plays for the Brooklyn Dodgers. They are a baseball team from where we were earlier today. The fact that Jackie Robinson is playing professional baseball is amazing-a breakthrough in America. You can plainly see, my young friends, that Jackie Robinson is a black man—the first one to play professional baseball." He took a breath, about to embark on an extended lesson. I was learning he had endless lessons to impart. "The truth is, America is not so different from any other country. It may be the best place to live but there are ruling classes here, just like anywhere else. In America the white people are in charge of everything. Most black people are very poor because they aren't allowed to get good jobs. When they do get a job they are often paid less for the exact same work as a white man toiling right next to him. In the deep south of this country blacks cannot use the same restroom or eat in the same restaurants. They are required to sit away from whites on public transportation and cannot attend many of the colleges. In nineteen forty-eight, just three years ago, a man from a southern state named Strom Thurmond ran for president of the United States on a segregationist platform. He advocated the complete separation of blacks and whites in society. In the northern part of the United States he is considered a 'bigot' or 'racist'. In the south, he is regarded as a hero. I don't think the American people will allow such a man to remain in any position of power." He paused, gathering his breath. "Ironically, many rich and powerful men from the south, while treating blacks like property, have fathered children by female servants employed on their family estates. But I'm sure *that* sort of thing has stopped. Even one of the founding fathers of this country, Thomas Jefferson, had children fathered by a black woman. Remember, slavery existed in this country less than a hundred years ago, and in the South very little has changed. After the American Civil War of 1861-1865 slavery was abolished throughout the entire country." A breath. "Blacks were freed from their white masters only to suffer another form of enslavement-poverty. They still lived on plantations. The cotton still needed picking. They served their former masters in every way as before but with two exceptions. The first and most obvious one being they could now come and go as they wished, as opposed to being hunted down and hanged from the nearest tree should one of them make a dash for freedom. A more subtle difference was the new responsibility of being a wage-earning employee. As slaves their masters had provided most of the items they needed. As wage earners they now had to procure these things for themselves. Pots and pans, cloth for clothes, needles to sew the cloth, all of these things cost money. Who do you think owned the stores to sell these things? A yard of cloth would cost a white woman eighty cents. The same cloth in the same amount would cost a black woman one dollar and sixty cents. On the pitiable wage they were paid there was no room in the budget for anything beyond the necessities required to survive. With no chance to save money there was no chance for a better life."

All of us followed his words with rapt attention except Mirko-he remained fixed on the television. Father Cuvalo was not finished.

"Little has changed in this country. In America money is freedom. If an opportunity for a black to make money is not available then in essence, they become slaves again. None of this is fair, yet it is a part of America which you will see more clearly the longer you are here."

Father Cuvalo decided we had absorbed enough for one day. Instructing us to find a patch of floor and go to sleep we willingly complied. The carpet smelt a little but the hotel had provided us with extra pillows and thin blankets. Being summer, the blanket was not needed as a covering. I stretched it out on the floor lying on top of it. Others followed suit; in no time the lights were out and I drifted off to sleep, my mind running over my first day in the United States of America.

A blink later the morning sun intruded on the darkness of our room. At six o'clock Father Cuvalo rousted us. I was already awake, rearing to start the day, as were the boys close to my own age. Bartholomew, older than most of us, kept snoring, only groaning when Father Cuvalo singled him out by gently nudging a foot into his ribs. How can he sleep so soundly? There is so much to do!

Soon we were dressed in our new duds and gathered in the hotel cafeteria for breakfast and prayers. After both were completed Father Cuvalo rapped his fork against his juice glass to get our attention. He quickly had it. All of us looked upon him as our lifeline in this strange land. I didn't know the language and could not read a word of English. The same was true for all of us. To a lesser degree the Grottammare Fathers were passengers on the same ship, the U.S.S. Ignorance.

"Today will be another busy one. We will be taking cabs to a Catholic orphanage in Sea Isle City, New Jersey. New Jersey is a state, the same as New York."

What? I thought New York was city! I raised my hand.

"Reverend Father Cuvalo?" I asked.

Father Cuvalo looked at me. "Yes Bernard, how may I help you?" he replied; resigned it seemed to my inquisitive nature.

"Reverend Father Cuvalo, I thought this was New York *City*. You just said it is a State. I thought cities were *inside* States and States made up America. Is this not so?"

"I see someone pays attention. Bernard, there is no rhyme or reason to why cities and states are named. You are correct though. This *is* New York City. New York City is a city *in* New York State. I know it sounds strange. There are even towns named after other states. For example, there is a town in the state of Missouri called California. California is a state at the western edge of America bordering the Pacific Ocean. There is even a town in the same state of Missouri called Mexico-another *country*! Now, back to the days schedule." Question time was obviously over and I decided not to test Father Cuvalo's patience. He quickly returned to his original topic. "Due to logistics we will spend approximately two weeks in Sea Isle City, New Jersey before leaving for Chicago, Illinois. When we get to Chicago you will stay at the Croatian Commissariat for a brief time before going to your new home, St. Joseph's College in Hinsdale, IL. While at the Commissariat you will be working in the printing shop-but I get ahead of myself. In twenty minutes we will convene in the lobby where brothers will be waiting to drive us to Sea Isle City."

Another car ride, this one longer than the last. The August sun was unforgiving, blasting us with pure heat. A sweaty, sticky hour melted away when Father Cuvalo tapped the shoulder of the priest driving the car saying something in English while pointing ahead of us. The driver nodded and we pulled into the parking lot of the building. Father Cuvalo told us to get out. We did. We stood on the blacktop wondering what was amiss.

Father Cuvalo enlightened us. "In America there are many places to eat and drink. We have stopped at the Sea Isle City Soda Fountain. They sell ice cream and flavored soda water. I will order a 'milkshake' for each of you. A milkshake is a mixture of ice cream and milk, and they are delicious. But be careful! They are also very cold, so drink them slowly. For those forgetting my advice woe unto you."

What did he mean by that? I wondered. We took seats inside. Minutes later boys our own age placed large glasses of a thick creamy mixture in front of us. They had funny looking paper hats on their heads making me smile. I dipped my finger into the contents of the glass placing a drop of the shake tentatively on my tongue. Delicious! I scooped *two* fingers in the glass without hesitation quickly slurping the milkshake from my fingers. Kind of a messy way to eat this thing I thought.

A long red and white striped tube protruded from everyone's glass. Favoring our fingers everyone ignored it except Mirko. He had pulled his out of the shake and was nibbling on one end.

"It doesn't taste very good," he said, spitting a piece on the table, "but I guess we have to take the good with the bad." He began chewing it so we followed suit. Soon all of us were chomping away on the paper tubes. I figured it would be best to get the unpleasant part over with first so I could focus on the yummy chocolate shake.

"They're hollow," I said to no one in particular. I pulled the tube out of the shake. It was clogged on that end, but the other end, protruding from the top, was definitely hollow. Father Vasilj was doing the same as me. Most of us had eaten almost all of it by the time Father Cuvalo returned from paying the bill. He stopped cold, looking at us chewing like so many busy little chipmunks and shook his head in dismay.

"Straws! They are called straws!" Father Cuvalo said in exasperation. "They are most definitely not for consumption! The straw is in your shake so you can suck on it and get the shake in your mouth-without using your fingers." He looked at my dripping fingers making a mess on the tabletop.

His gaze traveled the tables ending on a humiliated Father Vasilj. Now that we knew what the straws were for we got new ones and set about sucking the chocolate shake through them. I saw Father Vasilj smiling. So *this* is what it took to get that sourpuss to crack a smile. Father Kozo was sucking on his straw as if his life depended on it. His fat cheeks sunk in on themselves (as much as fat cheeks allow for that sort of thing) when suddenly he backed away from his shake holding his head in hands and whimpering in pain. Looking at him with concern we stopped sucking on the straws horrified at what was happening to him. Not exactly *what* was happening to *him*, but more concerned if the same thing could happen to *us*. Is this delicious thing some sort of poison? What's going on here? We all felt the same way-it was obvious as I saw the look on everyone else's face. Father Cuvalo looked up from his own shake when he heard Father Kozo whimpering and burst out laughing.

"I warned you to eat *slowly*. Shakes are very cold. They *are* made of ice cream after all. I did say woe be unto you if you eat the shake too quickly. Go slowly like myself and you can avoid a *smrskati smrsavati*. In America it is called a brain freeze." With a chuckle he returned to his shake. When we finished (Father Kozo was last) we climbed back inside the cars and twenty minutes later pulled up in front of the Sea Isle City Catholic orphanage.

Nothing changed from Grottammare. Vespers still took place every evening. Morning prayers were still the start of the day, short of waking and dressing. We found out from Monsignor Mandich we would be here at least two weeks until all the paperwork cleared and airplane tickets for Chicago were purchased. In the Catholic education system very little time is wasted. We began learning English. While very excited about learning my new country's language I found it to be very difficult. So many words mean the same thing! Read or read-to have done before or to be doing now. While spelled the same they were pronounced differently. This is impossible! Even with the help of Father Cuvalo interpreting I learned almost nothing.

"Slavi, go home," a group of boys hissed one evening at supper. It was in English so we had no idea what they were saying. We did catch Slavi though, a derogatory term for people of Slavic origin, or, incorrectly applied, for people of Eastern European origin. All of us felt the chilly reception from both the priests who ran the orphanage and the orphans themselves. They considered themselves real Americans and didn't want us here. Nevertheless, they had no choice. This was a Catholic institution, and as such ruled by Rome's directives. Father Cuvalo explained nothing could be done about the taunting, and besides, we were to be here but a short time anyway. Essentially, he told us we should ignore everything outside of learning and prayer.

"The sooner you learn English," he told us, "the sooner you will fit in and so avoid the contempt the average American feels for immigrants, though the majority are grandchildren or children of immigrants themselves."

I studied harder than ever, determined to master English. I already knew Latin, Greek, a smattering of Italian and of course, Croat. What was one more language? Two weeks went by in the rush of learning and the clock-numbing slowness of prayer.

Similar to the evening meal at Grottammare when Monsignor Mandich announced our plans to come to America, this time Father Cuvalo raised his glass of juice. In America, we learned, wine does *not* accompany every dinner. Children *do not* drink wine in America. Wine or not, Father Cuvalo raised his glass announcing what we had been waiting for. "The time has come for us to go to Chicago. We leave tomorrow! August 24th, 1951 is a day you will never forget. Your new home awaits!"

# CHAPTER XIV

## "Drexel Boulevard"

The day was, as Father Cuvalo foretold, a day I would never forget. We arrived at the airport early, driven in the same cars (by the same uncommunicative drivers) as the ones that picked us up in Manhattan and transported us to Sea Isle City, New Jersey. Leaving the earth behind, a rush of unbridled forward momentum pushed me back into my seat with strong, invisible hands. I was as scared as I was thrilled.

Monsignor Mandich was Executive in Charge of Seating. Arrived at by a method known only to Monsignor Mandich he assigned Mirko a window seat. *I* wanted a window seat! Alas, it was not to be. Squashed in the middle seat with Mirko on the window side and Thomas on the aisle my first plane trip was looking bleak indeed. Resignation was stomping to my door (in the heavy footsteps it's known for) when my good friend Mirko came through for me without realizing it.

"Branko, if we crash into the ground *you* will see our deaths-not I. I don't want to. Here, *you* take the window seat." Mirko was the same nervous friend I had met four years ago. With some awkward maneuvering we negotiated the switch. Woo-hoo! I was glad to take it! This gave me the chance to see outside the avion's windows. Ever since Father Cuvalo told us we would be taking a plane to Chicago I had lain up nights dreaming of what it would be like to leave the earth behind, soaring into the sky, traveling so fast!

My imagination was not as vivid as the real thing. As we lifted from the runway row upon row of houses, and street upon street upon street stretched to the horizon in a self-repeating vista.

Lifting from the runway details below my window unfolded at breakneck speed. In a small square of a backyard a child swung on a swing set. I knew that's what it was. Sea Isle City Orphanage had one. The boy pushed forward, propelling his legs downward from his back-swing arc, pushing them within an inch of the ground, then shooting them skyward as if to kick the sun from its path. A man and woman were engaged in a serious fight in the front yard of the same house. The woman was throwing clothes at the man. The man was waving his arms all about while attempting to catch his clothes at the same time. As serious as it was for them, from up here they looked silly, like actors involved in their roles.

As I was lifted above the earth the neighborhood I had seen but seconds before faded into more of the same. Soon a hundred streets, then a thousand spread out below me. The clock stands still for fascination. I was so engrossed in the unfolding panorama that in no time at all the view evolved into a patchwork of farmland. I was amazed how every field was a different shade of green or brown. Not one matched the other. The fields appeared as a large earth-colored quilt from this far up.

"Ladies and Gentlemen, this is the captain."

I jumped. The voice was coming from right above me! Mirko, I mean Mark, did the same. He leaned into me in a panic.

"Why isn't the captain flying the plane? We'll crash for sure now!"

We looked above our heads, spotting the round disk the voice was coming from. I looked above other people's seats noting they had the same cover. I whispered to Mirko.

"It's just a speaker Mark. The captain is in front of the plane, not crawling along inside the luggage racks talking to everyone one at a time." I gave him a reassuring squeeze on the shoulder.

The captain resumed, "Our cruising altitude will be twenty thousand feet. If you look outside your windows you'll see Pennsylvania. We will cross it, then pass over the states of Ohio, Indiana, and then into Illinois. We will be landing at Midway airport at approximately three o'clock. Please see your stewardess for any needs. Enjoy the trip, and thank you for choosing us as your carrier."

A click from the speaker signaled the end of the captain's welcome. I looked around for a stewardess. I recalled the term steward being a male aide. Stewardess made sense, I guess, since all of them *are* females. The captain said they would help us, and I was thirsty. I noticed them when being seated, but was so excited about the plane itself I paid them scant attention. Not so now. A stewardess saw my raised hand and made her way to me. She was exquisitely beautiful. Sparkling blue eyes gazed upon a world of less physically perfect specimens. Tall, with a lean body, her maroon colored uniform stretched taut in all the right places. Smooth, tan legs propelled her. Her hair was long and blonde, cascading in front of her face as she leaned down, the better to hear me. When she swept it back I picked up the scent of flowers- as fresh as any newly picked bouquet. She spoke, and I surmised she was asking what I wanted. But I couldn't answer! My mind could go no further than smelling her hair and looking into her eyes. Coherent thought and speech had retreated to a back corner of my brain. However, one word, the most important one, managed to squeak past my dry tongue.

"*Vodu*"

"He is asking for water." Father Cuvalo, ever to the rescue, had overheard the stewardess and my clumsy answer.

The most beautiful set of lips I had ever seen turned upwards, forming a brilliant smile. My heart melted. She offered me a cup of water. I took it gratefully, very aware of how close she was. I wanted to touch her hand but didn't have the courage. She gave me another smile, this one with a twinkle in her eyes. I guess I wasn't the first boy to grow stupid in her presence. She moved down the row, doing her job.

Beginning our descent to Chicago, a view opposite of our New Jersey departure unfolded outside my window. The fields lost the appearance of an earthen quilt, transforming slowly into individual farms. Soon the farms gave way to vast sprawling neighborhoods. Descending, the neighborhoods morphed into streets, and in a rush we dropped hard onto the runway of Midway Airport. With one last look at the stewardess who saved me from dying of thirst I disembarked the plane with the rest of my group. Together, with Monsignor Mandich firmly in charge we clamored into waiting cars. I was not as squished as in New York City so I got a better view of my surroundings. The streets, businesses and homes looked the same as those of New Jersey. Father Cuvalo interrupted my thoughts.

"We are on a street called Cicero," he offered.

Cicero! I was *familiar* with that name! Cicero, I recalled, was a famous Roman. Ah yes, Marcus Tullius Cicero. It was a little fuzzy-Grottammare seemed a century ago. I knew he was the greatest orator of the Romans, as well as a powerful politician. The one sure thing I knew was a phrase he had spoken to the Roman people, "Ask not what your country can do for you, but what you can do for your country."

Father Cuvalo continued, "We are going to the Catholic Croatian Commissariat. The Church, in Her infinite capacity of love for Her fellow Catholics, founded the Commissariat a number of years ago to help Croat Catholics in the United States. It is located on Drexel Boulevard. A boulevard is a major thoroughfare. It is a little south of downtown Chicago, hence not far from here. Your education in your new country will begin upon your arrival. We who live there call the Catholic Croatian Commissariat 'Drexel Boulevard'. Remember that. Oh, yes, another thing. Running a large operation such as this cost money. We help defray the expenses by operating a printing shop publishing a monthly newspaper for Croats living in the United States, Australia, South America and Canada. It is called *Danica*, or Morning Star in English. This leads me to yet another issue. You are *in America* now. The official language of this country, as you know, is English. You will fail in America without learning English. I am aware I've brought this up a number of times already, but I can't stress the importance of my message." He paused to let his words sink in. "You will hear less Croat and more English spoken as your studies progress. Some words in English don't conform well to the Croatian tongue. An experiment please. *Svjet* (Svee-et), as you know, is world in Croat. *Svjet* is no problem to pronounce. Bernard Dujlovich!"

I looked up rapidly, my shoes forgotten.

"How do you pronounce svjet in English? It sounds like this"

Father Cuvalo pursed his lips together, as if forming a kiss. Blossoming, his lips formed two petals of red. His top lip pushed up and out, his bottom lip thrust down and out. Lushly blinking, they retreated lip to lip. His pronunciation of the word concluded with an ever so slight click of his tongue against his teeth.

"W—O—R—L—D."

I heard the word in my mind, but my tongue wrestled against forming it. My lips joined the fight and when I spoke, it came out "v r o l d." Fifteen chuckles floated throughout the room bouncing off each other until a wave of laughter lapped wall to wall. Father Cuvalo rescued me from further embarrassment.

"Don't be so quick to laugh at Bernard my friends." Shooting stern looks at the fathers before resuming, visibly perturbed. "The same will happen to you-*all* of you. You must become fluent in English. It truly is the passport to being successful in this land. Only practice will help you shed the accent of your homeland, if you want to. There is nothing wrong with the language of our land. It's just that if you want to fit into this new country you must learn to read, write and speak English."

Father Cuvalo was an inexhaustible source of information. Launching into a history of Lake Michigan and Chicago he told us how Lake Michigan was formed, how downtown Chicago was essentially built on marshland, how most of the city burned in a huge fire and a dozen other trivial tidbits.

Father Cuvalo interrupted himself.

"We are arriving. The Commissariat is located at Forty-Eighth Street and Drexel Boulevard. Founded years ago it has helped many Catholic Croats gain a firm footing in the United States." Father Cuvalo droned on about the building and grounds; who donated this, who helped build that . . .

I was too busy taking in the expanding view of the grounds too fully absorb his words. A large, black wrought iron fence enclosed the grounds. Intricate groups of metal circles ran the entire top length of the fence. The fence consisted of an unbroken row of solid square bars at least five feet long from top to bottom spaced about four inches apart. I focused on a bar just ahead of the car and then let the next one draw my eyes and the next one, until they meshed into a solid wall of black. As I drew parallel to the bars the wall dissolved. It reminded me of my farm in Croatia, the same way rows of beans appeared and disappeared, leaving gaps of brown for a split moment-then again! Then again! It only worked when Joseph ran the horses for all they were worth past the fields of Ivanjska.

At least it doesn't have broken glass on top I thought, recalling the wall surrounding Santa Maria degli Angeli.

The main entrance to the Commissariat was an imposing double-gated affair, wrought in the same design as the fence. The driver of the lead car pulled in and stopped just shy of the metal bars. He got out, reached in his pocket and producing a large brass key. Walking to the gates he inserted the key into the lock. When finished he replaced the key in his pocket then pushed both gates inward on thick, uncomplaining hinges.

I couldn't believe my eyes. The main building was enormous! At least a hundred feet long and three stories tall it was constructed of immense limestone blocks which age had robbed of their original white. It must be hundreds of years old, or older! It was also very spooky looking. Almost all of the windows were covered. The ones that weren't projected a shiny, sinister reflection. There were no signs of life. There was no movement behind the dark windows and the ample front lawn was devoid of life. No cars occupied the large concrete driveway.

While driving from Midway Airport storm clouds had swept in low to the ground and running blue from the sky in ominous black waves. Zagreb flashed in my mind's eye. I saw myself, bundled against the cold, chin tucked, exiting the gymnasium for my spot by the Hungry Window. These same dead gray clouds had squished themselves to just above the earth on that day as well. Bad clouds, bad things.

We tumbled from the cars when they came to a halt. Directed by Father Cuvalo to line up for a quick tour of the outer grounds. The group started off but I was unaware, I had stopped to simply stare. A push on my shoulder brought me from my reverie. Father Vasilj leaned down whispering harshly in my ear as was his custom.

"*Idi*!" Move along!

I thought too much. My mind evaluated what I saw and then my imagination leapt up, eager to be part of the interpretation. The even expanse of grass, a tidily manicured plot on the northeast corner of 48th and Drexel, with cars whizzing past and people walking next to it on the sidewalk, performed its function as a grassy barrier between building and street. But this was not just a lawn, Catacombs, stuffed full of bodies, laced beneath it hiding a hundred secrets. The windows weren't windows at all. They were dark eyes peering from an immense stone body.

The bulk of the building pushed from the earth in a rush, forcing my eyes ever higher. Jutting from a corner of the main bulk a round turret shaped room caught my eye. Copper sheets formed a separate round roof for just the addition, reminding me of an Oriental rice farmer's hat. The sheets lay upon themselves forming a domed, pointed roof that capped the squat addition. The rounded, jutting room was composed of the same stone blocks as the main body of the building, but traveled only a third of the way to the top. One story up, taking the place of stone, a row of six small windows framed in white wood ringed the room. On the voyage from Halifax Monsignor Mandich pointed out a tall round building on the coastline, calling it a 'lighthouse.' This reminded me of that, except the earth had swallowed the main body of *this* lighthouse leaving only the windows and roof above ground.

On the far side of the building there was a similar round addition, but this one was three stories tall. It sported the same Chinese copper hat for a roof. At the tiptop a well anchored cross defied the wind, casting an unyielding silhouette, stark against the lesser black of the clouds.

Father Cuvalo was in teacher mode. "... and around this side of the administration building is the priests lodgings, as well as the print shop I spoke of . . . *Danica* is a very important publication for Croats all over the world."

He launched into a history of the main building. The structure, built for the Swift family, was once their estate until becoming church property. Very wealthy Americans, they made their fortune selling ham and lunchmeats.

"That's a lot of ham," a whisper floated to my ears. Thomas had come up behind me.

"Indeed it is a lot of ham, Thomas." We looked up, our smiles vanishing in a heartbeat.

How in God's name could he have heard that? I thought. He was at least twenty feet away and Thomas had whispered so softly that *I* barely heard him. This Cuvalo, I must be careful with him. Could he hear me now, hear my thoughts? He was looking directly at me with disturbing intensity. Shivering, I looked away.

Rounding the administration building two less grand buildings appeared. They weren't constructed of hewn limestone blocks. They didn't have rounded rooms with copper domes, soaring chimneys and defiant crosses. Simple yellow brick bespoke their functionality. Father Cuvalo gestured to the larger building telling us it was the dormitory for all residents, be they temporary or permanent. The smaller building held the print shop for Morning Star. A quick look inside the dusty windows revealed a distorted view of sleeping printing presses and stacks of paper.

"*Idite*!" Move along, all of you! Ever the hungry one Father Kozo prodded us as if we took too long (in *his* estimation) peering through the print shop windows, as if we were personally denying him dinner. Pushing us along he grumbled how long it had been since his last meal. Dinner came soon, to Father Kozo's enthusiastic pleasure. The food was similar to what I had eaten at Sea Isle City Orphanage.

Prayers followed dinner, bed followed prayers. With a sense of security previously unknown I sank into the comfort of an American bed. Dream-filled sleep took over with unobstructed permission. My dreams were not of Ivanjska this time but of a new place not defined by sight, or smell. It was a dream space floating on feelings, and they all were good. I didn't *see* anything; I just *felt* it, a diffusive joy permeating the core of my world perceptions. I'm sure I was smiling in my sleep.

Five-thirty comes early, even in America. My first day at Drexel Boulevard began the same as my first day in Grottammare—with prayer, and lots of it. Upon awakening, I shuffled about the bathroom with few thoughts beyond completing my hygienic tasks.

Dressed and ready for the day Father Cuvalo appeared in the doorway. He looked very modern in his black suit and white collar. Exiting the dormitory for the chapel the Italian gang of Reverend Fathers was waiting for us in the courtyard. They looked 'old world' with their brown robes and hooded cowls. Comparing the two priestly garbs I instantly preferred the American version.

Father Cuvalo took charge of our group leading us to the chapel, a small dimly lit room adjacent to the print shop. At this point Monsignor Mandich took charge. I think he was delighted with the opportunity to be in control again. Knowing him as I did I'm sure it was eating him alive, having to relinquish his authority to a priest of lesser rank. Mass was spoken, communion taken. My knees, well callused from endless hours in prayer, once again supported my weight in a never-ending bid for salvation. It was just another Mass.

Eggs, bacon and white toast followed prayer. After breakfast Father Cuvalo informed us our schooling would begin immediately. Filing into a small classroom on the second floor of the administration building Mark and I found seats by the window. I wanted to see outside since it always made me feel better. More importantly, the view gave me something to focus on other than the sleep inducing voice of a disinterested instructor.

Father Cuvalo, it turned out, was anything but disinterested. Passing out textbooks as he talked about America, the passion in his voice was infectious. We launched into the book, starting with letters "A", "B", "C". The hours passed quickly, and when lunchtime was announced the letters of the alphabet rattled in my mind like so many pebbles of sound.

After lunch we resumed where we left off. The letter "W" was a toughie for all of us. It was my turn to chuckle when my classmates pronounced it aloud. However, no one laughed when Father Vasilj messed it up. His sense of humor definitely did not extend to his own actions. I could scarcely believe it was time for dinner when Father Cuvalo closed his textbook.

With one last imparting in him, "I can see some of you want to learn. Others, I notice, have either no aptitude for English or you choose not to learn it. Let me make myself clear regarding this. You all have a choice. For those of you choosing to speak, read and write English you will advance within the Church. For those of you without the interest or energy to learn will find themselves on a boat to Argentina. There are many Croats living there where you can speak Croat all the time, never burdened with the complexities of English. You will also not be part of the priesthood . . . and Argentina is a very, *very* poor country. Without the Church you will have to learn a skill, get a job, pay for your food and the roof over your head. You will have to pay taxes. In short, you will almost certainly live a life of poverty. As I said, you have choices."

As he spoke he was slowly focusing, one at a time, on every single person. With some, he smiled and gave a nod. With others, Father Kozo included, he gave little more than a quick glance before moving on. When his eyes locked with mine I held my gaze firm and smiled. He smiled back. At that point I knew I was on the right path with this Reverend Father.

The days passed in a rush of learning. On the sixth day at Drexel Boulevard the routine changed. I settled in my seat, ready for another session when Father Cuvalo announced

"You are exercising your mind which pleases God. However, He is also pleased when you exercise your body. I wouldn't feel right if I didn't have a way for you to do that." The fleetest of smiles, then he added "Please follow me to the print shop." With that he exited the classroom into the hall and rattled his way down the steps.

When assembled outside, he turned to us. "The print shop is the lifeblood of the Commissariat. We are going to perform what in America is called a spring cleaning."

After unlocking a heavy bolt on the door we were ushered inside the print shop. A dank, musty smell assaulted my nostrils. It also reeked of grease and smelt of machinery. Huge silent printing presses squatted on bare concrete. Cobwebs crowded dark corners where the ceiling met wall. The building was maybe sixty feet wide and a hundred feet long with a low ceiling and miserly number of windows coated with a thick film of dust, defeating all but the strongest beams of sunlight. What a dreary place I thought.

"This is a dreary place, is it not?" Father Cuvalo asked us.

Quickly looking at him I was relieved to see him inspecting a piece of machinery. Whew! I was about ready to ask for that boat ride to Argentina. Scraping, scrubbing, washing, scrubbing, cleaning, scraping, scrubbing. With the exception of a short lunch break ten hours toiled themselves away in the gloom of the printing room. I couldn't believe it when Father Cuvalo said we were almost halfway done. Halfway? The floor was spotless! The windows glistened with the shine of a Macy's display. Cobwebs were obsolete in this newly improved world publishing headquarters. What else was there to do?

I found out over the next five days how much more we could accomplish. Not just in the print shop, but on the grounds, in the administration building, in the dormitories. By the time we packed for our trip to St. Joseph's College my back was aching from work and my mind was numb from the onslaught of learning.

# CHAPTER XV

## "Saint Joe's Time"

The time was at hand! Bremerhaven to New York to Sea Isle City Chicago, these were but stopping points en 'route to my final destination. The place I would be spending years at was now a quick car ride away. Leaving the Commissariat on a sunny Sunday afternoon we traveled west from Drexel Boulevard. The further west we went the more farms I saw. Mile after mile of fields steadily replaced buildings and people. After what seemed like an hour the car in front slowed, turning left off the main road onto an impossibly long driveway. I was not fortunate enough this time to be in the lead car with Father Cuvalo. Relegated to the third vehicle with Father Vasilj, he brought his dark disposition with him. Smiles and laughter felt uncomfortable around him and so chose to hide. There was the driver (a brother from the Commissariat), Father Vasilj and five other boys inside the car. Finally in control of *something* the good Father lost no time reminding us of his authority.

"I know you are all very excited about being in America." In a rare moment of openness he confided, "I share your enthusiasm." Back to the business of being a Reverend Father. "This is a very large place, with many things to do. Saint Joseph's College is a school as well as a fully functional farm. There are cows, chickens, goats, and horses. The Brothers here slaughter our meat, and gather our eggs. In addition, this is a farm with fields of crops which the Brothers maintain as well." Continuing on about duties and responsibilities he (predictably) rolled into his sin speech. I had heard it so many times I could recite parts of it word for word. Tuning him out I caught site of the main building as it rolled into view. The lines of the building sliced the cloudless sky creating a clean division of man and nature. At the top of the building a deep blueness offered itself for view, extending well beyond the scope of the human eye.

This building, this *structure*, could swallow the entire grounds of the Commissariat on Drexel Boulevard. It was enormous, composed entirely of red brick. Three stories tall I counted twenty-five windows stretching from one end to the other on the top floor. U shaped, each wing was half as long as the front. It reminded me of pictures I had seen of old English castles. Rising from the middle of the front portion a brick and limestone bell tower soared at least fifty feet above the roof with a large church bell hanging inside the three open arches that formed the belfry. The grounds stretched so far off I gave up trying to take in everything in at once. I knew I would have plenty of time.

The dormitories were no different from Grottammare, or even Drexel Boulevard. They were rectangular, as always, with bathrooms on one end and beds predictably spaced in orderly rows the length of the room. Father Cuvalo informed us we were to be split up into pairs, with each pair staying in a different dormitory.

The twelve of us quickly formed six pairs. It didn't matter which continent we were on. Mirko pulled my sleeve as incessantly in America as he did in Germany.

"Branko, we should pair up. I would feel much better." Mirko looked up at me in that helpless way of his.

"Oh, okay. If it makes you feel better." I squished my eyebrows together, the opening act in the muscular symphony required to perform "La' Scowl." Just kidding him my eyebrows retreated. I gave Mirko a friendly smile and gave his shoulder a reassuring squeeze.

Father Cuvalo explained his reasoning in brisk, yet compassionate tones. "There are only twelve of you left of the original fifty-two. You have come a long way and learned much from your time spent in Santa Maria degli Angeli, and the Church is proud of all of you. As I said, there were originally fifty-two of you. Time and circumstances have whittled your numbers to twelve. The main reason you are still here, if you will forgive my saying so, is that either your families cannot support you, or" a painful pause, "they are dead. I am sorry to say this out loud, but it is nothing you have not spoken of to each other or thought in the privacy of your own minds." Father Cuvalo seemed a kind man. He was troubled having to say things so obviously hurting his listeners. At the same time he had a job to do. "Saint Joseph's College is at the same academic level as what is called a 'high school' in America. There are eighty-eight other boys here. You are being divided among the other students to learn English more quickly. There are no girls at Saint Joseph's College." He turned toward a groaning sound coming from the back of the group. Mathew, the oldest of us, assumed a sheepish look when every face turned toward him. Father Cuvalo let it pass, continuing. "The course load here will be quite heavy. Learning English is of primary importance. I've already explained why this is so vital. I have spoken with Monsignor Mandich at length regarding what your daily activities included while at Grottammare. It will be almost the same here at St. Joseph's."

He launched into a detailed accounting of our day's regimen. As he rattled it off it was indeed similar to Grottammare's. Prayer, breakfast, schooling, lunch, prayer, schooling, free time, dinner, prayer and bed-in a nutshell. It was early September, the time when the school year started for kids in America. Our arrival was perfectly timed.

Father Cuvalo had gone off to attend to other arrangements leaving sourpuss Vasilj in charge. "Regarding dormitory assignments," the nasally voice of Father Vasilj reverberated in the main hall, "you have already grouped yourselves in pairs.

Please stand next to your partner. To my left," he pointed toward six older seminarians, "are student dormitory leaders. They will take you to your rooms and help you settle into the routine. As Father Cuvalo has mentioned numerous times, I suggest you study hard on your English if you wish to communicate with your fellow students. They do not, nor does anyone here, speak Croat."

With that said he motioned the closest student leader to the closest pair. Doing the same down the line we were quickly divided and on our way to our rooms. The boy leading us was tall, and big. I tried to thank him for his help. When I did he stopped and turned toward me.

"Dirty DP," was all he said. Turning from Mark and me he picked up his pace eager to leave us behind. Father Kozo had told me D.P. was the abbreviation for displaced person. A displaced person, he informed me, was one without a country. He was wrong! I have a country now-America!

Worry and the desire for sleep fought in my mind, and the effort involved in the struggle gave sleep the edge it needed. I was still exhausted from the work at Drexel Boulevard and was afraid I wouldn't be able to keep up the pace of class and prayer. But then I thought, I really don't have any option. *One* maybe, but living in Argentina didn't sound like much of an option. I had lived my share of poor. Resolving to do whatever was required of me to remain here, my eyelids gave into gravity, growing impossibly heavy, with sleep defeating worry yet again.

"Welcome to class. This is the first day of your freshman year. Some of you," the instructor threw a disapproving look at me and two others of the Grottammare gang, "should be in different grades, but due to a lack of English skills will start here." At this point he gave us three his full attention. "You won't get any special breaks from me. You're just D.P.s. You aren't here because you wish to serve God, only because the Church has placed you here."

He was an unremarkable man with an unremarkable voice. There was nothing about him hinting at greatness. To the contrary, his demeanor indicated there was little to expect beyond a reliable mediocrity. His animosity was visible in his eyes and tone of voice. I understood almost nothing of what he said but the intent was crystal clear.

I looked forward to lunch. It came and went, as did the day.

Eggs are eggs anywhere in the world, so breakfast had offered nothing new. Lunch, however, produced new and interesting foods. Things I had never seen before were plopped on my tray. I sat alone with American students at mealtime; all twelve of us did.

The other boys at the table slid on their butts and scooted their trays away from me as I sat.

Fine, be that way, I thought. Lunch was more important to me than making new friends. Two slices of bread occupied the side of my plate. A scoop of a deep red jelly-like substance jiggled next to it. Hmm, jam. I had first tasted jam on the Blatchford. It was sweet and delicious. Taking my piece of bread I smeared some of the ruby red jelly on it and started eating it like toast. When the other boys saw me doing this they giggled, poking fingers at me. In a flash a brother appeared at my table.

"Silence!" He whispered loudly.

All laughter ceased. I was introduced to a new rule. No talking was allowed for the first ten minutes and last ten minutes of every meal. Mealtime lasted thirty minutes, so any conversation to be had was ten minutes or less. The boys laughing at me had done so within the first ten minutes, hence the attention of the brother.

Father Cuvalo attended mealtimes with us. He was invaluable since he was the only person who spoke both English and Croat. He had come up behind me after the brother resumed his seat.

"Branko, what you thought was jam, I'm assuming anyway, is actually called cranberry sauce. Cranberries are mashed together and made into a thick sauce. You eat it with a fork, not by smearing it on bread. I don't want you worrying too much about doing things differently from your peers. These things will happen no matter how hard you try. As long as you remember how to do it correctly the next time you will be fine."

I looked up at him from my seat and gave him a smile.

"Thank you Reverend Father Cuvalo."

I returned to my meal. A long, round yellow object had been put on my plate in addition to the sandwich and cranberry sauce. I had no idea what it was. Disregarding my standard policy of observing others attempt something unknown to me before trying it myself I bravely sank my teeth into the yellow piece of food. The outside was tough and slightly bitter, but the inside was delicious! It was soft and squishy, sweet and creamy, and I couldn't eat it fast enough. Chomping on the outer part I didn't notice the boys poking fun at me until I had already eaten and swallowed three huge bites. Again, laughter rocked my table. We were in the middle ten minutes of lunch so no brother came forward to stop them from ridiculing me. I was turning red with embarrassment when a boy sitting two seats down reached behind the boy between us and tapped me on the back. After getting my attention he showed me how to eat the yellow tube. Leaning forward and watching him, he held it low in his left hand, while pulling down from the top of the tube with his right. The rough fibrous part came away from the yummy insides. He took a big bite of the soft treat inside and smiled at me.

"Bah—na-na," he slowly mouthed.

"Bah—na-na," I mimicked back. Following his motions I did the same to my banana, or what was left of it. Without the tough outside this banana was heaven on earth! After chewing a big mouthful I gave him a wide smile and told him thank you in Croat.

"*Fala*," he replied to my astonishment. "My name is Edward Vrdolyak." This bit of Croat spoken haltingly. "My parents are from Croatia so I picked up a little, but I was born in America. I hope to be a priest." With a smile of encouragement he turned back to his meal. I felt better just talking to him. His face inspired confidence in the viewer. Large, dark, wide-set eyes peered upon the world with a mix of intelligence and kindness most people didn't possess, at least not in my experience. A mop of dark hair topped him off. He possessed a chiseled thinness indicating strength and agility. All in all, he impressed me greatly.

A week passed in a whirlwind of books and lessons, services and vespers, meals and more meals. I was slowly getting a feel for the place. There were one hundred students enrolled at St. Joseph's College. Eighty-eight of them were American. Some were there, like Edward, because they wanted to become priests. Others because their *parents* wanted them to become priests, and a few who were orphanage veterans and this seemed the best course for them according to the Church.

I was happy to be here-the meals were always warm and filling. In spite of the grandness of my adventure the greatest benefit was still the meals. As unstoppable as a new day is, I met each one with a hunger satisfied only in the cafeteria and the classroom. My grasp of English grew with each passing day and the point soon arrived when the once incoherent ramblings of my fellow students sounded less and less like gibberish.

Money, and how to get it, seemed to be the main topic of lights-out conversation. I learned the importance of money from those late nights, laying in bed and listening to my fellow students. I didn't join in the conversation since I wasn't welcome to do so. I was never made to feel welcome, and beyond a few boys like Edward communication in English was limited to the classroom and the struggling conversations I had with Mirko and the Grottammare gang.

Money. Money, according to what I heard, was the passport to having anything one desired, if one had enough of it. The boys in my dormitory said they worked various jobs to get it. I resolved I would do the same, but I had no one to ask how to do so.

When we arrived here at St. Joseph's, the Grottammare Fathers and Father Cuvalo stayed for a few weeks then left. We received a short speech from Monsignor Mandich before they piled in a car to head back to Drexel Boulevard.

"My boys you are about to embark on a journey that will, God willing, conclude with your ordination as a priest in the Holy Roman Catholic Church. I hope to greet all of you as a fellow brother in Christ in the coming years. Sadly, a number of you will not become priests. Some of you are too lazy, too stupid, or too sinful. I don't know. There are many reasons. But I must stress, I think the biggest detriment to success in the Church would be the failure to learn English." He paused as if to impart some bit of devastating news to us. "We are going back to Drexel Boulevard to help other Croatians coming into the country. You will stay and learn. Focus on learning the language. Without it you will not survive here. There is no one other than you twelve that speaks our native tongue. You will be in contact with these Americans all day every day. Learn from them." He stopped. He took several deep breaths seeking air molecules to feed his lungs. Ten seconds later, his lungs satiated, he continued his dialogue. "The school term will be over in June. At that point you will come to live at the Commissariat for the summer then return here for the new school year. This will be the case until you graduate and move on to the next stage in your education. Now we must go. We will be back periodically to check on your progress. The Fathers here are only a phone call away. They have the authority to dispense punishment as they see fit. *You* must see fit not to do anything that would cause them to discipline you. Not only will they do so, but when we come back you will be getting a visit from us as well. Now, if you will excuse us, we must depart. Good bye and God bless you."

Lovely. Essentially, they were leaving us in a strange place where not one person spoke

Croat. How was I to ask for *anything*? My knowledge of English was next to nothing. It was the same for the rest of us. We looked at each other dumbstruck at what just happened. However, the moment passed. The trim silhouette of Father Cuvalo disappeared through the front door. A brother was on hand to make sure we went directly to our rooms. "Go! Move!" These were words picked up quickly. Words that were yelled or spoken more forcefully than others were always more quickly remembered.

Winter found us. Frost on the windows in the most intricate designs offered a sparkling distortion to the view of cold, barren fields outside my classroom. Autumn like weather had held but a tiny slice of the year. When we arrived at St. Joseph's several months ago the trees were bright green and heavy with leaves, which all too quickly turned to gold, then to nothing. Naked, skeletal branches sliced the winter sky where not so long ago a million leaves had cloaked their bony fingers. As Christmas came and went I focused on my studies, learning increasingly acceptable English with every passing day. The prescribed routine also gave me comfort in its predictability. Even prayer was looked forward to (a little bit). Stone floors didn't bother me like they used to. My knees, tender those first few thousand hours spent on them at Grottammare, were now calloused pads. I took the time spent in Vespers to further enhance my English skills, my mind running over the day's lessons.

I still believed in God-nothing could change that, but I knew I would never become a priest. The discovery of the secret death-room in Grottammare had taken care of that. I was sure I had more to look forward to than working with child abusers, hypocrites and killers. Father Cuvalo had made that much clear to me through his teachings about America. He taught me there were endless opportunities for people that spoke English. Never had I held such a strong resolve to do any one thing. I was keeping up with the rest of my class in speaking and writing skills. The Grottammare gang began coming to me when one of them was faced with an English problem they were incapable of solving. My teachers also took note of my progress and I was rewarded with praise when the Reverend Fathers came to visit us from Drexel Boulevard.

Months passed and the bony fingers of the trees grew green flesh. Flowers bathed the earth in color and the glorious miracle of spring unfolded a day at a time before my eyes.

The bulletin board in the main hall was no longer a jumbled mass of strange symbols. I studied it every day, not leaving until I knew exactly what every announcement stated. In early spring the words 'Baseball Tryouts' clicked into recognition. Baseball! I could try out for the team! Many of us loved baseball. Mirko understood the game by now and didn't pester me for explanations nearly as much. He peppered me with the occasional question though, which I happily answered. This was a chance for me to actually play baseball! As I read further I picked out the date for tryouts-March second. A fine spring dawn opened March second. I jumped out of bed eager to greet the day. It whizzed by. With classes completed I ran all the way to the baseball diamond. A group of boys were already there. Some were practicing pitching, some throwing and some catching. A few of the bigger boys strolled near home plate swinging two bats at once. That made sense I thought. Just think how easy it will be to swing one bat in a game if I always practice swinging two? I decided on the spot I would always practice with two bats, availability of bats withstanding. Just as I had my plan finalized to become the best baseball player in history a voice cut in on my thoughts, whooshing me from my dreams of glory to St. Joseph's College in the blink of an eye.

"Welcome. My name is Father Benedict. All boys trying out for the St. Joseph's Varsity baseball team for the first time please form a line to the left of home plate. You will be given an opportunity at bat." We did as he instructed, and only when we had done so did he continue. "By my count there are twenty-seven potential starters here today. There are only eight starting spots in baseball. Five of last years starting team are still here. That leaves three starting positions to be filled from a field of twenty-seven applicants. We will need a back up for every position plus two back-up pitchers. This means out of twenty-seven applicants I will be selecting only twelve. However, I *will* say the five returning players are not guaranteed their starting spots." I looked at them, standing aloof and apart from the rest of us. They heard him and their smugness vanished. Confidence never took a faster dive. "You have the opportunity to replace them. No one is indispensable, yet that doesn't change the fact that fifteen of you will not be picked."

He stopped speaking. Looking beyond us to a Reverend Father appearing on the edge of the field his attention went with his eyes. I took the opportunity to look at him closer. Father Benedict appeared to be in his mid-forties. Grey and black fought for his full head of hair. Grey held his temples, simultaneously gaining impressive ground on all fronts. Middle age was enjoying similar success around his eyes as well. The wrinkles around his eyes reminded me of a Chinese fan. Great amounts of time spent in the sun had given his skin a weathered tan; a saddle left too long in the sun. His eyes, however, possessed the bright blue of new birth. Nothing-life, cigarettes, guilt, wine, remorse of paths not chosen nor regrets of decisions made could dim the blue of his eyes. Returning his attention to us he summed up the tryout process in three sentences.

"If you can hit, catch and throw the baseball, and do it well enough, you play. If not, go try out for softball. First batter up!"

Softball tryouts were similar to baseball tryouts. However, softball didn't rate the attention of a priest, so I listened to a Franciscan brother this time. "If you can hit, catch and throw the softball, and do it well enough, you play. If not, go try out for volleyball. First batter up!"

Volleyball suited me. The coach giving his speech in the beginning never did say what we were to try out for if we couldn't hit and serve well enough to play volleyball. My teammates groaned when I was at the net but I didn't care since I got to play. It was enormous fun, and between practice, games, homework, prayer and landscaping, months slid by in a frenzied rush. The day came when classes were done, and on that day I was a sophomore at St. Joseph's college.

# CHAPTER XVI

## "A Summer (or three) of Repayment"

The thrill was gone. The Commissariat was no longer a mysterious building of secret rooms; its walls silent witness to important decisions. I was in a work camp. Our role in the summer months at Drexel Boulevard was quickly defined and punctuated with action.

"*Dobro dosli*". Welcome, the speaker said in Croat. Switching to English, he continued. "My name is Father Raguz and I am in charge of the print shop. There is much work involved in putting out a newspaper. The articles must be researched and written, approvals must be sought, blank copy ordered and received, inks purchased etcetera, etcetera. As I said, there is much involved in the production of Morning Star."

His eyes traveled to the door. Father Cuvalo was motioning him over with a wave of his hand. Father Cuvalo towered over him as they spoke softly to one another. Framed in the sunlight of the open door I took advantage of the break to study him. Father Raguz was a fireplug of a man. Stout, but without the fat of Father Kozo, there was the hint of swagger in his walk. He was speaking softly but with confidence. I got the feeling he was more of a 'hands-on' priest and less of a theologian. His face was not unkind with intelligent eyes peering beneath black untrimmed eyebrows. Every eyebrow in residence seemed to be taking advantage of their host's lack of attention. A meatball sort of face, his was round but solid, framing an expansive set of lips and a strong, surprisingly perfect nose. Were it not for his nose Father Raguz would have joined the immensely large sea of mediocre looking people. I looked at his hands. He feathered them up, down and across as he spoke in animated accompaniment to his speech. They were working man's hands. It was easy to see, even from ten feet away. They were black under the nails and scars ran in tracks on the back of his hands.

At that point I was sold on Father Raguz. He seemed like an all right guy. He turned his attention back to us. "I will not deceive you. The hours are long, and the work is hard. You will be loading paper in the presses, stacking heavy bundles, loading vans full of finished copy as well as keeping the print shop clean. You will work twelve to sixteen hours a day, six days a week. Of course there will still be time for prayer and meals . . . Also there is no air-conditioning, so get used to sweating."

A smirk touched ever so lightly on his lips and fled. "One more thing-you will not be paid for your work." There was no smirk this time. Noting how we received this news he assumed a lighter tone and added, "But on the bright side you will each receive a pint of vanilla ice cream every Sunday." This did nothing to raise our spirits which he again noted. He sighed, folded his arms across his chest and provided us with an explanation. "Nothing in life is free my young seminarians. Except of course, salvation." He added this last bit almost as an afterthought. "Do you have any idea how much it costs the Church to feed, clothe and house you since you arrived in Grottammare? The train rides from Grottammare, the boat trip from Bremerhaven-none of that was free!" Getting worked up, he took a short pause. Drawing in a deep breath he resumed less excitedly. "The two main parties responsible for your presence in the United States are The Red Cross and the National Catholic Welfare Committee. Both of these institutions expect to be repaid in full *from you* for the train and boat tickets. The clothes you purchased in New York cost money. The same with your hotel room, the meals, the taxi fare, even the milkshakes. Your work here will repay some of the cost." He paused letting this set in. Counting on him being a reasonable man I timidly raised my hand.

"Reverend Father Raguz I have a question."

"Yes. What is your name?"

Oh, geez, here we go again. "My name is Bran—Bernard Dujlovich," I answered.

"Okay, Bernard. You may call me Father Raguz, not Reverend Father Raguz. We are not in Italy. What is your question?"

"I am not wanting something for nothing, Father Raguz, but I was informed long ago that The Red Cross is an organization that helps people from donations they receive. If this is so, then my boat ticket was paid for through donations. So why are they wanting *us* to pay? If they are charging me for my ticket then what happens to the money they received through donations?"

"An intelligent question Bernard, and I have an answer for you. The Red Cross is a business, and like any business they want to *stay* in business. Their business is helping people. The truth is many, indeed, most of the people they help never repay them. It costs quite a bit of money to do what they do. If the donations don't equal the money they spend helping people then what? They will be out of the business of helping people for good. So they bill everyone and hope a small percentage actually pays them back. This is not unfair, is it?" He concluded the explanation quickly.

I was upset. How was I ever going to save money if I had to work ninety hours a week? That barely left enough time for prayer and sleep, but I was without a choice. Who could I go to? As nice as Father Cuvalo was I didn't see him being able to do anything about it. With no recourse early summer became mid-summer. Sixteen hours a day is a long time to work. The pounds dropped away leaving little but muscle, skin and bone. I was dead tired at the end of the day. We took work breaks for vespers and meals but that was it. I grew to look forward to evening vespers as a release from labor.

Sundays, our only day of rest, was usually anything but. Early in the summer, a dreadful routine was established.
"Listen!" Father Vasilj's voice rang clearly throughout the cafeteria. He spoke slowly since it was in English. "The church is in requirement for altar boys. You have all been learned how to do the task. Two are required for aiding the Fathers dispense Mass to the faithful at St. Jerome's Church. I am to be picking the two boys who have known English the most improved."
Known English the most improved? Oh brother, I thought.
"This is not just any Mass. Cardinal Samuel Strich, the Archbishop of the Chicago diocese will lead. Tomorrow is, as you are to be aware, Assumption Day. This is an honor to be chosen. Dujlovich and Krispic, you will be at the outside front at six o'clock in the morning to be escorted to St. Jerome's."
I looked up. I hadn't expected to be called, but I *did* know English better than anyone else (including Father Vasilj, apparently). Thomas and I exchanged glances that were part pride and part despair. Neither of us wanted to do it, Cardinal in residence or not. The hours we worked drained us of desire to do anything but sleep. Sunday came, as I knew it would. Five-thirty A.M. came, as I knew it would. Per the plan Thomas Krispic and I greeted the waking sun in front of the main entrance of the administration building. A quiet dawn surrounded us. The first rays of direct sun to bathe the new Chicago day electrified thousands of leaves into twice as many shades of green.
Precisely at six o'clock a smartly dressed Father unknown to either of us opened the front door of the Commissariat and stepped down the stairs.
"Follow me," he said not actually looking at us as while pointing at a long black vehicle.
He spoke to us as one commanding servants. And that's what we are I thought. The only reason they chose the best English-speaking boys was to showcase the fine job they were doing.

It was just another service, Cardinal Strich not withstanding, and the morning passed in typical grinding fashion. The sole benefit to assisting in this service (as I saw it) was the higher quality of wine employed for such an august presence. As altar boys we were responsible for many things; the stocking of the wine included. A Cardinal's wine rolls on my tongue with far greater ease than the bitter red of the common priest. I was not a novice in these affairs. I had learned a basic fact over the last five years. The higher in rank the presiding priest for the service the better the quality of wine consumed at communion. A Cardinal, a Prince of the Church, is very highly placed.

There is only one loftier position in the Church, held by one man: The Vicar of Christ, Successor of St. Peter, Supreme Pontiff of the Universal Church, Holder of the Fisherman's ring, Patriarch of the West, Primate of Italy, Archbishop of Rome, and Sovereign Ruler of the State of Vatican City.

Holder of the Fisherman's Ring sounded so mysterious. Popes have worn the Ring since the Fifth Century even though it is named after Peter the Rock. St. Peter, I knew, was foremost among the original twelve disciples of Jesus. Christ himself said to Peter, "I will make you a fisher of men." Peter was the first Bishop of Rome and first leader of the Holy Roman Catholic Church. He was the first Pope, but a Pope without the lavish lifestyle of the current Pontiff. Peter lived in the miles of catacombs laced beneath the streets of Rome on the run from Romans living above his head. He spread the Word of God by mouth; village-to-village, hamlet to hamlet, hut to hut. In the end he suffered a martyr's death in Rome itself, the seat of power of the Roman Catholic Church. The Fisherman's Ring, never worn by Peter himself became a symbol of Papal office in the Fifth Century. Crafted of gold and encrusted with jewels the rings are custom made for the current Pontiff. They are inscribed with his name, encircling a representation of St. Peter in a fishing boat. I remember learning the ring was destroyed upon the death of the Pope whose finger it adorned.

The drive back from St. Jerome's provided me a glimpse of America normally denied. I always knew a non-catholic existence was out there on the other side of the wrought iron fence of Drexel Boulevard, but until that mornings drive my curiosity to see it was minimal. I was too busy learning how to be an American to take interest in anything but learning, sleep and food. The drive lasted fifteen minutes, and in that time I saw enough interesting things to want to see more. I had been in Chicago for almost a year and had never gone beyond the gates of either Drexel Boulevard or St. Joseph's College, except to travel in a car from one to the other and back again. On the short drive what stood out immediately was the incredible number of black people I saw. They were everywhere. Some walked with a purpose, but most of them stood in shuffling groups of four and five on the street corners. Most of them were shabbily dressed. Poverty held court in this part of town. I saw black men slumped on the sidewalk, propping buildings with their backs as they grasped bottles of liquor. I spent four years in Italy watching priests drink themselves silly so I guessed it was probably wine. As a scrolling marquee of downtrodden people slid by my window I recalled Father Cuvalo's tutorial regarding the history of blacks in the United States. This was clear evidence of the truth he was speaking! It was a year ago, but I had thought many times on what he had said that evening in New York City . . . . "The truth is, America is not so different from any other country. It may be the best place to live, but there are ruling classes here just like anywhere else. In America the white people are in charge of everything. Most black people are very poor because they aren't allowed to get good jobs. When they do get a job they are often paid less for the exact same work as a white man toiling right next to him. In the south of this country blacks cannot use the same restroom or eat in the same restaurants. They are required to sit away from whites on public transportation and cannot attend many of the colleges."

The results of segregation was unfolding before my eyes. I realized racism existed in Chicago as surely as the southern part of the United States. I recalled a classroom lesson from early in the school year. Father Pheils Chifter was teaching spelling in English class. The lesson's goal was to teach us how words sound, and how to speak and spell them correctly in spite of how they are written on paper. We were instructed to write a sentence one hundred times.

"Negroes eat potatoes with mosquitoes and tomatoes." After writing it a hundred times I was positive I would know that sentence for the rest of my life.

Another memory flashed in my mind, an unpleasant one. I was walking to class, just leaving one and on my way to another. A black student came toward me in the hall. I hadn't seen him before that day. It was the closest I had ever been to a black person and any time I heard them referred to it was as nigger, or Negro. As he came abreast of me I wanted to be friendly, saying to him, "Hello nigger".

"What did you just say?" He turned, looking down on me. I mean he *really* looked *down* at me. Much taller, bigger and obviously ready to beat me to a pulp, I stuttered out an answer.

"I—I said, hello nigger".

His fist slammed into my face. I had no idea what happened. A bright flash erupted, coupled with a deafening thunder in my ears. Wavering blackness threatened to take over. My legs abandoned me and I fell to the ground in a heap. Through the ringing I heard him tell me I had better watch my mouth. Leaning low over me, his face three inches from mine, he told me, "My name is Simon, *not* nigger." Standing up and spearing me with a look of disgust he shook his head and left me lying in the middle of the hallway. I never called another black person a nigger after that. Simon reported me and soon enough I was standing, head bowed, in front of Father Chifter.

"I understand you are from Croatia. I realize your homeland is a country of intolerance. In America, at least in Chicago, we do not call black people *niggers*!" He said this in a vent of controlled anger. I knew nothing of black people. I wanted him to know, so I ventured to speak.

"I am very sorry Father Chifter. I did not know. Please understand I know nothing of black people. I did not mean to offend Simon. May I ask one question please?"

"Yes, you may" came the quick reply.

"Can you tell me if black people have black blood instead of red?" I heard this in Italy from a fellow seminarian.

Father Chifter exploded. "Black *blood?* Are you insane! They are the same as us in every way Bernard. The *only* difference is their black skin. You would do well not to repeat that question to anyone. I can see that your comments were made in ignorance, not in malice. Watch what you say Bernard. Now get back to class."

That was last year, and this was now. I'm fifteen, not so afraid of the world beyond St. Joseph's or the fences of the Croatian Commissariat. A week after the service at St. Jerome's Sunday offered itself up for sleeping, reading, talking or praying. I opted for none of those things. Determined to get out on the streets and see these black people up close I took advantage of the lack of supervision to escape the compound for a few hours. Unlike my graveyard foray at Grottammare, this time I decided to go it alone. Mirko was wrapped up in a game of chess with an older (and more successful) chess player. I looked at the game. Mirko had captured only one bishop and two pawns. His opponent held Mirko's queen and both rooks, one knight and four pawns. The game would be over soon I thought. I grabbed a book off a shelf and telling the Father in attendance I was going to find a shady tree near the back of the Commissariat grounds to study my English.

Leaving the book at the foot of a large oak I crept away, ever mindful of the eagle eyed priest that could be peering from behind any of the windows in either the dormitories or the main building.

I made it. Freedom! At last, I was alone on the streets of America. I walked a few blocks from the Commissariat, heading toward downtown Chicago. On my right an alley invited a look. It was narrow and dark, squished between two buildings at least three stories high. Peering in from the security of the main street I saw an old black man slumped on the pavement. Trash was scattered all around him and he didn't move at all. I was afraid he might be hurt or dead. I swallowed my fear and went the thirty feet or so into the alley to see if he was okay. The closer I got to him the surer I was he would sit up and tell me to move along. He didn't. When I reached him I knelt down next to him listening for breathing sounds. A rumble and rasp floated up from his lungs, making its way past slack lips. A filthy shirt covered his scrawny chest. From a distance he looked old, but up close I saw that was not the case. He was at least fifty though. His skin was loose around his neck and curly black hair covered all but the very top of his head. He looked ravaged. His pants and shoes were thin, coated with dust and various stains. Reaching out with one hand I gave him a tentative shake on his left shoulder while asking if he was okay.

"What? Whatchu wants?" His eyes flew open and he scuttled away from me. As he scooted on his butt a paper bag slid from the crook of his arm dropping six inches or so to the pavement. The sound of breaking glass. Red liquid pooled from the bag, instantly staining the cobbles to a ruby colored mess.

"You broke my wine! You broke my wine! How I'm gonna get mo now, huh? You owe me eighty cents! Gimme my money, gimme it!"

I stood up quickly and started running back to the street. The Lord was not watching over me that afternoon. Four black teenagers, all older and larger than me, were passing by the mouth of the alley just as the old man started yelling for me to give him his money. They fanned out in front of the alley, effectively blocking my escape. I didn't want to run the other way because the alley was long, and I knew they would catch me. I stopped.

The biggest one said "You better gi that ole' man his eighty cents. Whatchu doin' robbin po' black folks?"

My bowels were getting looser by the second. With clarity I recalled how painful that punch from Simon had felt. I stuttered a garbled reply.

"N-no! I was help—trying to help him, not rob him, I swear!"

They looked at each other, deciding I was lying.

The oldest one spoke again. "You was trying to rob that ole' drunk. Now you gonna pay!"

All four of them came towards me in a rush. The first punch was to my stomach. I doubled over, falling to the ground. Soon all four of them were punching and kicking my face, arms and body. Leaning over me, busy at their task, the stench of rotten breath and rancid bodies overpowered me. My breakfast of scrambled eggs came hurtling from my stomach to open air. Gravity defeated velocity, and my vomit splattered the shoes of one of the boys. When he saw what I had done he wound back his leg to deliver a mighty kick to my stomach. There was no barbed wire hole to scoot through this time. It was not dark and these boys weren't fellow Croats. The rest of my breakfast and all the air in my lungs expelled in a massive whoosh as his foot sank deep into my gut. I scrunched into a fetal ball.

"Damn, Tyrone, don't kill 'em! Les go!" They cussed at me a second or two longer telling me to keep my white ass in the white part of town. Their warnings made their way to my brain through a fog of pain. Finally opening my eyes to look around I breathed a sigh of relief that they were gone. Turning my head to look at the man I tried helping I saw him glaring at me with fury in his eyes, struggling to his feet. I didn't need another beating, and he looked like he *did* want to kill me. Every bone ached, every muscle screamed, and my head was a cavern of thunderous poundings, but I managed to get to my feet, staggering from the alley before he could get himself upright and in motion.

The gates of the Commissariat never looked so good. I found the book I had left under a tree, and when I reached it my legs went on strike. I collapsed to the ground, staying there the rest of the afternoon. What was I going to say? How was I going to explain the bruises and cuts on my face? Spiraling into panic, a year of pain whirl-pooled inside me. I let the pain out and cried like never before, but the tears were not flowing due to my injuries. I was no stranger to beatings. The fear of explaining *how* I got the scrapes and cuts, coupled with the bleakness of having no one to turn to promoted the torrent. They stopped only when the chest pains caused from repeated heaving, and the personal disgust of snot running over my lips overrode everything I was feeling.

I knew the police were not an option—it would involve the Reverend Fathers. Telling the Reverend Fathers was out of the question because it would involve the

Reverend Fathers. I finally settled on telling them I tried climbing a tree on the grounds and slipped while climbing it. As I fell, the bark scraped my face and I hit my head against a branch. It made sense. I had told one of the Fathers earlier I was going to read under a tree all afternoon. Evaluating my lie for possible flaws I couldn't find any. I decided that was my story and I was sticking with it.

When I went inside the dormitory I made my way to the shower room to inspect the bruises I was certain covered my body. Father Raguz was coming down the steps as I was going up. When he saw my face he stopped cold.

"Bernard, what happened to you?" he asked. His face showed concern, not anger.

I answered him with rehearsed perfection. "I was studying English under a tree near the back of the grounds and grew bored. I decided to climb it. I fell and the bark scraped my face on the way down. I'm sorry Father Raguz." I hung my head to show him I was afraid of punishment for the tree climbing, which I would happily accept to keep the real reason for the cuts away from them.

"Are you okay Bernard" he asked?

"Yes Father Raguz. My side hurts a little bit but I will be all right. I want to go see how badly the tree beat me up."

"Go right ahead, and see me if you need medical attention." He continued down the stairs and outside. I breathed a sigh of relief, void of even the slightest twinge of guilt for telling a priest a lie. Five years in the care of the Franciscans had taught me that telling the truth brought not praise for honesty but punishment resulting in physical pain.

Eleven other Croat students had come with me from St. Joseph's College at the beginning of summer. Seven of us left the Commissariat for school in the fall. Of the five boys not returning; two went back to their families in Croatia, two went to Argentina, and one simply disappeared. He was seventeen and I guess he figured he would be better off homeless and unemployed than spend another day within the confines of the Commissariat. Still a little sore around my ribs I scrunched into a car with six other boys, Father Cuvalo and the driver for the return to St. Joseph's College to begin my sophomore year. It was a short trip, and in no time at all we wound up the drive and rolled into the new academic year.

My grasp of English was growing stronger every day. I began to look at my studies as a way out of the Church. More times than I could count I heard the Fathers tell us that learning English was the key to success in America. I finally realized the truth of what they said. I wouldn't need the Church if I knew English. I could get a job, meet a girl, ask for directions and understand the reply. I could order food in a restaurant, give a cabbie a destination, and ask the cable car conductor how to go downtown. It was the best piece of advice I ever received from them.

It was a typical autumn Saturday at St. Joseph's college. Notre Dame was beating the stuffing out of Navy. Johnny Lattner was playing another outstanding game and the crowd roared its approval. The Fighting Irish won again and I knew it was going to be a better night than if they lost. Every Father, Brother and student crammed the auditorium on Saturdays to watch the Notre Dame Football team. After three months of Saturdays I looked forward to the games, but I still missed baseball. I didn't know English well enough during my freshman year to bother getting in any group settings other than class. I had spent most of the year in solitude. However, this was a new year and I had a renewed interest in baseball, ironically sparked by watching football.

Late November, beautiful in its dying, offered a day of low clouds in a special shade of gray found only on especially perfect autumn days. I was outside raking leaves (mountains and millions of them) when I noticed a car pulling up in front of the main building. I was happy to see Father Cuvalo emerge from the backseat. He saw me looking at him from the north side of the building. He smiled and waved at me. After getting his bag out of the trunk and setting it on the ground he began walking toward me.

As he came within earshot he said, "How are you Branko-I'm sorry, How are you, Bernard?" His eyes were smiling.

"I am well Father Cuvalo. It is good to see you again." I answered in English. I was very glad to have an adult to talk to that didn't berate me. I took the opportunity as it presented itself. I wanted to know why we were forbidden to watch baseball games so I asked him.

"Bernard," he replied, "The professional baseball team's players are almost exclusively Protestant. They are heretics, and the Catholic Church does not condone the activities of heretics. We allow you to watch Notre Dame Football because Notre Dame University is a Catholic institution. Any win by them is a win for the Church."

"I understand Father Cuvalo," I replied. It was not the answer I was looking for. I hoped he would say something along the lines of, "What! No baseball? This is an outrage! Bernard, come with me now. We'll get to the bottom of this and I will not leave until you can watch baseball *every night!*" However, imagination usually finds disappointment in the face of reality, and this time was no different. After mumbling how I understood I returned to raking the leaves.

"Bernard, my young friend," Father Cuvalo said as he placed a hand on my shoulder. I stopped raking but still did not meet his gaze. I didn't want him to see my sadness. He knelt down next to me. Swiveling his neck, he stole a furtive glance around the lawn to see if anyone was within earshot. No one was.

"You wear your disappointment like a banner for the entire world to see. You must guard against this. If others can divine your emotional state with but a glance you lose a large advantage when dealing with people. This is my personal advice only. However, I to am discouraged that the Church will not allow you to watch baseball." He leaned in close, as if the nearest Father, fifty yards away, might hear him. "It is a foolish policy, and indicative of the narrow mindset of the Church. Take heart my young friend, the day will come when you will not be so restricted." He stood abruptly as if worried he might have ladled too deeply in the pool of truth.

"So, young Bernard! Your studies; how are they progressing?" All business now.

"I am doing well. Thank you for asking Father Cuvalo." I answered.

"Bernard! You have a long way to go on these leaves, I suggest you put greater energy to your task." Father Benedict spoke harshly as he came up behind me. He must have popped around the back corner. I suddenly understood why Father Cuvalo had broken off his confidential advice so abruptly.

"Yes I will. Thank you Father Benedict". I renewed my leaf gathering efforts with the energy of one who knows he is not alone in despair. Not for the first time, I was heartened to know men such as Father Cuvalo existed in the Church. My feeling of gratitude did nothing, however, to change my feelings regarding baseball. I made a promise to myself I would somehow be able to follow the games. I didn't see one baseball game my entire sophomore year. It turned out to be a promise long unfulfilled.

My sophomore year folded itself into memory. The summer following the school year was identical to the summer before. June worked itself into September, and at sixteen years old I found myself (a little) taller and leaner, with a passable command of the English language.

Professional baseball was in full swing and while at the Commissariat from late May to late August I missed most of the season. The Church remained steadfast in the assertion that watching Protestants play baseball might somehow endanger our immortal souls, hence the ban was still enforced.

I was now a junior at St. Joseph's College. Only four of the original twelve refugees' were still enrolled with me. Mirko, to my great sadness, informed me early in the academic year that his family had contacted the Commissariat and mailed them payment for a one-way plane ticket to Argentina.

"Branko, I will miss you". Mirko was fifteen now, and the small boy tugging my sleeve on the dock in Bremerhaven, Germany had grown into a strong, stocky, confident friend. "You were always my best friend, Branko. I will never forget you. Perhaps you can visit me in Argentina, eh?"

Strong, yes. Confident, yes. Realistic, no. I answered in such a way to make him feel at ease with his departure.

"Of course I will come and see you Mirko-perhaps when I am out of Seminary. Goodbye, my friend, and God bless you."

"That would be good Branko. May God bless you also." He looked at me intensely. Perhaps he was not so naive after all. Turning to walk outside he didn't look back. The door swung shut behind him and Mirko was no longer a part of my living world. He stepped into a room in my mind. The room holds my mother, father, and all of my sisters-even Milan is there. The hungry window's first victim is there, and so is Andrija Borovich, the young girl raped by the Serbs also there is the captain of the Partisans that killed our livestock-reared up on his horse, although far in the recesses of this vast room. Sahar offers me a plate of steaming food for the thousandth time, always as kindly as that winter evening in Bosankska Gradiska. It was a room of ghosts. Some held honored spots while others sulked in the corners, banished by me until I saw fit to parade them up for inspection. Mirko made his way to the front row with ease. I saw him in my mind and smiled.

"Goodbye, my friend," I said softly to him, though he was already gone.

The year progressed. I was a junior, and as such, certain opportunities were open to me. As soon as school started I picked up a job at the bowling alley located in the basement of the Main building. These chances to work were available to juniors, but denied to sophomores and underclassmen.

The bowling alley had two full-length lanes. I manually removed the fallen pins still in the way from the first bowl and set them back up after the completion of a frame. It was dangerous work. The Brothers and Fathers were always considerate, but some of the other students were not so thoughtful. I had to reach into the set-up area to reset the pins and remove the fallen ones. When they saw me up inside the pin area, a few of the more obnoxious ones hurled their bowling balls down the lane at me. I scrambled and was lucky to avoid being there when they thundered in. I learned a bowling ball is very heavy. Made of hardened rubber most of them weigh around twelve to fifteen pounds. The racket the balls made when smashing against the pins was deafening from my perch above. I worked ten hours a week and earned coupons for my efforts. I traded them in for candy and a few trinkets at a bookstore on the grounds. I also earned coupons by shining the shoes of the Priests. As many hours as I worked I didn't earn enough coupons to get anything of value, but I finally came upon the solution that would allow me to follow the Major League Baseball games.

September breathed the first early-morning chills of autumn. My job in the bowling alley progressed frame by frame. I wrapped up another shift went directly to my dormitory to get ready for supper. There was only one other person there. He was a senior named John who didn't like me very much. He was of the group that rolled bowling balls with an eye to bean me. However, my desire to get what he was holding in his hands overruled my fear. My hand rustled around inside my pocket. It was stuffed full of coupons. I thought I might be able to swing a trade so I walked over to him.

"Hello John" I said with the least accent I could muster. He already called me an effing D.P., so there was no sense in fueling *that* fire.

"What do you want D.P.?" He stared down at me with disdain. John's attitude toward the final four Croat students was typical of the entire student body. *They* were Americans and we were the trash of Europe.

I swallowed.

"I have an idea . . . . I very much want the radio you are holding. I am working hard in the bowling alley. There are also many shoes I polish. I can offer you four hundred and thirty seven coupons for your radio. What do you think?" I held my breath. If he said yes I would be able to listen to the ballgames!

"Coupons! What do I want with worthless coupons?" He scornfully replied. "You D.P.'s are so stupid! You work so hard and all you get is a ticket worth a piece of candy. Don't you even know when you're getting scammed?" He shook his head, laughed a quick bark of amusement and turned away from me.

Oh great I thought. Now I had to break a rule I had set up for myself. I was going to let someone know I had a secret stash of money-*American* money. I was nervous about it though. If not careful I would put myself in the hottest water imaginable. The priests would gladly throw wood on the fire roaring beneath my boiling kettle.

Over the last year I had lifted a dollar here and a dollar there from the collection plates. Filled to the brim with hard, cold cash I would take the plates to the priest for counting. This usually involved walking down a hall to a room in which the priest waited for us to arrive. It was during this short walk that the occasional dollar bill found its way into my pocket. At last count this had occurred twelve times. It was my secret. I was scared to death to tell anyone what I had done, but I was not letting this radio go if I could help it.

"I have cash," I said simply and slowly.

John turned around when he heard the word cash.

"How much cash?" His eyes grew narrow. I'm not sure if he meant to, but he leaned in toward me as he asked. I backed up a step, suddenly afraid.

"Hopefully enough to buy your radio." My voice wavered. "How many dollars do you want for it?"

He looked down at me with contempt. Giving my question some thought he looked at the ceiling for minute then smiled and looked back down. He was at least six inches taller than me, so he literally (and figuratively) looked down on me.

"I'll tell you what D.P. This is the finest transistor radio made. It can pick up anything—even baseball games." His eyebrows rose tauntingly. "I know you can't afford it. You don't make any money, you're too busy saving *coupons*. But if you have seven dollars in *American* money I will sell it to you."

Seven dollars! I would gladly have given him all twelve! Wisely, I kept my expression neutral and answered just as evenly.

"Seven dollars is a lot of money, but I can pay what you are asking. Can we meet after dinner right here? I will have the money with me." I didn't want to get into my money in front of him. I had a feeling if I did that would be the last I would see of it.

He seemed surprised that I could afford what he was asking. It was obvious from his evil smile he thought priced the radio so high I couldn't afford it in a million years. He answered in a sly tone.

"Let's get it done now, Bernard. Why wait? You can listen to your precious baseball games right away—I heard the Yankees and the White Sox are playing tonight. What do you say?"

I was tempted, very tempted. Nonetheless I held firm, telling him the money was hidden and I wanted to get it after dinner. Dinnertime consumed itself, and shortly thereafter I found myself the proud owner of a transistor radio. That first evening was the most fun I enjoyed since walking down the gangplank to Ellis Island. The White Sox and Yankees were battling it out in the bottom of the ninth inning. I could *just*, and I mean just barely hear the game through my pillow. Other boys around me would be so jealous if they knew I had it. I was certain they didn't know about the radio since John wasn't supposed to have it either. Bedtime became a thing to look forward to. I was always in bed first, with the radio tucked safely between my pillow and mattress. While the other boys were whispering about the games I was listening to them. The season was in full swing and I spent as much time with my ear glued to the radio as possible. The starting times for ball games became the clock around which I built my day, and before I knew it the playoff season opened.

One evening a few weeks later, just before bed, I was getting ready for a big playoff game between the Washington Senators and the New York Yankees. Everyone else would be coming soon so I hurriedly tuned the radio while sitting on my bed, holding it low between my legs. Focusing intently I lifted it to my ear to fine tune the station, and just as I had it coming in perfectly another student walked into the dormitory, a crony of Johns. Great! I tried to hide it but my furtive actions only drew attention to myself.

"What's that, D.P.? What do you have there, eh? A *radio*? How did you get that?" He made a motion to grab it but I tucked it in to my stomach.

"It is mine. I bought it fairly and squarely. Please do not tell. *Please*?" I pleadingly looked up at him. I knew he had the power to cause me to lose my radio and put me in an enormous amount of trouble.

"You're in serious trouble, D.P." He turned quickly, yelling as he ran out the door, "Bernard the D.P. has a radio! Bernard the D.P. has a radio!"

I heard his voice fading as he repeated it going down the steps. As surely as the sun rises I expected a priest to storm through the door within a minute. I was off by at least half. It only took thirty seconds for Father Benedict to sweep into the room. My heart sank into a pool of dread. Of all the Fathers in residence Father Benedict held the most hatred for the Croat students. He made a beeline to where I sat dejectedly on the bed. There was no point in denying I owned the radio. Father Benedict reached down and snatched it out of my hands. I might as well not have been there, so little attention did I receive. He was far more interested in the radio. I had set the tuning to crystal clear reception. Father Benedict held it aloft, looked for and found the volume knob on the side. With his thumb he rolled the mini plastic wheel up and the announcer's voice floated into open air. It was the bottom of the second inning I glumly noted. The announcer's voice faded, not because Father Benedict turned it off, but because he was leaving the room with it glued to his left ear, thoroughly engrossed in the game. He was almost through the door when he turned back to face me.

"You will be dealt with tomorrow," he noted in my general direction. His mind was clearly on the ball game that was such a sin to listen to.

I spent the night wrapped in a blanket of my own making. Woven of fear, regret, and anxiety, it cloaked my spirit making the night a fearful and ugly thing. Demons of the past reared up and demons of the present were so real my sweat splashed them. The morning was a breached birth.

"Dujlovich, come with me now." A Brother I had seen only a few times roughed my shoulder, speaking insistently and immediately. The evening flooded back in a rush of events. Dread swam close behind—an angry, hungry shark eager for a bite of me.

I followed him out into the hall, down the steps, and along another even longer hall. The sound of our shoe soles slapping on the tile floor bounced off smooth walls. The Brother leading me said nothing. I looked at him as a jailer leading the condemned to his execution. He stopped at a doorway on his left, reached out and opened the door, then silently motioned me through it. Stepping inside the room Father Benedict directed me to a seat across from the desk he sat behind. The door closed behind me leaving the two of us alone. There was nothing in the room except for; us, a desk, two chairs, and a picture of Jesus on the wall slightly above and behind the head of Father Benedict. He skewered me with a glance.

"So Bernard, we meet again under similar circumstances."

I recalled the other circumstance he referred to. In the middle of my sophomore year, I was caught reading a book called "From Here to Eternity." There was no special reason for my reading it. I found it along the road bordering the north side of the grounds and thought the cover was provocative, fueling my thoughts of the opposite sex. It had a picture of Burt Lancaster and Deborah Kerr holding each other in a tight hug. Just as this time another student told on me, and just like that time Father Benedict was the priest in charge of my disciplinary action. He told me the book was a sinful piece of literature because the author described scenes with sex in it. The book was on a ban list composed by the Church. I was reading the last few pages when I was caught, and nowhere did I read of any especially graphic sex scenes. The only one that sprang to mind was when Burt Lancaster and Deborah Kerr were on the beach kissing-that was it though. However, a ban is a ban, so according to Father Benedict penance must be paid. I spent a month scrubbing pots and pans in the kitchen after dinner when everyone else had time to study and goof off.

"Yes, I'm sorry Father Benedict," I answered.

"What shall we do with you Bernard? You seem to have a problem following the rules we have established. First the book, and now a radio! You know of course the radio will not be returned to you. I destroyed it this morning."

Uh-huh. Destroyed, I bet. If destroyed meant keeping it for oneself. He must think I'm dumb. He hadn't been able to get the radio out of his ear long enough to bother talking to me last night.

"Sorry means nothing." he continued. "You said you were sorry about the book. You were punished for that and yet now you are discovered with a transistor radio that you know is forbidden. I see no option but to assign you three months of kitchen work effective tonight after dinner. Further, due to the seriousness of your offence, expulsion is not out of the question. Your case will come up before the Vicar-General for resolution. You may go." He dismissed me with his eyes, looking from me to the door and back again. When I didn't get up immediately he sighed and looked toward the door yet again. I left, retracing my steps straight back to my room.

I felt I was getting off easy with the kitchen assignment, so the three months passed in a series of fourteen hour days composed of learning, studying, prayer, and lots and lots of scouring pots and pans. Nothing ever came of the expulsion issue. I doubted Father Benedict ever presented my case to anyone. He picked up a transistor radio for free and was leaving it at that.

The summer of 1954 was a hot one. Back for another round of work at the Commissariat (my third) I hoped the Morning Star was out of business and the presses were silent. This was not to be-Morning Star still pumped out bundles after bundle. Fifteen-hour work days drained me of energy until sleeping, eating and working meshed into a haze. Sixteen years on earth and I was no further along than I was three years ago. My English was better than ever so I had no problem understanding and conveying my thoughts in the native tongue of my new home, but I still had no money and very few experiences of American life beyond the confines of the Commissariat and St. Joseph's College. In September I would be a senior. After that I could make the break for freedom. At eighteen years old the Church lost the right of guardianship over me and I could leave if I so chose. I spent hour upon hour dreaming of the day it would happen.

Toward the end of the summer Father Vasilj, now a Commissariat regular, announced we would be going to the Chicago Opera House to see a play called A Midsummer Night's Dream. It was a magical evening. Another eventful evening followed a few weeks later. Father Cuvalo announced over dinner he was taking us to the Chicago Symphony to listen to Handle's Messiah. The music was hauntingly beautiful.

Why now? I wondered. Why, after all these years are the Fathers being so generous? After thinking it through I decided it must be because there were originally twelve of us to pay for as opposed to the three now remaining. In addition, I was one of the younger boys in my group when we came to America, hence all of us were at least sixteen or seventeen years old now. As such they might safely assume we would have a greater appreciation for opera or symphony than we would as young boys.

Soon enough summer was over and I climbed into the car for my last trip to St. Joseph's College. I was sure I would not be coming back for another summer of hard labor at the Commissariat so I gave it an especially long glance as we pulled out of the gate and headed north on Drexel Boulevard. There were no tears and my throat didn't constrict at all. Relief was the only emotion I felt.

My senior year progressed in typical St. Joseph fashion. Grinding my way through classes and prayer the days blended until May-then the blending came to a halt. In early May, about a month before the school year ended, an announcement was posted on the main bulletin board outside the dormitory rooms. As I read it I became increasingly excited. This was what I was waiting for! The notice was directed to graduating seniors only. In a nutshell, as graduating seniors we were directed to inform our principal instructor of our intentions after graduating. The options listed (for two of the three of us remaining) included returning to Drexel Boulevard for the summer, then enrolling at a Catholic University in the St. Louis area with priesthood the goal. The only other option was to leave the Church and strike out on our own. The choice was clear and simple. I informed Father Benedict within the day. It was not pleasant. I found him erasing a chalkboard in his classroom. Rapping lightly on the doorframe I entered the room.

"Excuse me, Father Benedict, but I am here to advise you of my future plans."

His back still turned from me he industriously rubbed the eraser up and down, back and forth. The silence grew in volume. I was already nervous and this didn't make it any easier.

"And what are your intentions Bernard?" His voice was dry and disinterested. He really did hate me.

"I have decided to leave the care of the Church. I will go on my own and do the best I can in my new country. I am very sorry I do not want to become a priest but I feel this is the best path for me." I was still at the door. My knuckles were shiny white, so tightly was I gripping the doorjamb.

Still not facing me Father Benedict's words floated across the room.

"You're an ingrate. The Church has paid for your education, fed and clothed you since you were nine years old. Now, at the first opportunity to get away, you take it. Well, go then. Goodbye, Bernard."

I said nothing in reply, just turned and walked away. The next three weeks floated by, and at the end of May I was driven back to the Commissariat with the other three original students. Once there I also explained my decision to Father Cuvalo. He was not pleased but did wish me luck. I had no desire to say goodbye to anyone else that was present. I was still seventeen and could not legally leave, so with my travel bag slung over my shoulder I stole through the front gate of Drexel Boulevard and into a new chapter of my life.

# CHAPTER XVII

## "A Day in the Life of a Newly Freed Man"

Summer. Glorious, warm, sunny, smiling, free summer. The weight of the years dropped from my shoulders as effortlessly as the Blue Jay's feather floating to the ground in front of me. The yoke of oppression I had lived under for the last eight years lifted with the ease of dandelion puffs dispersing on a breeze. Father Vasilj had no power over me now. Father Benedict could ask me to scrub pans for a thousand years and I could simply walk away from him. *This* is the true measure of freedom I thought. Freedom, however, I quickly learned is a double-edged sword. Sure I could say no to Father Vasilj. I didn't have to rake leaves, scrub pans or wash lavatories, but I *did* have to eat. I had to have a place to lay my head at night. I realized I had taken these things for granted with the Church, but now that I was on my own I fretted with a nervousness bordering on the hysterical. My thoughts centered on finding a place to live.

After sneaking away from Drexel Boulevard I turned right. I had always come from this direction when returning from St. Joseph's so I knew I was on the right track. Finding a phone booth was the first thing I needed to do. A printer for Morning Star had offered to help me find a place if I ended up leaving the Church. I scrunched through a wad of papers and found his number. I didn't have any loose change for the phone call but the self-donations from the offerings had accrued over the last year into a tidy roll of fifteen one-dollar bills. Going around the back of the filling station that I came upon I separated one bill from the money roll then shoved the roll deep in the bottom of my old suitcase. I didn't want to walk in fumbling with a fat roll of money. Yela's innate mistrust of people had rubbed off on me. I had seen more than one person beat to near death for their stupidity in showing those around them an especially delicious parcel of food. In the camps there is no room for morals in an empty stomach.

Walking back around to the front of the place I looked up at a sign anchored high above the ground on a pole. I was pleased to see it was red, white and blue. It spelled Standard Oil. I had seen other signs just like this one on trips back and forth between Drexel Boulevard and St. Joseph's College.

A man in a pressed green uniform looked up when the doorbell clanged. A millisecond glance at me told him all he needed to know, a chore performed fifty times a day. A small oval patch was sewn onto the left breast of his shirt. It had a white background with a red border and an embroidered name that spelled Ron. Ron was non-descript in every way.

"Hello Ron," I said. "May I please have change for one dollar?" I thought I sounded like an American but in the four seconds I spoke he deduced I was an immigrant, and (in his mind) treated me accordingly. He shook his head, mumbling something about damn foreigners, as he took my outstretched dollar bill. He held it up to the light, inspecting it as if I was trying to pass off some other nation's currency. Satisfied, he popped open the register and handed me three quarters, two dimes and a nickel. Thanking him I retreated out the front door and went to the phone booth on the side of the building next to the restrooms.

The phone call cost a dime. I winced. Even though it was just one dime I only had fifteen dollars to my name, so it made me ill spending *any* of it. The phone rang twice after the operator connected me to the number before Andy Urban answered.

"Hello? How may I help you?" His voice came through the earpiece with crystal clarity.

"Andy, this is Bernard Dujlovich from Drexel Boulevard. How are you?" I tried my hardest to be very polite to him. He held my immediate future in his hands.

"I'm fine Bernard, and how are you?" He seemed genuinely glad to hear my voice so I continued with more confidence.

"I am well Andy. Thank you for asking. I am thinking you are wondering why I called. I am remembering a conversation we had last year in the printing room. You told me if, when the time came and I decided to leave the Church, you would help me with a place to live, at least temporarily. This is why I am calling. Can you still help me?" I quickly continued, "I left the Commissariat one hour ago and I am at a Standard Oil filling station on Forty-Seventh Street." Rarely did so much depend on a response. I held my breath with the same anxiety I felt in Bosanka Gradiska while waiting for Sahar to come to the door.

Relief flooded through me.

"Of course the offer is still good Bernard. Can you make your way to the Lincoln Park neighborhood?"

"Yes I can," I quickly answered. I had no idea where Lincoln Park was located but I would crawl there if I had to.

"Good. Go there and ask for directions to a little tavern a few blocks south of Fullerton on Clark Street. Anyone living in the area will know of it. I will be waiting for you there. When do you expect to arrive? Will you be taking a cable car or a cab?"

He spoke so rapidly I had trouble keeping up. I got flustered; suddenly scared I couldn't do this.

"I am four blocks from the Commissariat Andy. How many miles is the Lincoln Park neighborhood from where I am?"

"Many. You need to catch a streetcar heading North on State Street. Tell the conductor you want to go to Lincoln Park and he will help you. Bernard I'm glad you called. By the way, you may have to transfer to the Clark Street streetcar. It's a little confusing. Now I need to make a few phone calls myself and get you set up. More than likely you will end up near where you're at now. It will take you at least an hour to get here so I will see you there this afternoon. Good luck! Bye now."

I started to thank him again but he rang off the line immediately after saying 'Bye now'.

Going back inside I asked Ron when the next streetcar came along.

"Every half-hour." He returned to his newspaper. I dreaded to ask, but I had to!

"Excuse me, Ron? What direction is Lincoln Park?"

He looked up, clearly annoyed. Not answering in words he pointed. My eyes followed his finger. My gaze had no choice but to stop at a Coca-Cola machine on the far wall. It was full of bottles of ice cold Coca-Cola glistening invitingly inside a glass door. They were only twenty cents each. I fingered the change in my pocket telling myself it was a long walk and a hot day. It didn't take much convincing. I walked over to the cooler reached in and pulled out a bottle. It was *so cold!* I held it to my forehead rolling the wet glass back and forth. I closed my eyes, lost in the sensation when Ron rudely interrupted.

"You gonna buy that or just heat it up?"

My eyes flew open. "I'm sorry. It just feels very good on such a hot day. Yes, I will buy it." I handed him a quarter and he handed me four cents. *Four* cents? I asked him why I did not get five cents back.

"Taxes! Don't you have taxes where you're from? You probably pay in chickens or something." He was clearly irritated. He asked me to move along. "Just head north." Opening his newspaper with a flourish he snapped it, covering his face. I got the message he was sending.

"Thank you Ron. Goodbye," I said, purely out of politeness. He didn't answer. The bell on the door jangled behind me on my way out.

My feet had their marching orders from one portion of my mind, so with another portion I concentrated on the next big hurdle I had to overcome-finding a job. If I wanted to eat I had to work. I planned on asking Andy Urban if he knew where I could get a job. I was hoping he might have a good suggestion. I knew a job would take care of my other concerns such as clothes and shoes and the like.

I needed to get my bearings. The sun was near its zenith, so I had to trust Ron at the Standard Oil. I started walking. And walking. And walking. After a half an hour of trudging, my bottle of coca-cola long since consumed I dragged my tired feet to a bench in front of what must be a streetcar stop. I paid the conductor the fare and gratefully found a seat to melt into. I knew I had at least an hour before reaching downtown so I closed my eyes for a quick visit to dreamland.

"Downtown Chicago! All off for downtown Chicago!" The conductor's voice returned me from wherever I had been in my dream. Opening my eyes a solid wall of buildings climbed above the view outside the car's windows. Stretching as I stood I made my way to the conductor. When he finished speaking with an elderly lady he turned to me.

"Excuse me, sir, but I need to get to the Lincoln Park neighborhood. Do you know which car I should get on to go there?" I was proud of the way I asked.

"Sure sonny. Go across the street and get on the car heading for Clark Street North. It will take you directly there." He dismissed me, already listening to another question from the person behind me.

I did as he instructed and sure enough the streetcar clanked to a stop at my feet. I paid the dime fare and settled in for another ride. This one was shorter, but far more interesting. My back and forth trips from St. Joseph's had offered little but farms and fields stretching off to either side. Here, in the heart of the city, a vast and incredibly busy Chicago unfolded outside my window. I almost pressed my face against the glass from excitement. Bicycles, motorcycles, buses, cars, trolleys and pedestrians wove in and out of each other. It was the most activity I had ever seen in one place. Banja Luka was a sleepy village next to this. Even Zagreb was a remote backwater compared to the never-ending activity of Chicago.

"Lincoln Park! All off for Lincoln Park!"

I took my cue, stepping onto the pavement below. I went to the first person I saw that looked friendly and asked him where the tavern on Fullerton was located.

"This is your lucky day young man! Look yonder!" His left arm swung into the space occupied by my head. I backed out of the path of his arm, following his pointed finger to a sign above a green door that said Tavern. It was indeed my lucky day.

"Thank you very much Sir." I said to the little man that helped me. Rarely did I meet someone *I* thought of as little.

The tavern was a smoky, dimly lit place. Laughter and smiles floated wall to wall, dispelling the initial gloom I felt walking through the door. I squinted, as if squinting would miraculously supply more lighting. Just coming from outside where the sun's brilliance revealed every detail this land of shadows seemed like another world inhabited by creatures of some dark region I knew nothing of.

A man leaned over a large table covered in green cloth. He held a long stick that tapered to a blunt point at one end. Using the small end he softly rapped the stick against a white ball. The white ball rolled slowly toward a red ball. Tapping it ever so lightly the red ball fell into a hole in one of the corners. I hadn't even noticed the holes. As I looked more closely at the table I saw there were six holes, one in every corner and one in each long side at the midway point. The game looked fun and I resolved to learn it. Busy studying the next shot the man was about to take a tug on my shoulder broke my concentration.

"Bernard, it's good to see you again my friend!" Andy Urban had come out of the shadows. He looked much the same as last year. He had a handsome ruggedness about him. His black hair was thick, sweeping to just above his shoulders. He always had a smile on his face and his brown eyes were ever twinkling. I very much enjoyed his company on those long summer days. Several years older than me he was a failed novitiate like myself. He was also a crude man prone to vulgar jokes. He told me more dirty jokes than I could ever remember. The one I *did* remember (from beginning to end) was particularly funny since it involved Catholic priests. Most of his jokes were about women so I missed the punch line most of the time. This one, though, was very funny. I tried not laughing when he told it but couldn't help myself. He told me the joke at the end of a very long, hot day. He and I were the last two people in the print shop. My mind was imagining how soft my bed was. Andy came around the side of a printing press I was sweeping under.

"Bernard, I have another joke for you. Do you want to hear it?" He asked.

"Of course Mr. Urban. Your jokes are always very funny."

"Okay here it is. A priest and a Rabbi are walking down the street. They both look over to a young boy playing with a toy fire engine. The Priest looks over at the Rabbi and nudges him in the ribs. 'Hey, Rabbi,' he asks, 'Do you want to screw that kid?' The Rabbi looks over at the priest and says, 'Sure, but out of what?'"

Andy started laughing from his belly up. The laughter formed a wave that bellowed forth in gusts. "Out of what! I *love* that joke!"

I couldn't help it. My belly gave birth to its own wave of laughter and soon both of us were bending over, holding our stomachs and trying not to make too much noise. I'm not sure if his laughter was infectious, or if it really was a funny joke.

He pulled me to a booth and pushed me down on the seat, nudging me while sliding in across from me while drinking from his glass of beer.

"So Bernard, tell me about your departure from St. Joseph's." Not a dozen words into my answer he interrupted me. "Listen to this Bernard. I was standing behind Father Vasilj when Father Cuvalo told him you were leaving. Vasilj shrugged his shoulders and said nothing. He is soulless that one. Father Cuvalo seemed genuinely sad about it. I know he liked you. So! You must be wondering if I have found you housing? I have!"

He stopped speaking long enough to take another swig of beer. He held his hand up palm forward. A belch rumbled forth and with a sheepish smile he said, "Excuse me, Bernard. This beer is very good."

Dismissing his burp he continued, "I know an old Lithuanian couple, Kazys and Judita Venclova. They own and operate a boarding house. Most of the boarders are

European. The Venclova's are crusty, I warn you! However, the rent is only twelve dollars per week. That is very reasonable. I must ask you—you *do* have twelve American dollars to pay for your first week?" He looked concerned. I gathered he didn't have a spare twelve dollars should my answer be no.

"I have fourteen dollars and fifty cents. Thank you very much for helping me Andy. If I may ask, can we please go there now? I'm tired, it has been a very long day." I actually liked being here, but the smoke from all of the cigarettes was stinging my eyes. I couldn't understand why people *chose* to inhale smoke into their lungs. It made no sense at all.

He stubbed out his cigarette into a solid looking glass ashtray. It was a Pall Mall. He always had a pack of Pall Malls with him. I had swept up dozens of the crumbled red packs over the last three summers.

"Of course we can go now Bernard. You must be tired-say! This is your first day of *true* freedom in America." He looked at his almost empty glass. "I think we should have a beer to celebrate! What do you say Bernard?" It was obvious he didn't want to leave but I thought my eyes probably hurt more than his longing for another beer.

"I would like to very much Andy, but if it is okay with you I really do want to go." I answered slowly. I was afraid he was going to tell me good luck and then stay right here.

"Okay then, we go." He stood up while reaching for his wallet. Wallet in hand, he went to the bar to pay for his beers as I went outside. Five minutes became fifteen minutes and I was still waiting. I went back inside to find him holding a half finished beer and talking to another man. I waved. He looked surprised, then embarrassed. With two mighty swigs he drained his mug then said goodbye to his friend and headed toward me.

"I'm sorry Bernard. I haven't seen that man in a while and he bought me a beer. What was I to do?"

"It is okay Andy," I answered. It really *was* okay with me. He was helping me so much I didn't know how I could repay him.

We took a streetcar back down south near the Commissariat getting off near sixty-third and State Street. We hopped off and walked to the front of a large three-story home. Marching up the steps Andy knocked on the front door. A very old man opened the door. An equally old lady came up behind him. Andy Urban bid them a good evening and introduced me.

"Mr. and Mrs. Venclova, this is Bernard Dujlovich the young man I spoke with you about earlier today."

Mr. Venclova looked at me and said, "Hello. Please come in." He spoke slowly and carefully.

Andy took this opportunity to leave. Wishing me good luck he bounced down the steps and headed back in the direction we had come from. Probably going right back to the saloon.

"Please, do you have first weeks rent?" Mr. Venclova inquired. I handed him twelve dollars. He counted it slowly handing it to his wife only when certain he did indeed receive twelve dollars and not a penny less. "Thank you. Now please follow me to room. It is on third floor."

I let out a silent sigh. As slow as *he* walked it would be a week before we finally reached the third floor.

What seemed like one week later he opened the door to my room, motioning me through. For the first time in my life I had my own place. I could lock my door and tell people to go away if they knocked on it. I felt powerful-the king of my destiny. The room was small. Faded yellow wallpaper provided little color. One window looked out onto the street below. A single bed invited from one corner and a small bureau rested in another corner. That was it, except for a medium size Crucifix on the wall at the head of my bed. I expected Mr. Venclova to leave but it was not to be. With a frustrating lack of speed he carefully walked to the bed, slowly turned around and gingerly sat on it. He stared at me. Never one to break a stare I returned his look.

"Mr. Urban tells me you left the Church. Why?" He asked somewhat harshly.

I knew most Lithuanians were devout Catholics so I took a moment to think about my answer before replying.

"Mr. Venclova, the Church has housed, fed and clothed me for eight years and I am very grateful for that. But please understand, I did not ask to become a priest. They chose me for novitiate schooling when I was nine years old. My mother Yela let them take me to Italy so I could get out of the refugee camps in Austria. I did not know at the time I would end up in America. I am very glad I did, but as much as I am grateful to the Church I believe I can still lead a devout life without becoming a priest. I hope you understand."

He shook his head, staring at the floor. "As you said, this is America. The best thing I have found in America, and I have been forty-seven years here, is that this is land of choices-so yes, I understand."

I felt an enormous relief. It was important to me that he understood why I did what I had done.

"However, I would like *you* to understand few rules we have." He was all business now. I listened intently.

"No drinking, no coming in late at night unless from work. No loud noises, no loud radio, no females and no parties. These are rules. What *we* will do is wash your clothes if you leave them outside your door. Oh, rent is due every Friday at five P.M. sharp. If you are late two weeks in row you must move immediately." He crept to his feet and ambled to the door. Before turning the knob he reached in his pocket and fished out a key handing it to me. "This is key to room. Do not lose it. Goodnight." Opening the door he stepped into the hall and ever so carefully closed the door behind him.

The room was proof of my independence and I loved every crack in the ceiling and every stain on the wallpaper. It was mine, mine, mine! Looking at the bed I felt it only fair to give it a test. I stripped to my underwear and stretched out on it. Never in my life had I enjoyed such a degree of privacy. I luxuriated in it. Weaving my fingers together behind my head and staring at the ceiling I reveled in the moment until my mind rudely hurled a thought into my cloud of joy; dispersing my good feelings in a puff. I was unemployed.

I had to get a job! I decided nothing was more important. I had to eat, pay rent, and buy clothes and toiletries. None of these things was free and I only had a little over two dollars after paying my first weeks rent. Starting early tomorrow morning I would begin applying at every business I came to until someone offered me a job. I was confident I could get one-Father Cuvalo had drilled his message regarding the benefits of speaking, reading and writing English. I allowed my eyelids to give up their fight against gravity and with glowing anticipation of things to come I allowed sleep to conquer me.

Clanging steel wheels rolled in and out of my early morning dreams . . . Trains pulled out of Zagreb-people screamed the names of relatives lost in the crush of bodies. In my dream I stumbled and that was all it took. With my footing gone I fell to the ground, immediately torn from my family as a thousand pair of feet continued a frenzied dash for the rail cars. One train was overflowing with refugees and a bell's ringing signaled it was pulling away. A bell was ringing? Trains don't have bells . . . something is wrong.

My eyes flew open. The ringing sound traveled from my dream into wakefulness. The sound of clanging wheels also made the leap from dreamland to reality. I stumbled from my bed and went to the unwashed window. Peering through it to the street three stories below I spied a streetcar, the source of the clanging and ringing bell. It was already rumbling down the street to the next stop. Reality forced itself to the front of my mind and dreamland faded into nothingness.

A job. I had to find a job. Enjoying every act involved in getting ready for my day I was soon dressed and ready to begin my search in earnest. I bounced down the stairs, hopped the front steps to the pavement, looked around and smiled at my new life. Another streetcar had passed in front of my building while I was getting dressed so I assumed they came by often. Good fortune had deposited me directly in front of a stop, so hopefully I wouldn't have any trouble getting to and from work.

I decided the best course was to start on foot. I pointed my feet in the same direction as the cable car. Wherever my feet led the rest of my body inevitably went as well. The morning passed without me applying for a single job. There was just too much to take in. It *was* my first *full* day on my own, and although I knew I needed work, in spite of that, I allowed myself the luxury of doing nothing but enjoying the sunny Chicago morning.

Morning became mid-afternoon when my stomach rumbled, demanding satisfaction. I giggled to myself realizing I had a *choice* in what to eat. This was another first. Every day for the last eight years I'd had no say in what I was going to put in my stomach. I felt lightheaded I was so happy. Looking up and down both sides of the street I realized I could walk in any one of the numerous restaurants and order *whatever I wanted!* Choosing a place at random I went inside and sat at a table. A waitress came to me within minutes and took my order. She brought the food and when I was finished she even removed my dirty dishes! I am king of the world! People are serving *me*! Meatloaf and mashed potatoes never tasted so good.

She was good looking, I noticed. I admired the way her hips swooshed inside her tight uniform. When she took the last dirty plate off my table she asked if I needed anything else. I shook my head back and forth, the universal indicator for "No".

Thanking me for coming in to eat she scribbled on a pad of paper, following her quick marks with a circular swoosh. She tore the ticket from the pad placing it face down on my table. I knew it could be only one thing-a bill, something I had to pay for. I didn't mind the responsibility though. I looked forward to it. The amount was one dollar and twenty cents. I drew out a wad of one-dollar bills and fumbled for exact change. I laid it on top of the check and waited for the waitress to walk by. Eventually she made her way down the row of tables toward me. When she came abreast of me I picked up the money and pushed it in her path.

"Thank you for the nice meal Ma'am." I wanted her to know I appreciated the good service.

She looked at me as if I were weird, accepting the money I offered. She glanced at the bill, then what I had given her. Her brows furrowed. Something was wrong! I had not paid less than I owed! Looking up from the money, her lips stretched tight in a frown.

"You foreigners!" She exclaimed. "Don't you tip wherever you're from? Geez! Me and my babies gotta eat ya know?"

Not giving me time to reply she moved to the next table.

What did she mean? What is a tip? I asked myself. I knew I had messed up somehow. I made a note to myself to find out what a tip is. I left quickly, embarrassed for a reason I had yet to learn.

Toward the end of the afternoon and seven job applications later I tiredly decided one more application wouldn't hurt my chances. Continental Can, Inc. loomed in front of me. Sighing, I walked up the path to the front door and stepped into the blessed coolness of the air-conditioned interior. The outside door opened into a very small room. Two steps brought me to a sliding glass window. On the other side of the glass six or seven desks populated the space, all of them occupied by busy business people. Phones were ringing and muted conversations made their way through the glass. A matronly looking woman sitting closest to the window spotted me and, scooting backwards in her chair, slid the window open.

"How may I help you?" Very polite, but her manner indicated she had important things to do and this interruption had best be worth the trouble of her address. I swallowed hard. Sweat literally popped out on my forehead.

"Hello. M-my name is Berislav—I am sorry, Bernard Dujlovich. I am in need of a job. Do you have any openings for workers?" My honesty must have derailed her. She paused, looking at me in a less mechanical light.

"Please have a seat," she said.

I did as she asked. This was going well. So far every one of the seven people I inquired for employment with had handed me a job application telling me they would 'pass it along.' The same woman appeared in the sliding window, beckoning me with her right hand. I went to the window. Her left hand held a standard job application. She handed it to me saying, "Please fill this out, I will do my best to get you an interview."

An interview! I was getting an interview! My legs had trouble obeying my minds order to stillness. I prayed (conveniently, I admit) for God to grant me this job. I filled out the application in my best handwriting. Turning it in to the woman she asked me to have a seat. I did precisely as she instructed.

Ten minutes passed. Twenty. Thirty. Beaten down by rejection I just, and I mean *just* decided I was going to leave when the only door other than the front door cracked open and the woman I spoke with earlier motioned me inside saying softly, "Mrs. Spahn will see you now." She turned left, taking for granted I would follow her down a carpeted corridor leading away from the main office area. She led me in quick silence to a part of the building reserved for the elite-managers, presidents, people who hired people. Three offices down on the left she turned stopping just outside the door. Swooshing me through the door with her hand the invisible current of air she created propelled me inside, and with two steps I stood before a desk occupied by a middle-aged woman.

Mrs. Spahn was a composition in severity. Her hair was drawn-*winched* back into a small tuft at the base of her neck. The rest of her mirrored the theme-from make-up (mathematically applied), to jewelry (a work watch, devoid of design), to clothes (a razor—cut gray blazer with equally linear skirt).

"Why do you want a job?" she asked, a whisper of German roots creeping through.

I was not accustomed to this direct approach. I had not gotten this far in an interview yet. I faltered, answering slowly, mindful of proper English. "I need a job. I just graduated from St. Joseph's College in Hinsdale." Dummy! She asked *why* I wanted a job. She already knew I *needed* a job. Geez!

"Where are you from?" she asked. I may have graduated from school in the U.S.A. but she knew I wasn't born here.

"I am from Croatia, Mrs. Spahn. Until yesterday I was a ward of the Catholic Church. I graduated as a senior two days ago. I have already found a place to live and a way to get here every day. I will not be late and you can count on me to do a good job." This summed it up. I offered more information than she requested but I wanted the job so badly I could taste it. I could hear my heartbeat thumping in wait for her answer.

She didn't give me the job but instead asked another question. "How old are you?"

Dear God, I said to myself, I prayed to you for this question *not* to come up! Why has it then? Are you there? Do you even care about me? These thoughts and a hundred others similar in content bounced inside my head with no answers stepping forward to silence them.

I answered evenly. "I am eighteen."

"Hmmm . . . you don't look eighteen." She mused.

Mrs. Spahn was a good judge of age. I lied to her as I lied to everyone who asked my age. I *was* free of the Church but only geographically. I turned seventeen less than two months ago. Until my eighteenth birthday arrived I was legally a ward of the Church. When I informed Father Benedict of my decision to leave the Franciscans only I knew I was leaving within days of my graduating. The Fathers simply assumed I would stay under their umbrella until I was eighteen. When I left I did so without fanfare.

The Reverend Fathers, I had not doubt, were very curious as to where I was at this very moment. I prayed Andy Urban would tell them nothing. I didn't think he would since his job would be terminated on the spot if they knew he had helped me.

Making a decision to leave the Commissariat was not an easy one. I knew if I went back for another summer at Drexel Boulevard I would end up working without pay for twelve hours a day, *then* leaving. I chose to hasten my break from the Franciscans mainly for that reason. If I was going to work my fanny off I wanted to earn money for doing so, plain and simple.

"I am eighteen Mrs. Spahn. Please give me a job. I will not disappoint you." I gave her my best 'Puh-leese?' look.

A pregnant pause enveloped the room as she scrutinized me, looking in my eyes, at my hair and my clothing.

"Okay, Bernard. If you are here tomorrow afternoon at two-thirty P.M. you can fill out the required paperwork and begin training on the production line at three-thirty P.M. Your work-shift will be from Three-thirty P.M. to Eleven P.M. Your salary will be one dollar and ninety-five cents per hour. That is your hourly wage but you can also earn a bonus for the number of units you produce. The harder you work the more money you will make. So, do you want the job?" She asked as if the question were a formality only. Her lips took an upward turn and her eyes thawed ever so slightly.

Do I want the job? Do I want to eat? Do I want different clothes? Do I want to pay my rent?

"Yes Mrs. Spahn, I want the job and thank you *very* much for this. I will be a good worker, you will see." If I could have hugged her I would have.

"Okay then. We will see you tomorrow. When you arrive ask for me and I will have your papers ready. Good-bye Bernard." She lowered her eyes to a piece of paper on her desk, picking it up and making a point of studying it. Silently indicating the interview was over I thanked her again and exited her office. Retracing my steps, I let myself out through the anteroom and made my way to the street.

I held my head higher and walked taller with a newly invigorated spine. My feet fairly floated on the sidewalk all the way back to the rooming house. Mr. Venclova sat on the front porch so I informed him of my employment. I expected him to congratulate me on my efforts.

Not even raising an eyebrow he answered, "I would expect nothing less. Rent is due in six days." He returned to his newspaper.

A little deflated (but not much-I had suffered far more severe rejections than this) it occurred to me I should remind Andy Urban not to say anything to the Fathers. I hoped he would be at the tavern on Fullerton so I left and headed up the street. Getting in touch with Andy was only one reason for my wanting to go back to the Belden. I also wanted to watch people play pool. The tavern had an atmosphere of genuine happiness that I wanted to be a part of. I was employed! This was a momentous day! I decided on the spot to see if they had *Sljivovica* behind the bar, even though they probably wouldn't serve me since I wasn't old enough.

A seemingly endless quilt of puffy clouds extended far beyond the horizon, doing a fine job of keeping direct sunlight at bay. It made for a cooler afternoon, hence a more enjoyable outing. My luck on the day held. After getting off the streetcar I stepped into the darkened interior of the tavern, spotting Andy Urban in the same position at the bar as yesterday evening. He was deep in conversation with another man and his beer was half full, just like yesterday. Were it not for the color of his shirt I would be pressed to find any difference at all between this evening and the previous one.

Smoke swirled in vaporous clouds under low hanging lights above the two pool tables. The row of booths lining the wall opposite the bar created a line of murky enclosures, each one living on crumbs of light offered by a small table candle.

When I got Andy Urban's attention he motioned me to follow him. We walked to one of the booths scooting across from each other on the cushioned benches.

"So how was your day, Bernard?" Andy asked me. He seemed genuinely interested so I served up the good news with a smile on the side.

"I got a job today Andy!" I couldn't help but blurt it out.

"Good for you Bernard! We must celebrate!" Andy looked up and spotted a waitress. "Patty!" He motioned to a waitress ten feet away that was heading in our general direction. She stopped directly in front of us. Her dress was cut shorter than any I had seen, revealing milky white, smoothly toned lower thighs. My breaths came closer together. My gaze traveled up. The neckline on her blouse hung low enough for me to see the swell of her breasts pushing against each other. I was trying not to gawk but failing miserably. Andy was watching me all but drool over Patty.

Suddenly the candle sputtered, gasping for life. Ten seconds later, it gave up and died. "Oh let me get that," Patty chirped. Standing on her toes, she arched up, placing her thighs against the table's edge then leaned down the middle of the table to reach the candle. Her body was directly between Andy and me. Her blouse fell very low, creating a large, dark open space for me to look at. A dark space. Light! I need light! My mind screamed. Dear God, if you truly love me . . . .

Reaching out with his left hand close to the table but in front of her blouse Andy said, "Patty, see if it will restart." Suddenly, in a glorious moment of illumination light sprang from his Zippo lighter revealing *everything* in its radius.

"Andy Urban! Shame on you!" she said, pulling her blouse close and standing up at the same time. I was horrified! What if she calls the police?

"Oh, no," I moaned.

Andy looked up at her smiling and very relaxed, considering. "What are you talking about Patty? I just wanted to see if the candle could be relit. You don't think . . . Oh, my goodness, Patty."

Patty looked down at him, a playful smile lighting up her face. She darted a glance at me, then back at Andy. He threw me a wink. They were just playing, I realized. Thank God.

"So Andy, what can I bring you and your friend to drink?" she cheerfully inquired. Apparently having her breasts on display for a drooling idiot didn't bother her in the least.

"I would like a Hamms draft and the same for my friend Bernard." He quickly replied.

I broke in before Patty could leave. "Excuse me Miss, but do you have *Sljivovica?*"

Looking down at me she put a hand on one hip and said "Slivo-what?"

"That is okay." I said quickly. "A Hamms beer would be perfect. Thanks to-thank you."

I told Andy all about my interview with Continental Can, Inc. Two hours and two beers later I wanted to get back to my room so I told Andy that. He signaled for the check. Patty brought it over and handed it to him as she said "Two dollars and forty cents, sweetie."

He reached in his billfold pulled out three dollars and handed the money to her, telling her to keep the change.

She shushed her hand toward his head. He leaned back, laughing.

"Bye, Andy," she wrinkled her nose at him and grinned then looked at me. Bending down toward me she whispered softly "Bye, Bernard," while making no effort to draw in the front of her blouse. The new candle was burning strong and bright. My legs were putty and every breath a fight for completion.

"B-bye." I croaked. She stood upright, whirled around, and was gone. I love American women! I looked over at Andy when Patty left. He was smiling smugly. Embarrassed, I changed the subject.

"Andy, I purchased lunch for myself today at a restaurant. When I paid my bill the waitress who was taking care of me said I did not know how to 'tip'. What is a tip? She seemed upset-I did not pay her less than the check amount so why was she mad at me?" I really wanted to know. If I'm going to fit into my new country it is essential I know the customs.

"Bernard, a tip is extra money you give a waitress, usually ten to fifteen percent of whatever the check amount was. That's how they make their money, not from their hourly wage. What you did is 'stiff' her, or not leave a tip. Depending on where you are some waitresses will say something to you, and some won't." Leaning back on his bench he smiled, saying, "I'm glad you ask questions. If you don't know something just ask. Most people are friendly, if you approach them correctly."

"Thank you for your help Andy." I told him.

I was ready to leave. The smoke was getting to my eyes again. I pushed my empty beer mug toward his side of the table. It scooted further than I intended and stopped just short of dropping into Andy's lap. Embarrassed I exclaimed, "Andy, I am very sorry! I barely pushed it!"

"Bernard, Bernard, relax. You just drank two beers. Do you think you are not a little tipsy?" He asked.

"Perhaps you are correct Andy. I am leaving now, and thank you again for the help you have given me."

Scooting from the booth, stepping through the front door, slowly walking to the stop, silently gliding up the steps, I slipped into bed. My eyes closed gratefully and Patty appeared in my mind, bending down to say goodbye to me again, and again . . . I counted my first full day on my own as a success.

# CHAPTER XVIII

## "The Daily Grind"

Another spin of the earth in its daily rotation brought light directly to, and through my window. My first waking thought was that I have a job. A big day for me. My bed felt wonderful but I had many things to take care of. My teeth were not going to clean themselves and I had no toothpaste. I had no toothbrush, nor towels, razors, shaving cream, underwear, T-shirts or a host of other necessary personal items. As much as I wanted to save my money I knew I had to part with some of it for these things.

Hitting the street I decided to explore my new neighborhood before heading to Continental Can at two-thirty. Striking out in the general direction of my new job I watched Chicago street life play itself out yet again. Kids yelled for their moms, husbands yelled at wives, cabbies yelled at each other and blacks hung out, appearing to do nothing. I did notice though that they were not yelling. They talked in small groups collectively laughing with the deliverance of a joke's punch line. It struck me that they were probably the poorest people I saw, but also appeared to be the happiest-if laughter was an indicator of happiness.

Rexall's Pharmacy was a busy place. The door was never lonely as hands pushed or pulled on it continuously. Finding everything I needed in one place was a blessing. I made my purchases and took them back to my room. It was noon by the time I got back to the boarding house. Hoping to miss the Venclova's I stole up the steps, deposited my purchases on my bed and just as quietly descended the stairs. My luck ran out. Mr. Venclova was just opening his door as I went past it. I told him hello as I made my way to the front door.

"Bernard, please wait a moment," he said. Oh great, I thought. Now I'm in trouble. I knew why. One of the rules he had laid out two nights ago was that I not come in late. "Bernard, I explained that you are not allowed to come in late. Last night you did just that." He looked upset, but I didn't know how to accommodate him.

"I am very sorry Mr. Venclova. I am trying to get my affairs in order. I start my job this afternoon and will be working every night until eleven in the evening. It will be difficult for me to be here early enough to suit you. As much as I want to be here, it will be difficult. I hope you understand."

"You need to come here directly after work. We will not tolerate you showing up late, drunk and noisy." He was serious.

"I will not be coming in drunk. You have my word Mr. Venclova. However, I must go now or I will be late for my first day of work. Goodbye now." Scooting out the door I didn't hear his reply.

Continental Can, Inc. loomed in front of me, not as a job prospect this time but as my first real employer in America. I knocked on the small glass partition window for the second time in two days. I was informed Mrs. Spahn was not at work today, but after a short moment of confusion (and panic for me) the required paperwork was handed to me. Instructed to have a seat and fill out the papers I took a full sixty minutes to complete them. One laborious hour later I knocked softly on the sliding window partition holding up a handful of completed forms.

"Take a seat," the woman taking my application told me. An hour later a hard looking man summoned me. Obviously not an office worker he led me into the bowels of the production area. Grey summed up the color of his uniform and disposition.

"Wait here, I will get a trainer." No hello, no welcome to Continental Can, no nothing. A few minutes later he returned with a burly brute, a man with pig eyes and the grin of an idiot. "This is Jim Clover, your trainer. Listen to him and you may make it here." Without introducing me to my trainer he turned around and walked away, leaving me with the man-child.

Training consisted of Jim Clover showing me which button to push and when to push it. The machinery was huge, loud and intimidating. Jim Clover showed me the machine I would stand in front of every day for eight hours. Within one hour I decided I needed to find another job, but I listened to him and did the best I could. This was my first job and I was determined to be the best gasoline can maker I could be. By the end of my first shift I was clear on my duties. My function was to place the small threaded can opening piece on top of the gas can, then to push a button sending a signal for the machine to weld the part onto the top of the can. It was tedious, repetitive and awesomely boring. My first eight hours turned into three months worth of eight-hour segments.

Over the ensuing months, when not working, sleeping or going to Mass, I took every opportunity I could to explore Chicago. Every day that passed helped me become more American-like.

According to the Venclova's I came in too late at night, and in general did not conform to the rules they had painstakingly spelled out to me on my first day under their roof. Why was I not home immediately after work? Why was I not at the early Mass? Endless! After months of explaining my actions to them I finally decided I needed to make a change.

Walking slowly down the street away from the Venclova's I played out my exit in my mind, performing a post-mortem evaluation of our conversation.

I knocked.

"Mrs. Venclova," I said after she opened her door with *just* enough space to assign status as actually 'open', as opposed to a threaded union of door and doorjamb.

"Yes Bernard," her voice fought its way through the crack. The tension, strangely enough, had no trouble swimming freely between us in spite of the door.

"Mrs. Venclova, I am here to inform you I am moving out. My rent is paid in full and I have cleaned my room." Nervously, almost glad of the door between us, I reached in my pocket, fished out my room key and held it toward the narrow gap. A shaking, liver spotted, bony grasping thing snuck through the suddenly increased door opening fetching the key from my hand. It quickly retreated to its lair before the door itself retreated to its former position. It was lucky, whisking my hand back outside by the narrowest of margins. "You have my key. Thank you for allowing me to live here. Now, I must go. Goodbye."

I turned, reaching for the front door knob.

"Bernard," a male voice stopped me firmly in my tracks. The door did not save me this time. Mr. Venclova did not talk behind doors. He stepped into the hallway with Mrs. Venclova bravely following him. We were cramped in the small foyer. "You can leave if you wish, of course. But I am telling you the city is a wicked place. Satan lounges on the streets, looking for young people such as you, ignorant of the world. You must go to church! Do not go to pool halls or burlesque shows. Gambling and lust are the devils tools! Remember what I have said. Now goodbye, and good luck." Not interested in anything I might wish to say he shooed Mrs. Venclova inside their apartment and then followed her, one studied step at a time. Once inside he began turning around, positioning his body seemingly one degree at a time until facing me directly. Without words he slowly and softly pushed the door shut. I was dismissed. I dismissed them as well. The Venclova's joined the room in my mind; while not in the light they were still well ahead of the Partisans, yet well behind Mirko and many others.

"Hhmmmm." I thought. Pool halls of course relate to gambling. Therefore, 'burlesque' must refer to lust. 'Lust', in my opinion, related to females. This was the sum total of what I considered 'useful information' from Mr. Venclova's parting words of wisdom. A millisecond later I had my answer. I knew who could tell me where I could find a burlesque show! Brendan Lally was waiting for me at the Y.M.C.A. in Roseland, my destination. He was one of four bodies on the same machine crew as me. Roseland was at least eighty blocks from Continental Can, so it would take me over an hour to get to work on the streetcar, but Brendan had his very own car and had offered at times to give me rides to and from work. He stayed at the Y.M.C.A. and through dinner conversation I learned it was less rent than where I was living. I was trying to save money and considered this a good (and timely) opportunity to do so.

Brendan Lally is a very nice man. Around thirty years old he held a positive spirit captive, allowing the joy of its existence to channel through him to excellent results. He stood at least six-foot three-inches tall, and when I looked up at him, unless he was looking down at me, my view consisted of a light brown goatee. The rounded balance of his chin, nose, cheeks and eyes leant themselves to a sturdy, evenly framed picture of a smiling, confident man. Serious laughter burst (rarely and fleetingly) from the twin oceans of his blue eyes indicating a depth of introspection not often (or willingly) displayed. His mouth was never still for long, forever floating tidbits of wisdom, facts, and observations to any willing ear. I was always willing. Listening is learning, and I was *always* interested in learning *anything* about America. Unless I knew what was neat, how to act on the subway, how much to tip a waitress, how would I ever be able to meet an American girl? When it came to answers Brendan was my man.

The Roseland Y.M.C.A. was a haven for displaced men, many barely able to afford the weekly rent. The small rooms occupying a ten by ten foot square cube of privacy held a single bed and small dresser, leaving almost no room to walk. As small as they were the rooms were amply large to hold the failed dreams of most of their residents.

I did not include myself (or Brendan) in that group. There *were* young and eager people, like me, striving to become Americans. The majority of the residents however were sad, tired looking old men. Some of them were sad, tired, old looking, young men with life beating them daily-a gut pounding that stopped only with sleep. Wine brought sleep, and many of them spent an unhealthy percentage of their days and nights in the nether-land of dreams.

Brendan met me in front of the Y.M.C.A. at 11:00a.m. per our plan. I spotted him immediately. His shoulder propped the building's east wall, but he took a chance the structure would remain standing without his support and carelessly left his post to greet me.

"Bernard, good to see you!" Bending low on one knee and flourishing his arm in a benevolent sweep toward the front door he bid me welcome. "Welcome to the last refuge for refuse. The rooms are spacious, the food available in copious quantities, and the women-well, there *is* lots of food." He grinned at his sarcasm in that funny style that was his alone.

"Thank you Brendan." I replied. Employing words I was completely unfamiliar with many of his sentences made zero sense to me.

My workday, beginning at two-thirty in the afternoon and ending at eleven P.M., seemed cut and stamped from a machine so little did it change. On rare occasions I sat for half an hour in the car with Brendan picking up windshield time (as he called it), and listening to him expound on a variety of subjects. His comments to me originated from newspapers he read, television shows he watched and people he talked to. Not once did I get out of his car knowing less about America than when I got in.

For eight and a half hours (less a thirty minute lunch) I operated as a human extension to the gas can machine, and the reason why happened on Fridays. Not only was it the day before the weekend, it was also payday. My checks had grown steadily over the last four months. When Mrs. Spahn had mentioned my salary would be one dollar and ninety cents per hour I knew exactly what she meant.

Salary, I recalled from one of thousands of Grottammare learning periods, is an ancient word deriving from the days of the Romans. Salt, or 'salarium', was issued to Roman soldiers for health reasons, and in Northern Africa salt was so rare it was used as a form of currency by which laborers were paid. The word salary is the modern day carryover from that practice.

'Piece work' was the phrase she mentioned that I was not familiar with. It didn't take long to understand the concept. The more cans we (as a team) produced the more money we made on our paycheck. Brendan explained the value of being paid this way, proving it to me by showing me a low production paycheck and a high production paycheck. Within several months our team of four made more money than the office personnel computing our paychecks.

I shuffled into the parking lot with a hundred other employees. We all waited for a silver truck to pull in the lot. Thillans owned the truck and it was full of money. When Thillans arrived the sides of the truck unfolded to reveal a bank on wheels. They charged a percentage of my check for the service of cashing it but I grudgingly had to pay as I had no bank account. I assumed banks were only for rich Americans and as I was neither rich *nor* American, so I never even tried to get an account.

1955 surrendered to the inevitable succession of years and was no more. 1956 brought with it many new things. Every day that passed offered a different experience. While the predictability of my working life plodded on a day at time for months on end the exact opposite took place during the hours I did not work.

"Minsky's Burlesque Parlor is the place for you Bernard!" I had finally asked Brendan about burlesque shows and he told me where Minsky's was located. I hopped on a streetcar to find it, hopping off in front of it when I did. Unsure of myself in this new part of town I looked around my new surroundings. Blacks hung out everywhere. Neon lights glowed in a disturbing mix of red, blue and sickly white. Prostitutes fed on slow moving cars.

Minsky's Burlesque Parlor loomed in front of me. Entering through a large black door I stepped into a wide darkened room. Rows of theatre style chairs lined a large center stage. I was looking forward to seeing the beautiful women I had seen on the pictures outside. Minsky's had a lighted cart set up in front with posters of awesomely sexy women in varying degrees of undress. All I had to do was walk through the door and see the rest of them! I settled in a chair, waiting for the next show to begin. A curtain at the back of the stage rustled and a leg tauntingly appeared through a break in the heavy curtains. Music, a slow jazzy number, floated to me on speakers from both sides of the small stage. The leg grew into a thigh performing a circular holding pattern with the rest of her teasing behind the curtain. "Come on, come on!" yelled men sitting around me. I joined in and soon we all urged her to step from behind the curtain. "Let's see!" At last she stepped all the way onto the stage!

Ugh! Where were the women from the pictures out front? This one had thin legs and looked great behind the curtain. When the rest of her followed onto the stage the illusion of beauty fled. There is no allure in fat and she had plenty of it. Her body resembled the upper half of a walrus I had seen at the Zoo. She didn't have tusks, but might have if she opened her mouth wide enough (which I didn't want her to). Thick black hair hung about her heavily painted face in disinterested strands. A worn out dress, three sizes too small, skinned itself around her thick, pipe shaped torso. Her breast (thankfully still concealed) jiggled wretchedly inside the cheap top. She reached behind herself to unfasten her brassiere. I left before it happened. With one longing gaze at the fictional women on the posters in front I turned and left Minsky's forever. Mr. Venclova didn't have to worry about me hanging out in burlesque halls if this was the quality of women inside them. Nothing changed for me though-I was still set on meeting a nice, pretty, American girl. I knew before I walked inside Minsky's I wouldn't find one there, but I still hoped to see a *pretty* American girl.

Years of waking at dawn had ingrained itself. I found myself with almost seven hours to fill prior to work, but this was about to change for the worse. I received less than favorable news on a Friday afternoon while waiting for the Thillan truck so I could cash my check. Brendan and I waited together in the rain.

"Bernard, I have some bad news for you, but on the bright side, it's good news for me! I am leaving!" Rocking triumphantly back on his heels he beamed, dispersing the gloom of the rain. My occasional ride was leaving the Roseland Y.M.C.A. Great! We traveled fifty blocks north from the Roseland Y and seventy-five blocks west to Continental Can, and it took a little over thirty minutes in a car. In a streetcar it took almost an hour!

"You see Bernard," he said, leaning in to me to make sure I heard, "There are opportunities for hard workers in the oil fields of southern Illinois. There are oil wells everywhere! I have a job waiting for me, and if I work hard and save I'll be able to buy my own rig and then I'm gonna get rich! Filthy rich!" The pay truck pulled in and the milling confusion always surrounding Thillan's arrival was no different this Friday from any other. Brendan faded into a collage of brown and black jackets.

"Good bye Brendan," looking up at him as I said it. Two weeks and one day had passed since he gave me the news. It was now Saturday morning and the time arrived for him to drive to Olney, Illinois. I was really going to miss my friend. He had taught me so much about America just by being himself. I couldn't have learned as much in a hundred classes dedicated to the subject.

"I hope you strike it rich in the oil business. Remember me if you do." I grinned up at him. He grinned back.

"And goodbye to you, young Bernard". He often called me that even though he was only about ten years older. Climbing into his car he dropped it in gear, and with a final energetic wave outside the driver's window, he pulled into busy traffic and disappeared. I didn't imagine I would ever see him again.

Shortly after Brendan Lally left town I made plans to quit my job at Continental Can, Inc. I found myself having to leave for work at 2 P.M. to arrive safely by two-thirty. Sometimes the streetcars broke down or an accident in the traffic ahead pushed them further off the schedule.

Returning to my room in the late evenings took well over an hour. A Chicago street car is no place to be after midnight. My first several late night rides taught me many things about people. Clean, well-dressed people, many with briefcases, used the streetcar. Some were not so well dressed, especially at night. A few dirty men (of the Y.M.C.A. flavor) staggered up the steps and swayed down the aisle, bumping people's shoulders or arms along the way. I couldn't believe how rude they were by offering no apologies.

On an especially damp and chilly night I sat halfway down the aisle on the left watching the dark buildings slide by outside. Raindrops clung for dear life on the outside of the streetcar's windows creating a fast moving, beautiful thing to see if watched with an eye for such things. The feeble light of the overhead street lamps gave birth to a hundred more tiny buildings, each one compressed in a single clinging raindrop. Dying within seconds another hundred were born anew, and so on, block after block after block.

On this night all of the seats were occupied. A tired looking old black man lurched down the aisle. I fervently prayed he wouldn't stand next to me. As was more the norm than the exception my prayer went unanswered. He came to a stop, standing directly at my side. Not ten seconds passed before the old man doubled over in a fit of coughing. The wheezing sounds he made in his bid for air was disgusting. He must be deathly ill, I thought. Spittle from his hacking misted in the air in front of him with the more solid particles landing on the right arm of my jacket. Disgusted, I didn't want any more of his insides on my clothes, I offered him my seat. Still coughing violently he waved his arm in my general direction as way of thanks. Mid-way through our switch he launched a torrent of vomit. Yellow and red, a steamy, chunky, putrid smelling mess covered the front of my shirt. A few particles clung to my face. I almost added my own vomit to the mix.

"Ahm s-sooory, mann." He looked up at my shirt then made the effort to look in my eyes. The whites of his eyes were not white at all but a sickly yellow laced with a fine network of blood vessels. Beneath his eyes bags of tired, mottled skin lay packed and ready for a journey. Saying nothing he looked down at himself. Opening his much cleaner jacket, he extracted a flat bottle with an inch of dark colored liquid swimming in the bottom. A drunk! I just gave up my seat to a drunk who threw up on me! I must be the dumbest D.P. in Chicago I thought. My jacket was ruined, and when I got off the streetcar I tossed it in the first trashcan I came upon. The notion that all Americans are good people simply because they are Americans followed my jacket into the garbage.

Continental Can, Inc. saw the last of me two nights ago. Another shift and another eight hours of noisy boredom were shattered as Jim Clover let loose a scream. Splattering blood and his nearly severed arm prompted me to make it my last night. Nothing involving machinery is foolproof. As I saw it one second of not paying attention led to his being maimed for life. That was enough for me.

Unemployment was not an option. I could barely survive with a full time job! Scouring the want ads in the newspapers I noticed an ad for a 'shipping clerk.' The company name was Honeywell Corporation located in the vicinity of Ohio and Clark Streets. The interview was no less scary then my first one at Continental Can but ended with equally positive results. I started two days later.

The building was a monstrously large four-story brick structure. Told to report to the third floor for my first day of work I timidly asked the elevator attendant to take me to it. He was a fat, sweating, smelly beast of a man. At his feet in the corner I noticed a small stack of squished cardboard boxes. As new days traveled into past days the small pile of crushed cardboard boxes varied in size, color and height, but nonetheless was present every single day. When I left at five o'clock I usually saw him leaving the parking lot with them tucked under his arm. I wonder what he does with all of those boxes? I asked myself. I never did ask *him*, and he never volunteered a reason. I figured he must be an immigrant. Only an immigrant would do something so stupid. Sometime thereafter I found out he was a Polish immigrant.

My luck with the girls amounted to nothing more than a pile of fears. Fear of rejection, fear of feeling stupid, fear they would not like a D.P., these and a hundred other fears formed a mountain too high for me to crest. My time at Honeywell, and all my feeble efforts to meet girls there, bore no fruit. I took a pay cut going to Honeywell but figured I would be able to meet more people, which would give me the chance to speak more English.

I moved from the Y.M.C.A. and found a boarding house closer to work. Honeywell was a solid job, and while I moved periodically my job remained a constant. Nineteen fifty-six faded into fifty-seven, then eight. A promotion to customer service brought a little more money but little changed in my pursuit of fun.

Weekends, I discovered, were nothing to look forward to for poor, displaced people such as me. Theaters, musical concerts, sporting events, fine dining; all of these things cost money, and what little I earned went to paying my bills. I always had ten cents for the streetcars though. One day in my citywide travels I happened onto a German soccer club. It was a private club, for men only. They *did* play soccer, but after a few weeks of hanging out with them I decided they drank beer and shot pool more than anything else. The third Saturday I went was not dedicated to soccer at all, but exclusively to drinking. After downing an unknown number of beers I became one of the staggering, swaying drunks I so despised on the streetcars. Two days later the world came back into some form of focus. My legs found themselves again and the pounding in my head departed for another drunk's skull to continue the relentless beat. No more 'soccer' for me after that day.

It was the heart of summer and the heat was a living, breathing thing. With the efficiency of a master torturer the heat melted its way deep inside to my core. When there it neatly collected all of my energy, then fled the building, leaving behind a drained husk. With an eye toward a different type of fun (one that didn't involve alcohol) I began frequenting a bowling ally not to far from my flat. The main attraction for me was not the bowling but the air-conditioning. I blessed the person who invented it every time I walked inside the place. The entire business, from spotless ashtrays, to clean smelling, disinfected bowling shoes reflected a personal goal of hygienic excellence. The driving force behind this well run establishment resided in a finicky, sickly, tight-fisted, well-dressed Greek man. This was his domain, and if one wanted to work for him one had best do as instructed. I noticed he had no personal hang-ups when it came to firing people. More than one barmaid fled the building in tears by the time he was done ripping into her. That was not my business however. I was there to bowl and keep out of the heat.

After spending some time there and speaking with fellow bowlers I learned a building behind the bowling alley was once called the Arlington Street Garage. I was told the gangster Al Capone had said hello to his competitor Bugs Moran in that very building. He used bullets instead of words. Bugs' gang was massacred. Al and his boys had dressed as policemen to do the deed. I peeked a few times at it but never investigated further. Buildings of death I had seen before so there was no compulsion to check out another one.

One bowling league night per week became two, then three. My game increased in skill for all the practice. Long after air conditioning was no longer required my game continued to get better. After a point I started entering money tournaments and was fortunate enough to win some. I went to bed at night dreaming of playing alongside the great Bob Carter on television. Losses, wins, losses and more losses followed the higher I climbed in the limited world of neighborhood bowling. It finally dawned on me I would never be good enough-I didn't have what it takes to play with Bob. The game would go on without Bernard Dujlovich I decided. Nonetheless, frustration scored a strike in me. Lugging my sixteen-pound ball out the front door of the Diversey Bowl, it was heavier than any time before. I was through! The Chicago River gleamed in the moonlight. A thought occurred to me. The river could do more with my ball than I could-I would never use it again. Inserting my fingers into the bowling ball's holes I swung my arm back, pendulum style, then forward, then back and forward again, and with a mighty heave-ho let loose my ball into the night. What a throw! It arced up, up and over the water, at last descending to the surface of the river. Kerplunk! A heavy thunking sound swam up from the river to my ears. A fountain of water erupted where the ball had entered. Satisfied with my final bowl I left my dreams of stardom on the muddy floor of the Chicago River and turned for home.

Bowling three nights a week takes a lot of time and money. When I quit bowling I suddenly found myself with a surplus of both. Walking the neighborhood one evening after work I noticed a group of people around my own age playing a game involving a large ball. Lonely for some company I wandered over and asked what they were playing. My accent marked me for what I am.

"It's called sixteen-inch softball foreigner. Go home to your own country!" one of the guys yelled over from the field. I turned away, cursing my aloneness. Just as I started walking away a hand came to rest on my shoulder.

"Wait, don't go!" It was a *female* voice! "Don't listen to him-David Scott is a jerk."

I turned around to face her as she lifted her hand. "My name is Cookie. My boyfriend," she pointed to a handsome guy twenty feet away, "is Tom."

"Hello. My name is Bernard Dujlovich. I am from Croatia. It is neat to meet you." I spoke slowly and carefully. I was trying out the word 'neat' for the first time on someone else so I wanted it to sound natural. My heart deflated a little when she had pointed to her boyfriend but Cookie beamed at me with such an honest, open friendliness I was glad to know her on any terms. Tom walked over when he saw his girlfriend talking to me. I expected him to tell me to get lost. Steadying myself for the rejection he disarmed me completely.

"Hi Cookie, who's this?" pointing at me. He didn't look angry, jealous, or negative in any way.

"Tom Custer, meet Bernard Dujlovich. He's from a country called Croatia, in Europe." Tom looked me in the eyes, stretched out his hand, and when my hand found it's way to his he pumped it warmly.

"Nice to meet you, Barry." He looked at me and asked, "Is Barry okay instead of Bernard? Bernard sounds kind of square."

"Barry is great!" I answered. I rolled it around in my mind . . . Barry, Barry. I definitely liked it and decided on the spot to adopt it as my first name.

Tom looked at Cookie and told her, "I know where Croatia is. We *did* go to the same history class, remember?" He was kidding her, and the love they obviously felt for each other took its own special moment, pulling them into a private room as strong as it was invisible. His eyes found their way back to me reluctantly. "Croatia, eh? Boy, you guys had it bad during the war. Say, you're not a Nazi, are you?"

"NO! Of course I would not to be a Nazi." He flustered me and my well-constructed sentences crumpled into a disorganized pile of immigrant-speak. "Please do not be thik—thinking this is so."

"Hey, Barry! I'm sorry! I was just razzing you." Laughing he patted my shoulder with his hand in a friendly and reassuring way. "You can hang out with us if you want. Not all the guys are so ignorant. Come on over!" He turned reaching for Cookie's hand. Her hand floated to his and as naturally as breathing they joined as one.

Alcott Playground flew to the top of my 'places to go, things to do' list. Summer, for all its blustery heat, faded like a lamb as September rolled into October. I met other couples there over the course of several months. Jim Campbell and his girlfriend Pat were every bit as nice as Cookie and Tom. In the early evenings ten or twenty of us played sixteen-inch softball, sat on the benches and drank beer. A nearby store sold three quarts for one dollar. There was always someone old enough to buy it for us and one dollar was a good price for the fun. The cops usually left us alone, though we felt their presence. Driving past they always slowed to a crawl, peering at us as if we were criminals. Bottles found their way behind backs and the cops moved on.

After three years of working in the same building five days a week it was inevitable, I would meet people and they would become my friends. Still not sure of myself I was happy to have anyone pay attention to me. A fellow I worked with named Brad offered to take me out after work for a drink. I gladly accepted. The day was extra long, made so by anticipation.

"Hey Barry, lets go!" Brad appeared behind me, then in front of me, and I ended up breaking into a light jog to catch up. He knew exactly where to go, and in no time I found myself in the dark corner of a tavern sipping on a cold beer. Two of his friends showed up slipping in the booth with us.

"Barry, these are a couple buddies of mine. Eugene, Snooker, meet Barry."

Eugene looked over at me and said "Hello Barry. How are you?" The way he looked at me was not right. I didn't know *why* it seemed creepy, it just did. Snooker looked up and raised his eyebrows in greeting then returned to his inspection of the tabletop. Many beers later the four of us wove our way outside where we dispersed.

Similar evenings followed and the four of us became friends. One such evening, a few months later, Brad brought up the idea of the four of us getting a place together.

"Think about it guys! If we get a three-bedroom place we will save money on the rent and utilities. Plus we can party as much as we want!" That sold Snooker.

"I'm in." was all he said. Snooker never talked much. He seemed to be either depressed and surly or mellow and nice. There were few variances with him.

"I can share a room with Barry" Eugene offered. He still gave me the willies a little bit even though I had known him for a while now.

"Uh, that is not a neat thought" I spoke up, maybe a bit quickly.

"What's the matter Barry, you don't want your fudge packed?" Brad said, then he and Snooker burst out laughing, reaching up and slapping their hands together.

Eugene threw a nasty look at Brad saying, "Be quiet! You *promised* you wouldn't do that!"

"Oh," I uttered stupidly, realizing the origin of my discomfort. "It is definitely not a neat plan guys. I will sleep on the couch, that will be fine with me, thank you." My face felt as if it were on fire. I clumsily reached for my beer just to do something else.

Brad and Snooker, if I thought they were laughing hard before, were now almost rolling out of their seats. When they reigned in their mirth Brad grinned at me telling me everything would be fine and I was welcome to the couch. That sealed it, and within two weeks the four of us had our own place near Clark and Fullerton. Moving was no longer a novelty for me. Over the last three years I had moved a number of times and had become an expert at packing my things into as manageable a bundle as possible.

Life was fun on Clark Street. The four of us bummed around Chicago looking for girls to meet but never really had any success. We tried the ballgame figuring girls *must* be at a baseball game. Wrigley Field held forty-five thousand fans but when we went there were only two thousand people in the entire ballpark. It was a Wednesday afternoon and most folks were working. A hot dog vendor walked the bottom row pushing a cart in front of him. The cart was a rolling hot dog cooker, grilling them right in front of him as he made his rounds. They smelled delicious. I decided to try one. I flagged him down and he rolled over.

"I would like a hotdog please" I told the vendor. He was an old man and his eyes were never far from the action on the field.

"Fine day for a ballgame, isn't it son?" He asked. Twinkling eyes and a warm smile were offered with my meal. "How about that Joe Garagiola, eh?" His enthusiasm was infectious. A wide smile lit up his face. As old as he must be I figured he worked the hotdog stand just to be able to see the games for free. "Enjoy sonny," he said before moving along.

"Thank you! I will." I replied to his retreating back.

Good times don't last forever and the time spent living on Clark Street was no exception. I pushed open the door and entered my apartment. Snooker yelled "Hold on! Don't come in here-I'm naked!" Oh. No problem, I thought.

"Okay." I answered loudly enough for him to hear. I just hoped Eugene wasn't in there with him.

Five seconds later Snooker rounded the corner. I looked at him, puzzled. How could he get dressed that fast?

"Wow man, you sure dress very fastly—quickly," I told him.

"Mind your own business Barry," he snarled. He was rolling his sleeves down to his wrists. Just before pulling them down I noticed several red bumps on the inside middle of his arm.

"Are you okay Snooker? Your arm looks like it has a rash." I wanted to help if I could.

"Man, you really are stupid. It's heroin man-really good high. Me and Eugene do it all the time. If you want I can hook you up. Whaddaya say Barry?"

Heroin? I had heard of it and knew it was a dangerous drug people injected into their arms. Not for me, no sir-ree!

"Thank you, but I will pass." I gathered up a few things and left immediately. I had been thinking about getting a briefcase and a leather jacket for some time and decided on the spot I would get them today. James Dean had a leather coat and he was the neatest looking American guy I could think of. Surely the women will like me in it, I told myself. I wanted the briefcase because whenever I rode the streetcars there were always people on board carrying them. They must be very important people I thought. I can do that!

I made it to Maxwell Street and found a store that had both items under one roof. I made my purchases then decided to stroll around in my new slick looking coat. It was brown and shiny. It was a bit hot for a coat that day but I didn't mind. I felt very American. Maxwell Street was a beehive of activity. Blues musicians strolled the sidewalks picking out complicated sounds on guitar and singing in nasally drawls. Most of the songs (the ones I understood) seemed to be about women leaving their men, or men staying drunk too long and losing their families I stayed out late that night not wanting to go back to Clark Street. I finally arrived home around eleven o' clock. Just as I fished my key from my pocket and put it in the door lock two policemen approached either side of me and informed me I was under arrest.

"What? Under arrest? What have I done? I have done nothing wrong I swear to you!" I was as scared as I had been on the train with the Hungry Window. Yanking me by either arm, my heels scraped the floor, (Father Kadirin all over) they dragged me inside my apartment. One of them let go of my arm long enough to grab a chair. He shoved me into it even as the other one was wrapping my arms behind me and taping my wrists together. In twenty seconds I was trussed for their disposal.

"Don't play dumb with us boy. You'll only make it harder on yourself. We need you to tell us where your buddies are." He pulled a small notepad from his right front pocket which he flipped open. Thumbing through the first several pages he found what he was looking for. "Your roommates . . . Brad, Snooker and Eugene. Where are they?" He was not smiling. His meaty face and small eyes radiated nothing but contempt as he towered above me.

"I swear officer, I do not know. They are to be living—they live here, but I do not know what they are doing . . . ." I looked up. "What have they done?"

He ignored my question. "Oh, so that's the way you're gonna play it, eh? Well, we got a jail cell full of men who would love to meet you. Let's go." With my wrists winched tightly behind my back my mouth opened and closed like a fish stranded out of water. They made a terrible racket hauling me down the steps, clumping and thumping loudly as if to announce to everyone that they were making the streets of Chicago safer-another villain removed from the view of decent law-abiding folk.

"What do we got here, Charlie?" a booking officer at the Sheffield station house asked the closest cop.

"Accessory after the fact Paddy. Seems," he looked down at his notes, "Berislav Doo-low-vich has taken up with robbers. His three roommates robbed a neighbor's apartment on Fullerton. They took some money, and get this-a dog! This guy," jabbing a thumb at me, "claims he doesn't know a thing. Gee, imagine that, not knowing anything about it! Never heard that before, have we Paddy?"

"First time, Charlie, first time." They both shared a chuckle over Charlie's exceptional wit.

"Excuse me," I butted in, "I really do not know what they are performing-doing. I left earlier today and went to Maxwell Street to buy a new coat. I left because Snooker was taking the heroin."

"Save if for the judge, D.P." said Meaty Face. "Right now we're going to book you." He must have noted the blank look on my face. "Book you-we're going to book you. That means we will take a copy of your fingerprints, take a picture and charge you with a crime."

My world, already a fragilely constructed house made up of a job and roof, started sliding into an abyss of pure dejection. I was going to lose my job! I could be deported! Sent away! I would not become an American-ever! The fear of the future was a python squeezing me for all it's worth. When the cops finished 'booking' me they lead me to a cell. Fear of the future took a backseat to the fear of the present. The jail cell was twenty feet square with cinder block walls and a concrete floor. Several benches were bolted to the walls. A toilet bolted to the floor, very much in the open, completed the dismal picture. One wall of steel bars enclosed the cell, just like in the movies. Thankfully, it was empty. Within three to four hours Brad, Eugene and Snooker joined me. The police had tracked them down in short order. Friday evaporated along with Saturday and then Sunday. Monday morning the police hauled all four of us in a paddy wagon to the Cook County jail and threw us in the holding tank. My bowls turned to butter when I saw the number of men inside it. All of them were black. They were mean looking and they were all staring at us, the only whites to join the party. Several of them smiled as I was pushed inside the cell. Feeling as puny as a human being can I scooted in between two sleeping men sitting on the floor with their backs against the wall. They both reeked of booze. I was relieved since they probably wouldn't wake up. My reasoning was sound, and the morning passed with a slowness reserved only for misery. Brought before a judge that afternoon I was told to appear in court in thirty days. Eileen, Brad's girlfriend, found out where we were. After posting a ten-dollar bond for Brad and me she explained what had just occurred as we left the jailhouse.

"Thank you many times Eileen. I cannot say how grateful I am to you for helping me." I was gushing in my gratitude.

"It's okay Barry. Anyway, here's the deal with you. The judge ordered you to reappear in thirty days."

I moved my stuff out of Clark Street the same day and moved to a boarding house very close to Honeywell. The months accumulated, seasons had their way with Chicago, then nineteen fifty-nine demanded new calendars for all. Work became the gauge by which I lived my life. There was work and there was non-work. The grind was eating at me and I instinctively knew I needed a change. Spending most of my time alone (still burned by my association with Brad, Snooker and Eugene) I took to watching movies at the theater. They were everywhere. The marquis above the entrance of one spelled "From Here to Eternity." I had to see it, if for no other reason than to find out what happened at the end. Burt Lancaster and Deborah Kerr came to life on the screen. I remembered reading the book and as I watched the movie the book unfolded in my mind. It was nice to see the ending.

Another night I went to the Biograph Theater. The movie playing was called "D.I." It starred someone called Jack Webb and was about a drill instructor in the United States Marine Corps. Mesmerized by the action I sat transfixed the entire movie. Unwilling to surrender the experience I watched it again. They were the toughest, meanest, most hardcore men I had ever seen and I wanted to be one of them. By the time I walked out of the theater I decided I would enlist, so I did just that.

Berislav Branko Dujlovich USMC Okinawa 1961

# CHAPTER XIX

## "Private D.P. Dujlovich"

What am I doing here? Why did I join the *Marines*? Am I completely insane? I asked myself thinking back to just a few days ago when I walked into the United States Marine Corp recruiting office. I now had trouble convincing myself of the correctness of my decision.

I poked my head inside the door. A tall, strapping man stood to greet me. He wore an immaculate blue uniform with several rows of medals strapping his barrel chest. He was a picture perfect Marine. Close-cropped light blonde hair crowned an angular, hewn from granite, jaw. Evenly spaced, cornflower blue eyes smiled at me. Sweeping his arm invitingly to a chair in front of his desk I succumbed to the power of the uniform, sitting without a peep.

"So, you want to become a Marine?" he quizzed as he sat back down. "Why?" he asked, following his first question with another before I could answer. It threw me off kilter. I wasn't sure how to answer so I replied simply.

"Yes, I do want to become a Marine. I love America. This is my new country." It was a little more than I intended to share but my nervousness begat child-like constructed answers.

"You're *not* a U.S. citizen? Is that what you're telling me son?" He leaned forward on his desk impaling me with his eyes. The cornflower blue turned glacial. "Where are you from? What Country are you from?"

My bowels were swimming. My heart thundered in my chest, my sweat glands jumped into overtime and my voice squeaked out, "Croatia."

"Oh! Croatia!" The glaciers melted. "Well, at least you're not a German or a commie. Are you a citizen yet?" he asked again, this time not as menacing as twenty seconds ago. I answered I was not.

Propping his elbows on his desk and lacing his fingers beneath his jaw he smiled and asked, "How would you like to become a citizen of the United States of America *immediately*?" He leaned forward again, this time with true concern for my wishes. He really wanted to help me!

"I could become a citizen right away?" I asked him. This was too good to be true! Since my first glimpse of the Statue of Liberty from the deck of the U.S.S. Blatchford this was what I dreamed of. Now here was this huge *marine* implying I could become a true American. I jumped at it. "What do I need to do to become a citizen right away sir?" I asked.

"Well, I'll tell you how. But first, my name is Gunnery Sergeant Vigue." He stretched out a meat hook sized hand. "And you are?" I hastily offered my left hand to shake his right hand, just as quickly pulling it back and offering my right. His paw-sized fist enveloped mine, shaking it up and down. My arm could have been attached to a mannequin, so little control did I have over it.

"My name is Berisla—Barry Dujlovich." I quickly answered.

"Well Barry, here's how it works. I'll make it simple. If you join the marines and commit to a four-year hitch you will be made a citizen as soon as you get out of boot camp. You're not a marine until you get out of boot camp by the way. Just because you join and *go* doesn't make you a marine-only graduating will do that. But we *will* make you a true blue American when you graduate." He paused. "Whaddaya say, Barry? Do we have a deal?" I said yes.

The results of that answer brought me to where I was now, on the tarmac of the San Diego airport waiting for the marines to pick me up. Spring weather in Southern California is a combination of paradise and sun. Cloudless blue skies stretched ever so lightly above me. The temperature floated in the mid-seventies and the salty smell of the Pacific wafted inland on waves borne on the ocean's winds.

At the edge of the airfield I spotted the strangest trees I had ever seen. With a branchless arching trunk the very top of the tree spread out to a canopy of long thin leaves. Hundreds of them formed a barrier to the sun. I gawked with the ignorance of an Ellis Island refugee. Turning to the nearest recruit I asked, "Excuse me, but what are those trees named?" I pointed to one. Again, my accent doomed me.

"They're called Palm Trees, you stupid D.P." The biggest and oldest recruit answered. The marines in Chicago that organized our flight had appointed him the leader of our group by virtue of his age.

"Thank you very much" I replied.

"Don't thank me you dumb refugee. You're nothin' but a D.P. The marines don't need no displaced persons. We're *real* Americans, not World War Two leftovers like you. You shouldn't even be here." He spun around to talk to others more like himself. People had turned to listen to him as he spoke to me. A ring of faces oozing animosity pounded me causing my face to turn hot and red under the assault. "This is going well," I muttered. Turning away I retreated from the main group waiting for the bus to take us to the Marine Corps Recruit Despot, or M.C.R.D., as I overheard on the airplane flight.

My thoughts again traveled to a completely different time in my life, all the way back to yesterday. I reviewed the previous day's events in my mind. I pictured my room-a dingy twelve-foot square slice of poverty. Faded crème colored wallpaper splotched the walls in sporadic fashion. Where that layer ended an earlier version of the same drab shade tiredly assumed wall-covering duties. A small window opened on a narrow alley crammed between two tall buildings. It was starved of light, offering dim views of trashcans and the occasional glistening of a broken wine bottle. The room, the view and my life were rolled into one sad ball of abject despair. When I first came to America my hopes soared higher then the Empire State Building. My future was as bright (in my mind) as New York City at night. The last three years had fallen miserably short of those wonderfully optimistic plans. Always broke, I had few friends, my job was going nowhere and my living quarters showed just how little distance I had traveled for all my efforts.

With a smidgen of guilt for skipping out on my rent-and little else in the way of regret I packed my few belongings in a travel bag I had purchased. Tip-toeing down the hall, slipping down the back steps, gingerly creaking the ancient screen door open with just enough room for me to slip through, I left the boarding house for the next grand adventure in my life.

The vehicle conveying me was now pulling to a stop in front of my group, forcing a halt to yesterday's review. A door opened at the front of a lusterless green bus disgorging a short, ramrod straight, fighting machine named Drill Instructor Willey.

"My name is Drill Instructor Sergeant Willey and you worthless maggots belong to *me*!" he shouted. Loudly. Placing his hands on his hips he reviewed the Chicago contingent of hopeful marines and continued, "I've been making Marines for *five* years and I have *never* in my life seen such a rag-tag, misfit, thoroughly pathetic group of women! You should all go home *now*!" He stopped. Assuming a lighter air he asked, "Who wants to go home to Mommy? Huh? Who doesn't think they have what it takes to become a *marine*? Who!" No arm crept skyward.

Where was the nice marine that signed me up? What happened to the smiles, the encouragement, the helpfulness? What the *hell* had I signed up for? I rolled the phrase 'what the *hell*' on my tongue. It was a useful bit of slang I picked up from Snooker. Very American sounding I thought.

Drill Instructor Sergeant Willey occupied a miniscule portion of the universe. At five foot—four inches tall his muscular frame nonetheless commanded a boundless degree of respect from my group of hopeful marine recruits. His close cropped hair ventured no further than the marine who recruited me. Penetrating, intelligent brown eyes locked in with disturbing intensity on whatever he looked at. His skin was deeply tanned. Maybe he was naturally swarthy, or maybe he spent a lot of time in the sun-I had no idea. What I did know (instinctively) was that Drill Instructor Sergeant Willey is not a man to be crossed. Muscles rippled smoothly under the surface of his smart khaki uniform. His forearms were not as big as Popeye the sailors but seemed close. He was a serious individual, and he had no problem conveying the enormity of his task. He waited five seconds before resuming at full volume.

"Get on the bus! Now! Move it! Move it! Move it!" Swinging around to the back of the group he began physically pushing the recruits in the rear toward the bus door.

We clambered inside assuming the first available seats. Underway, the rumbling of the bus's motor was no match for Drill Instructor Sergeant Willey.

"Welcome to the Maine Corps! Thirteen weeks from now at least a quarter of you will be back home with mommy, hiding behind her skirts because you weren't man enough! For those of you that *do* graduate boot camp you will wear the uniform of a United States Marine-a member of the finest fighting force to ever walk the planet! You will know how to shoot a rifle-how to survive in the rough with nothing but a knife-how to kill a man twenty different ways-how to be fearless-and if required, how to die with honor!" He paused, not to let his comments sink in but to take a breath. "For the next thirteen weeks ladies I'll be the most important person in your life. I'm your mother! I'm your father, brother, sister and priest! You don't take a shit without me saying yes! When and *if* you graduate boot I will be the person you thank when you're hunkered in a ditch with bullets whizzing a foot above your head. If you listen to me and the other drill instructors *you may stay alive in battle!* You will sleep in mud, eat dust for breakfast, exercise 'till you want to die and march more miles than you can count. But by the time we're done with you you'll have so much pride in being a Marine that no accomplishment in your life will *ever* exceed it." Drill Instructor Sergeant Willey continued his less than encouraging tirade to the gates of the Marine Corps Recruit Despot of San Diego, California.

The same trees I saw from a distance at the airport were now directly above and all around me. The military base was enormous. Our bus deposited us in front of an unremarkable building. Wasting no time Drill Instructor Sergeant Willey screamed at us to get off the bus even as the engine exchanged its chugging for silence.

"Out! Out! Get off my bus maggots! Form a line to the right of *him*!" His finger jabbed at Jason, the recruit in charge of our group from Chicago. Jason's eyes popped at the command. He was just as unsure and frightened as me, I realized.

"You worthless pieces of crap! If I was offered a nickel I'd sell all of you!" he screamed as we fumbled, scrambling off the bus. A recruit around my own size stumbled to the ground while being pushed from behind as he stepped down the bus's steps. Drill Instructor Sergeant Willey noted his clumsiness and with several long strides was at his side. "Get up you clumsy idiot! Can't you get off a bus without tripping? Are you crippled? Are you stupid? Get in line little girl!" The recruit turned red with shame. He quickly gained his footing and ran toward the forming line. "**Wait**!" The command from Drill Instructor Sergeant Willey froze him in his tracks. Reaching him immediately he spun the kid around by his shoulders and then shoved his own face within an inch of his object of torment. Spittle landed in droplets on the kid's face as Drill Instructor Sergeant Willey screamed. "What's you're name girl? I want your name *now*!"

The kid was terrified. His mouth opened and closed just like fish I had seen in pet stores. No sound came out.

Still in his face Willey continued screaming. "Do-you-want-to-keep-your-balls? Well! You better answer me *right now* or they'll be swinging from the rear-view mirror of my car by God!"

Gripped in obvious terror the recruit answered, whimpering, "I-I'm sorry."

"Your name is I-I'm sorry?" Drill Instructor Sergeant Willey gave him a look of utter disgust then rammed his hand into the kid's chest sending him sprawling butt first on the concrete. "Sit down Private I-I'm Sorry! You don't have what it takes-I can see that already." The kid looked up at him, reduced to a whimpering, scared little boy. Not through with him Drill Instructor Sergeant Willey leaned down again only inches from his face. Turning up the volume of his voice he screamed madly in the boys face. "Get up! Get up! What the hell are you doing on the ground Private I-I'm Sorry? Get in line before I kick the living shit out of you! I *swear* if you don't get it together I'll make your life a living *hell*! You'll be praying for a bullet by the time I'm done with you-now *get-in-line*!" Private I-I'm Sorry didn't need to be told twice. Scrambling to his feet he literally ran the ten feet to the end of the line.

The screaming never stopped. Drill Instructor Sergeant Willey hustled us through our processing. The top of my head was reduced from a healthy, overgrown farm of hair to a harvested field of barren skull in thirty seconds flat. Every personal belonging I owned was taken away. My clothes, after changing into supplied green fatigues, were unceremoniously deposited in a trash bag and hauled off along with everyone else's. I kept my mouth shut and moved as fast as I could to do everything asked of me.

In the afternoon Drill Instructor Sergeant Willey introduced us to his boss, Senior Drill Instructor Staff Sergeant Fitzgerald, who seemed to enjoy yelling just as much as Drill Instructor Willey.

"Recruits, listen up! This man controls your destiny! He can send you packing with the stroke of a pen. And he listens to *me*! Do I make myself clear?"

"Sir, yes sir!" rang every voice with enthusiasm.

He carried on at the same volume as his drill instructors, promising this and threatening that. "Sergeant Willey is correct! If you don't do *exactly* as I say when I say it your ass is grass, and I have the biggest lawnmower in town! You will not think or question our orders! You are not paid to think! You are lower than whale shit at the bottom of the ocean! Do you read me? Do you *read* me?"

"Sir, yes sir!"

Mealtime arrived, and what came as a shock to many of the recruits was the same old thing for me. The only sound allowed by the Marines was the clank of forks on metal trays, or a cup being sat on the table. Talking was not an option. Looking at anything other than my plate was not an option. The food *was* good though. As was my habit I gauged my situation on the availability and quality of the food I was eating. Aside from screaming drill instructors and the sheer misery of my surroundings I *did* enjoy mealtime. Not only was the food filling and delicious it was the only reprieve from the undivided attention of my tormentors.

Thankfully at last, the day ended. We were herded inside just as night, two shades shy of darkness, crept forward to claim the next eight hours. Barracks life was not so far removed from my memory, but the barracks itself was very strange. The building resembled an enormous round metal can laid on the ground long ways- except half of the can was buried in the ground while leaving the other half above. Thankfully, we slept in the upper half. Once inside the 'Quonset hut' we were instructed to select a 'rack', or bed, and after another ten minutes of yelling, threats and promises of misery the lights were extinguished, followed by blessed silence.

"What the hell have I gotten myself into?" I asked myself again in the darkness. "Oh Dear God" I prayed, "Please let me out of this. I'll do whatever you ask of me. Please Lord, I'm sorry for finding the babies, I'm sorry for leaving the Church, I'm sorry for looking at women. I'm sorry for all of the bad things I've ever done-just please, please help me get out of here!" My mind fell into the land of dreams even as I prayed for divine aide. Assuming His (for me, anyway) customary policy of non-intervention my prayers did indeed go unanswered. The morning arrived, announced by the crash of two trashcan lids slamming together. The clanging sound brought me out of my rack in a flash. One particularly sound sleeper (a tousled head revealed Jason) ignored the wake up call by snuggling even deeper into his blanket. This was a serious mistake.

"What the *fuck* do you think you're doing?" Drill Instructor Sergeant Willey had spotted Jason digging deeper in his bed. Running to the foot of Jason's bed he ripped the covers off his body in one mighty jerk, tossing Jason to the floor in the process. "You little fuckstick! You think you're at home? Do you? What are you doing? You're in *my* barracks shithead! Get your sorry ass off the floor, put your thoughts of Linda Lou back in your pants and get dressed!"

Jason, so rudely separated from his dreams, snapped to his feet and stared straight ahead. He had a comfortable ten inches in height on Drill Instructor Sergeant Willey so when he looked at the wall in front of him his tormentor was a screaming demon coming from somewhere below. Drill Instructor Sergeant Willey was foaming at the mouth, shouting at the top of his lungs how by the time he was through with Jason he would either be a lean, mean fighting machine or a loser making milkshakes in Podunk, Idaho for the rest of his life.

"Is that what you want? You want to make milkshakes? Answer me Private Milkshake!"

"No sir!" Jason yelled into the wall.

"No sir? No sir? When a marine asks you a question you begin with sir and end with sir! Do you understand me, Private Milkshake?"

"Sir, yes sir!" he answered, with feeling.

Drill Instructor Sergeant Willey reached up and grabbed Jason's left ear. Yanking it savagely downward Jason's head followed. With Jason's head cocked at an angle and his face grimacing in pain Drill Instructor Sergeant Willey blasted one final scream into the seized ear. "Get with it Private Milkshake or you're **outta** here!" Releasing Jason's ear with a snap and a shove he dismissed him and moved down the line, tormenting anyone who caught his eye.

I discovered many things as the week progressed. There is a correct way to walk and an incorrect way to walk. There is a right way to ask a question and a wrong way- a smart way to march and a stupid way to march. In the early dawn the yells and insults of other company's drill instructors floated over the huge concrete parade ground. My unit was but one among a dozen, a tight collection of little green ants methodically plodding first to the left, then to the right, or was that to the right, then left?

"What are you doing!" my other drill instructor screamed an inch from my nose. "Do you have two left feet? Do you even know your left from your right, Private . . ." he looked down at my chest to the name sewn above the left pocket. "Doo-loh-vich. What kind of name is that? Where are you from, Doo-loh-vich?"

"*Sir*, the private is from Croatia, *sir*!" Short answers worked best I learned. Any recruit stupid enough to attempt a conversation with a drill instructor found himself wishing he were never born. The typical result of these attempts was an hour of personal fitness training, or PT, at the hands of a D.I., it was a thing to be feared. Jason had become a favored recipient of PT time. A merciless sun, the dustiest patch of Southern California to be had, and a screaming maniac berating him the entire time had reduced Jason from the cocky punk that disembarked in San Diego a week ago into a timid young man scared to death of screwing up. And he is an *American*! I thought. I prayed every day to remain invisible but my feet had betrayed me and brought me unsought attention.

"You're one of them displaced people, eh? A fucking D.P.! Hey Sergeant Willey, we got us a D.P. here!"

Drill Instructor Sergeant Willey sauntered over standing next to my tormentor. They both inspected me in a new light.

"Sergeant Hall, did this D.P. say where he's from?"

"He said he's from Croatia Sergeant Willey," he answered.

"Croatia! You goddamn Nazi! What are you doing in my marine corps?" Drill Instructor Willey yelled in my face. Not waiting for an answer he turned away, muttering about immigrants and something about Nazi lovers. My face burned, and if not for the fact I would pay dearly for speaking I would have jumped on his back and tried to beat the stuffing out of him.

Drill Instructor Sergeant Hall towered at least eight inches above me. I felt the spray of his spittle on my newly shaved skull. "Is that true, D.P.? Are you a Nazi lover Private Dujlovich? I'm watching you Private D.P. If you're not an *exceptional* recruit I'll personally run you out of here so fast your ass'll be waiting in Croatia for the rest of you to show up. **Do you read me, Private D.P.**!"? He was getting so worked up his chest started quivering. Taking two steps back his face came within range. It was red, very red. His nostrils flared, twin bellows pumping bursts of anger. An unremarkable looking man, the level of rage he exhibited made him anything but. I had never seen anyone as mad in my entire life. There was only one safe course of action- comply, utterly and completely.

"*Sir, yes Sir!*" Ramrod straight, eyes forward, stomach in, I fervently believed in God at that moment. He would help me! He had to because, God knows, no one else was going to stand up for me.

"Sergeant!" The sharp command broke the back of his rage.

Drill Instructor Sergeant Hall's neck swiveled left. He immediately barked "Officer present!" His body followed his head and the drill instructor stood at attention, facing our company commander. Small as he was, Captain Swift stood well within the shadow created by Sergeant Hall, but nonetheless, he was clearly in charge.

"It's time to get the recruits tested," he told him. Turning to us, Captain Swift began speaking in the same efficient tone of voice as when he introduced himself on my second day here. "Recruits, today you will be engaging in a battery of written and oral tests designed to find your strengths and weaknesses. With this information the Marine Corps will put you where the Marine Corps feels you will be most useful. You cannot fail this test! Some recruits who take this test end up at Officer Candidate School but most of you will be infantry. Infantry soldiers are the backbone of the Marine Corps. Without the infantry *there would be no Marines!* Do I make myself clear?"

"Sir, yes Sir!" I bellowed my response with every member of my training company. I *wanted* to be in the infantry! Why do anything else?

A full day of testing followed Captain Swift's short speech.

Several weeks passed in a nightmarish haze of screaming D.I.'s, banging trashcan lids, cold mornings, ten-mile marches, and a hundred other manifestations of hell on earth. At the end of yet another march we were informed of our job descriptions. This would determine the course of our time spent in the marines—*if* we graduated boot camp.

"Private D.P.!" Drill Instructor Sergeant Willey bellowed.

"Sir, yes Sir!" I quickly called out.

"You will be assigned to a combat communications platoon"

"Private Milkshake!" he called out, quickly moving down the list.

"A communication platoon?" I thought. "A *communications* platoon? Are they crazy?"

Of all the assignments I could have drawn the marines placed me in a job focusing on communication. I couldn't understand why in the world they would place *me*, an immigrant with communication *problems*, in a combat communications platoon where lives depended on my speed and accuracy.

Graduation day arrived and the past thirteen weeks of my life were squished into one meaningful moment. When the time came, when the General announced I was now a United States Marine, I felt an unequaled swell of pride. It was just like Sergeant Willey claimed. Sergeant Willey also claimed many other things. He claimed I was a Nazi—lover, a fucking low-life D.P., an idiot and a worthless immigrant. But all of that was behind me now, and all I could think about was becoming a citizen. I had not forgotten Sergeant Cornflower Blue Eye's promise.

Families surrounded proud, newly minted Marines. Happiness floated tangibly in the air.

It was a thoroughly festive occasion, and I never felt so alone. There was no one to congratulate me, no hugs, no, "I'm so proud of you, Barry". There was just me, looking at everyone else.

Leaving the parade ground I made my way to the Adjutant General's office. It was set I was to become a United States citizen immediately upon graduation. Savoring my immanent elevation I proudly (and ramrod straight) walked across the parade ground. Making my way inside the large stucco building I found a clerk and explained my situation. I then did what every serviceman is instructed to do when making a request outside normal channels-I waited. An hour passed. Two hours passed.

"Private Dujlovich, Lieutenant Curtright will see you. Follow me." A nameless, faceless corporal led me into the bowels of the building. Stopping at a cubicle to his left, and equal in size to fifty others I passed, he announced my presence to the officer sitting inside it, handed him a slim manila folder and retreated.

Second Lieutenant Curtright was a large, doughy non-descript marine. An office functionary, it was obvious from his waistline he had not endured the marches of a recruit in quite some time. Shuffling papers with a contrived impression of importance he looked up as I stood at attention directly in front of his desk. His furrowed eyebrows indicated this had better be of paramount importance; he was a very busy marine after all.

"At ease Private. State the nature of your request." He imparted this in flat military fashion. Not looking at me his focus was on the manila folder the corporal had given him. It contained a sheath of papers. As he reviewed its contents I might as well not have been there. My eyes traveled to the folder's tab. In small typewritten letters I saw it spelled, 'Dujlovich, Barislav' Huh! They were taking me seriously. This encouraged me to push ahead. Fresh from boot camp I still crept in the shadow of fear when it came to dealing with superior enlisted men and officers. I was not a true blue son of American soil. As a displaced person I was looked upon in the same low regard as black recruits. We were less than nothing, undeserving of praise or reward, viewed as inferior soldiers.

"Sir," I began. "Thanks—thank you for seeing me. Sir, when I joined the Marines my recruiting officer told me I would be made a citizen of America automatically from graduation of boot camp." I paused and then plunged in. "I graduated today Sir, and I am now here to become a citizen of the United States of America." For emphasis on how important this was to me I added, "I am very proud to be a Marine, Sir. I would be even more proud to be a United States Citizen." I stopped talking. I had made my case.

The silence grew in volume with every unanswered second. Bzzzzz . . . ZZZZZZzzzz . . . a fly joined our ranks. It became quickly apparent that strafing runs of the Lieutenant's desk had to be the fly's mission and it performed a number of skillful sweeps before the quick palm of Second Lieutenant Curtright slapped it out of the sky. Grounded on the battlefield of the oak desk it attempted to regain its addled senses but a mighty shadow of unavoidable death, the palm of an annoyed Lieutenant, fell from the sky and the fly's attempts to return to duty ended in blackness and utter annihilation.

Wiping the carcass of his foe from his hand he looked up at me.

"You came here from Chicago, yes?" He asked.

"Yes Sir, that is correct." I answered quickly.

"I have bad news for you marine. I've reviewed your file. Legally, you're a displaced person. You are not, and cannot become a citizen for three more years, marine or no marine." He paused as he saw my jaw drop. This was not fair!

"Sir, I was promised by my recruiter that when I grad-"

"Listen up Marine! I don't care what your recruiter told you. That's not my concern! What *is* my concern is that you report to Camp Pendleton fourteen days from today. Do you understand me Marine?" His face, an unhealthy complexion even when calm, was darkening. Red consumed his features and I feared purple was just behind it. It suddenly occurred to me this would be an excellent time to take my leave.

"Yes *Sir*! Thank you sir." Throwing him a smart salute I performed a precise left face and exited the cubicle.

Anger is an expensive emotion, a ladle of poison, a thousand tentacles of subtle weave and cancerous intent, bent upon the destruction of purity and good intention. Shedding my garments (those soul-covering restrictions we all must wear, lest we go mad) I dove into the sea of anger. Indignities flooded back, and I welcomed them. The sting of Joseph's leather belt burning across my back. Milan's foot crashing into my gut. Yela's precision blows bloodying me. Father Kadirin whipping me with vigor undiminished by the years. Father Benedict roasted in my mind to an even hotter flame. *He stole from my dormitory with* my *radio glued to his ear!* Rage burned upon the kindling whittled from my bitter heart. I was powerless, my goal of becoming an American as unfulfilled as my desire to keep my radio.

Sergeant Cornflower had lied to me. The lie, coupled with my rage, fanned my anger into a boiling volcano I fought to keep a lid on. I walked. Miles of walking will lower the temperature of any temper.

I exulted in one fact. I was a *MARINE!* A full-fledged, dyed in the wool, true-blue honest to God United States Marine. I didn't see Drill Instructor Sergeant Willey after graduation day, but if I did I could call him Sergeant Willey (not Drill Instructor God Almighty May You Not Smite Me Sergeant Willey). I could even call him an asshole if I wanted. I would have been eating dust if I did, but I *could* get away with it and not spend time in the brig.

While many of the marines in my training company went home during our two-week leave (to wherever home was) there were a number of us that for one reason or another chose to stay in Southern California. For us remaining marines our primary mission for the next two weeks was to cram as much fun into fourteen days as possible. All of us were young, gung-ho, and ready to conquer the world. I was in the best shape of my life. My muscles proudly rippled on command. I could march ten miles non-stop. I could shoot a rifle, arm and throw a grenade. I learned how to march in tight formation, how to salute and how to never say no to a challenge.

One week into my two-week leave my greatest challenge was how to keep down another shot of tequila without losing my lunch all over the floor of a Tijuana bar. The place was crawling with marines and sailors. I quickly learned Tijuana, Mexico was a Mecca for marines and sailors off ship and on leave in San Diego. Some of the sailors went wild. Setting foot on land for the first time in three months with a pocket full of money earned from time spent at sea. They seemed determined to lose their virginity as quickly as they could part with their money. Whores, booze, vomit, sweat, flies and heat combined to convince me that while this lifestyle was fun for a short time, it was not for me. Soon enough I looked forward to returning to active duty.

Camp Pendleton, California oversaw my change from a teenager into a strong young man. I climbed telephone poles, learned how to disarm land mines. I learned ten different ways to kill a man. I hoped they would never come in handy. Others from my training company were here in Camp Pendleton with me, while a number were dispersed to various points depending on their individual training requirements. Through all of my training I listened to my instructors and did as I was told. Two years later, at the end of my time at Camp Pendleton, all of my reviews indicated I had grown into a solid marine.

'The Rock,' Okinawa, sweated a mile off the starboard bow of my troop transport ship. Two weeks of rolling decks, long chow lines, inspections, exercise and more exercise punctuated an unpleasant time spent at sea. But now I was here!

Tight quarters and a few extra activities make for lots of conversation time in the evening. I listened to a hundred while traversing the Pacific Ocean.

"Oh my God, the women, Geno, you won't believe the women! For *two* dollars you get them for a whole *hour*! They'll do anything you want. Why I heard one guy . . ." a voice floated from across the small room.

"Hell *yes* it's a tropical island. The place rains every day, it's *always* humid as hell . . ." came another.

"Damn straight you can get sex diseases! I knew one guy who knew a guy whose balls grew as big as *grapefruits*! . . . . I'm *not* lying!" My bunkmate two racks below me defended himself loudly.

And so it went for thirteen nights and twelve days. When we dropped anchor and headed ashore the hookers were ready and waiting, just like I had heard. Stepping foot on land for the first time in two weeks I blessed the stationary benefits of solid ground. Declining an offer to hit the bars I decided to walk along the waterfront instead. I wasn't sure how long we would be here so I wanted to see as much of Okinawa as I could, which couldn't be done inside a whore house. The women *were* exquisitely beautiful though. With hands deep in my trouser pockets, and my view the ground in front of me, I was fully absorbed when a voice to my left drew me from my visions of Okinawan women.

"Excuse me, mah-reen, shoe shine, yes?" My head followed the direction of the voice. A small oriental man in his middle years sat at the foot of a large black chair sprouting a footrest built onto the bottom of it.

A jagged scar divided his left cheek neatly into two segments; drawing my eyes like a magnet. I couldn't look away. He was very humble, bowing as he asked again if I wanted my shoes shined. I am a marine! Of *course* I need my shoes shined. Rustling inside my pants pocket I welcomed the sound of jingling coins.

"Yes, I would like my shoes shined. Thank you." I answered him.

He swept his arm from me toward the chair. I stepped up and sank into it.

"How did you get that scar," I asked rudely, still having difficulty ripping my eyes from it. The scar originated above his hairline scathing an angry diagonal slash downward across his forehead. Not satisfied with the damage, it continued on the same trajectory decimating his left eyelid to the point of non-compliance. Tearing through the meaty part of his cheek it lost its viciousness only after slicing the plane of his jaw and encountering air. He was thin but exhibited a sinewy system of movement acquired only through physical training and discipline. A sharp jaw line framed thin lips not given easily to smiling. His eyes possessed an unusual mixture of sadness. Sorrow roamed freely about his face but it was a sorrow tempered with resignation.

He answered in halting English.

"This scar, yes, my scar. Why do you want to know how I got this scar?" He asked.

His question threw me off. Why *did* I want to know? Because it must have an interesting story behind it, I thought.

"Something serious must have happened to you and I am interested in what it was." I answered honestly.

"This scar," he answered slowly, "is my reminder of a debt I can never repay. God has placed this mark on me so that every time I look into a mirror I relive my crime"

He seemed content to let it rest there but this only intrigued me further. I wanted to know the whole story. What crime?

"What crime did you commit?" I asked.

He seemed not to hear me. Industriously working polish into the top of my shoes my question went unanswered. A few minutes passed and I assumed I had touched on a topic he had no desire to discuss. Looking out on the waterfront numerous ships lined up at port, utter chaos held in check by ropes and chains.

"I was a soldier." He said this with an air of defeat sprinkled with defiance. "This," he pointed to his face, "happened near the end of World War Two. My superior officers chose to strike at Americans by using suicide soldiers to deliver bombs to airplanes and ships. I considered it an honor to die for Japan. I thought all Americans were evil barbarians whose only mission was to destroy my homeland. I did not know better! It was what I was taught!" His voice grew tight and speaking became a labored affair. "The day was like this one." Turning around to face the ocean he swept his hand across the horizon encompassing numerous ships of war, bobbing beneath a dark gray sky on the edge of giving birth to black. He had my undivided attention.

"My superior officer asked for volunteers. I stepped forward with two of my comrades. He had explained to us how we were losing the war and our only hope for victory lie in the hands of us, warriors in the traditions of samurai and seppuku. To die with honor, he told us, is the greatest achievement in life." While he spoke he applied and removed shoe polish, rubbing industriously, seeming completely undistracted from his task for the weightiness of his dialogue. Finishing his last sentence he hung his head and stopped speaking. His muscular shoulders thrust upward and retreated several times, the result of deep breaths and his effort to regain composure. Steeled, he looked up into my eyes. The black shoe polish was thoroughly removed as his hands speedily swiped a fresh cloth in front, on top, on the back of my shoes.

"A huge military transport ship full of soldiers was coming to rape our wives and sisters. I was told they tortured Japanese soldiers and killed for fun. I saw it as my duty to kill as many of them as I could. I climbed into a boat loaded with explosives and rammed it into a troop landing craft. Just before I hit them I set off the bomb. The force of the explosion ripped my boat in half. It happened in half a second but a piece of metal ripped across my skull. The blast shot me forty feet into the air and I landed far away from the two boats. The troop landing boat was filled with fifty marines, I was told later. Twenty-seven of them died." Remorse grabbed his tongue. He relived the scene and his heart plummeted to a (for him) now familiar depth. "They found me in the water, the Americans, and brought me on their ship. They sewed my face back together and gave me a new chance on life. You Americans, I learned, are not evil people who want to destroy us! I learned the true meaning of forgiveness and kindness from you, my sworn enemies. I also learned that what I was taught was wrong. I killed twenty-seven of your comrades and yet you nursed me back to health. That is how I got my scar."

My shoes glistened, as well as my eyes. I had forgotten he was even shining them. He stood up, backing away with a slight bow.

"You are completed. Please have a nice day."

My mind was not running on level tracks. His story threw me off and unbalanced my day. Pulling myself together I asked what I owed him for the shoeshine.

"You owe me nothing, sir. It is my pleasure and honor to serve American G.I.'s." He turned from me, politely ending our association. Following his gaze down the pier I saw two G.I.'s making their way toward us. I reached out with fifty cents in my palm but he ignored me. Shrugging I returned the change to my pocket. As I walked away and the two marines drew closer the indebted ex-soldier's voice floated to me. "Excuse me, mah-reens, shoe shine, yes?"

Okinawa was now behind me and Hong Kong was my new destination. Okinawa was an island of rocks and rugged earth with few people. Hong Kong, I quickly saw, was just the opposite-an island of solid people with the earth peeking through in random spots. I heard that Hong Kong is the most densely populated city on the face of the planet. A number of my fellow marines lost their hearts to the beautiful Chinese women that, just as in Okinawa, were waiting for us to hit the waterfront. We called them Suzy Wongs after the woman in a movie starring William Holden. In the movie he was a soldier (like us) he was stationed in the Orient (like us) and he fell in love with a gorgeous Oriental woman (like several of my crew). A few marines went A.W.O.L. (absent without leave) to be with their new loves.

Where there are new loves, there are old loves. The old loves, named Becky, or Paula, or Gina, still dolled up and went to the soda fountain on Friday nights. They went to work at the bank, or the dry cleaners, or the factory. Life went on, with or without their man.

Professions of love and commitment, sincerely spoken and felt to the core of one's heart, lose meaning with the passing of months. My fellow soldiers who swore undying love to their gals now eagerly looked forward to getting off ship so they could buy a whore and release the urge that grows in all human beings, often stronger than any vow of celibacy. The same urge held true for the Becky's and Gina's back home. At mail call one or two soldiers would receive a 'Dear John' letter. In most cases the recipient of a 'Dear John' letter was heartbroken. A few were relieved, and some even rejoiced. Most of them made their way to a bulletin board hung on a wall for just that purpose. It helped the ones who received a letter to know they were not alone in their rejection.

One marine was devastated when he received his letter. He opened it with a smile, expecting news of home and sweet words from his honey. I watched him as he read. The light of happiness in his eyes extinguished itself within seconds. His smile retreated with it. By the time he carefully folded the letter and placed it in his shirt pocket tears streamed freely down his cheeks. Saying nothing, he stood up and exited the mess hall. I followed him. A particular flavor of somberness in his eyes worried me. I had seen the look before in the camps and on the trains. It was a look of pure and utter defeat; despair strong enough to douse the light of hope. Despair so great it disengages the drive that keeps us getting up every day to go to work and partake in conversations we have no interest in. Hope is the force strong enough to keep the wheels turning on a life with nothing spectacular in the offing. His wheel had stopped turning.

Following his back as he wound his way into the bowels of the ship I found him in the corner of the boiler room with the letter in one hand and a knife in the other. He spotted me as I came into the room. He knew I followed. I looked down at the knife. He looked at my eyes looking at the knife. He held it up, pointing the blade directly at his heart.

"Go away Dujlovich." He told me this without anger-a monotonic command. I am a private-he is a private, so there was no fear of disobeying a superior's command. I stayed.

"I am sorry for your bad news Frank. Please do not do what you are planning to do." I spoke softly to him, remaining where I was. "I too know of despair. I have no family left, no friends and no sweetheart back home. You do. If you do this what will your parents think? What about the girl who wrote the letter? You are a marine! Many of us have gotten letters the same as yours. You must fight the urge to end your life. I have seen many people kill themselves, and you know what?"

"What?' He bitterly asked. (At least he was talking to me, and not sticking himself with the knife).

"When those people killed themselves all of their sorrow went with them. They were looked upon as dead bodies, weak dead bodies. No one will care that your gal has found someone else. Your memory will be a stain for whoever that woman is-your family will miss you and curse you for your weakness. There will be few tears shed at your funeral. You must not do this!" I thought of a great compromise. He still had the knife pointed at his heart, though now he held it aloft without such imminent intent. "If you still feel this way in two weeks then do what you must do. But please wait a while and think it through. Life is a gift from God and there should be nothing so tragic that you throw God's gift back in his face." I stopped speaking-if I kept rambling he might go ahead and do it just to not have to keep listening to me. My words struck a cord inside him. The knife clanged on the metal deck and his agony found release in a new flood of tears. I went over to him, kicked the knife away, and put my arms around him. His tears soaked my shirt. The dam holding his pain crumbled under the assault.

"I love her! Oh God, what will I do?" He spoke in choppy sentences between sobbing, torn from a wounded heart. "Her smiles will never be for me. Now she loves another man! I *hate* the marines! I *hate* the man who took my Linda!" He muttered, yelled, cried and sobbed for twenty minutes at least. After a time he regained some control. Suddenly embarrassed at being held by another grown man he backed away from me and stood on his own. Looking in my eyes he sought to speak to me but had trouble finding the words.

"Thank you Barry. I will not forget this. Please keep it between us." He looked at the knife in the corner, looked at me one more time, then quickly left the boiler room to the boilers, the knife and me. I walked over and picked it up. Slipping the knife in my pocket I retraced my steps topside. Retrieving it from my pocket and leaning over the deck railing I held it over the water and let it go. The South China Sea accepted it with but a ripple of protest.

Climates are different the world over. Some places have no winter, some no summer. Many countries do not enjoy autumn or spring. As a world traveler I knew this to be true. For the residents of Chicago, Illinois four summers had blasted heat on them and three winters had gripped the city with icy fingers, wrapping it in frozen blankets of snow.

Four years in the marines had changed me. I had a broader view of the world and life in general. Compassion had nurtured a solid spot inside me. Skepticism had found equally firm footing in my heart. The United States Marine Corp taught me the value of effort and the rewards that come with it. It also taught me that racism is a river that runs deep in almost everyone. Called a D.P. until the day I was officially discharged, half of me thanked the Corp while the other half cursed it. I departed Chicago for boot camp in April 1959. I returned to Chicago in January 1963. Walking taller, standing prouder and speaking better English than ever before I nimbly bounced down the steps of a 'Sante Fe railroad passenger car. I set foot back in Chicago as a United States Marine and I felt there was nothing I couldn't accomplish.

# CHAPTER XX

## "Chicago—Round II"

"Eugene and Snooker are *dead*?" I couldn't believe it, but Eileen had no reason to lie. She and Brad sat across from me in a booth at a local saloon.

"It's true," Brad said. "Snooker died of a heroin overdose and Eugene was shot to death in a drug deal that went bad. It's just as well you left when you did Barry."

Brad had changed for the better. His hair was shorter and he looked cleaner. His clothes were not so shabby. They both wore wedding bands so I suspected Eileen had something to do with his new and improved appearance. We spent an hour catching up on old times and another hour updating each other on new times.

"So, Barry, what are your plans now that you're a damn M*arine*!" Brad always liked me and I had always gotten along with him the best of the three. Eugene and Snooker had spoiled our friendship over the short time we lived together.

"I have already spoken with Honeywell. My job is waiting for me." I answered simply.

My plans had not progressed beyond finding employment. Only in town for two days I had secured a weekly room with the intention of moving after my job situation solidified. "Also, I am applying for citizenship tomorrow. Before I left M.C.R.D., I spoke with the A.G.'s office. They told me I was now eligible to become a United States citizen."

"That's great Barry! But what's the A.G.'s office?"

"I'm sorry," I said. "It is the Adjutant General's office. It is where all the lawyers are."

We chatted a little longer then I excused myself. I was starting work at Honeywell tomorrow morning and wanted to be at my sharpest.

Honeywell had moved to Lincolnwood, Illinois so for the first few days I had a devil of a time getting to work. It reminded me of before I went in the Marines. I quickly settled into my old routine at work, but that's where the 'old' routine ended. My English skills were greatly improved and I no longer feared women (as much). I gained instant respect from men and women alike when they learned I was a Marine. I told stories of my time spent in the Orient and held intelligent conversations with my co-workers instead of retreating to a corner to listen to others talk.

Most importantly, this time I had *money*. My last year in the Corp had been a mildly profitable one for me. While my fellow marines drank their pay I stayed in the barracks and read. When they gave their money to whores for an hour of satisfaction I held onto my cash. The problem with spending money is that you spend it. When it's spent and there is no more the party's over and that's where I came in. I was stationed in Olongopo Zambales, Philippines. The girls were beautiful and there wasn't a lot to spend money on except booze and women. I did both, but not in the crazy way most of my comrades did.

A marine came to me asking for a loan. "Hey D.P., if you give me five dollars I promise to give you ten back on payday." That sounded like a hell of a good idea to me. I loaned him the money on the spot. He paid me back just as he said he would. The word spread and soon I was loaning money out several times a week, and making back double what I loaned.

Money can buy anything you want if you have enough of it. Walking down Clark Street several months after getting back I spotted the most incredible car I had ever seen. Asking the dealer how much; I listened to how perfect this machine would be for me, how neat I would look driving it, and how the girls loved a guy with a car before finally getting around to the price.

"For three hundred dollars you can drive it off the lot."

I returned the next day, and twenty minutes later I was behind the wheel of a pink 1957 Ford Thunderbird convertible. Things were looking up! With my car I could ask a girl out without feeling like a dolt. Many girls sat in the front seat of my T-Bird and a respectable percentage 'sat' in back. We listened and danced to Elvis, Johnny Cash and Buddy Holly and the Crickets. The girls I spent time with were American girls and I learned more about them from every date I went on.

My approval papers came through from the Federal Government three months after getting back from San Diego. The test I had taken immediately upon my return to Chicago indicated I could read well enough, speak English well enough and write the language well enough to become a citizen of this great country. Sergeant Willey was wrong-I felt more pride at that moment than ever before. Tears flowed down my cheeks as the Judge proclaimed me an American. I never felt such conviction as when I took my oath of citizenship, and I never partied as hard in celebrating it.

A co-worker at Honeywell told me they were moving out of their apartment and recommended to the landlord that I move in when he vacated. I did. It was a nice one-bedroom, not the usual one room dismal cube I was accustomed to. I loved it, and in a blink of an eye almost a year passed. As successful as my personal life was I began feeling stymied at work. I still labored in the customer service department. It was the same thing every day, just disguised in the form of different complaints. After a month of tossing it back and forth I worked up the nerve to ask my Department Head if I would at some point be promoted, or at least moved to a position somewhere in the company that held greater responsibility.

"Well Barry, customer service is a very important function here at Honeywell. You do an excellent job so I don't want to lose you to another department. I'll tell you what-I will let you know if anything opens up. Is that okay with you?"

What could I say? No! It's not okay! I don't want to be stuck doing this every day for the rest of my life! I had a strong intuition such a reply would not endear him to my plight.

I answered politely, "I understand. Thank you for listening to my request Mr. Cameron." Turning from his desk to exit his office I hoped he would say he was just kidding and of course he had an opening. That was not the case.

Joanna Western Mills billed itself as the largest window covering company in the entire country. They were not lying. In a short time Honeywell was just a memory. The people at J.W. Mills were wonderful with a vibrant atmosphere, this was a place I knew I could grow at and succeed. However, I began my career with J.W. Mills in customer service, just like at Honeywell.

The very best thing to come out of my five years at Joanna Western Mills was my association with Donald Manna. Donald Manna owned National Window Shade, Inc., the oldest and one of the most respected window-covering firms in Chicago. Chicago is a money town and Don had the right idea when it came to clientele cultivation. He went after the money, plain and simple. As one of the larger clients in the Chicago market Don Manna frequently visited the J.W. Mills warehouse meeting with myself and my sales manager. Sometimes he wanted to walk the floor where the shades were produced. I learned more about window coverings by listening to him than I did in a hundred classes dedicated to production, installation and sales. A few years passed, and Don Manna and I developed a relationship extending beyond business. I looked up to him-his knowledge, his acumen as a businessman, and most importantly, his example as an honorable man.

Gradually I came to realize I didn't *have* to work for a company my entire life. If I had the drive, the balls, and a plan I could go for it own my own. He (unknowingly) gave me the drive and the plan-I already had the balls. But big moves don't happen overnight. I had a goal and plenty of time to realize it.

Don became the father I missed. I became a sort of 'unrelated' son to him. He invited me to his house on holidays. I had a little bit of money and a car (another one-I totaled my T-Bird almost a year ago while daydreaming of a girl) but I was still pitifully shy on true friends. He filled that gap. I went to his house not only on Catholic holidays, such as Christmas, he also invited me to Jewish holidays reserved for his family only. I had not felt so much a part of a family unit since the days of frogs and snakes in Central Croatia so many years ago.

National Window Shade, Inc. had been servicing clients since 1900. Sixty-six years is a long time to be doing the same thing for the same families, although now it is the sons or grandsons of the original clients. He taught me the value of excellence in every endeavor. He showed me (through practical application) that the adage 'You get what you pay for' is not just an expression. He helped me understand it's the *customer* that puts food on the table, not the salesman. He made me realize the value of courtesy. He introduced me to a different class of people-not better, just wealthier. In short, Don Manna changed my life in every conceivable way, all to the better. Don worked hard for his dollar and he knew how to enjoy what he earned. On a sunny afternoon he picked me up for a second ride on his boat. The Diversy Harbor; large immaculate boats, bobbing patiently for their wealthy owners had always been a place I was nervous to even be around. This afternoon I was going for my *second* time!

Don picked me up promptly at two o'clock. We motored down Lake Shore Drive with Lake Michigan on our left, making small talk about the latest shades on the market and other trivial asides. I was about to thank him for having me out on his boat when a thunderous crash from behind sent me flying into the windshield. The light of day was abruptly extinguished.

Swimming upward through layers of unconsciousness I opened my eyes with great effort. I was in a white walled room. White sheets covered my bed and body. White shades hung from the window. A stunningly cute nurse, dressed all in white, asked me how I felt.

"*Kakosi?*" How are you? She asked me.

"*Dobro*" I answered. Fine. The fog still hovered-I didn't realize she was speaking (or I was answering) in Croat.

She beamed a smile, melting my heart. "*Dobro*," she said back to me, again with a large smile. She turned and quickly exited the room.

I couldn't believe my luck! The Croat speaking nurse was American-yet she spoke Croat! I couldn't get her out of my head. Staying awake and waiting in vain for her to come back. She didn't, but a doctor did.

"I'm afraid you've pinched your sciatic nerve. We need to keep you here under observation. I understand the person that hit you has insurance and has already agreed to take care of all of your hospital bills. Now, if you'll excuse me." Without waiting to see if I had any questions he did a swift about-face, exiting the room. My back was killing me but I was glad to hear the hospital was keeping me for a bit. It meant I would hopefully get to see the nurse again.

The next day, around the same time, my Croat speaking vision of loveliness returned. This time I was in possession of my wits and asked her how she knew Croat. She told me she was born in America but her Grandfather was from Croatia so her parents spoke it fluently. She admitted she didn't know many words, just the basics. She came every day to tend to me and by the time I was discharged, ten days later, I knew she was the girl for me. I met her parents and thought they were perfect. Several months later she whispered to me, "*Ja te ljubim*". I like you, or love you, depending on the intent.

"*Ja te ljubim takoder,*" I love you also, distinctly conveyed my whisper back.

That sealed it. Lee and I were married at St. Barbara's Church in Brookfield, Illinois. In 1966 all of my dreams were coming true. I had a good, solid job and now an American girl for a wife. Every day we spent together was a blessing to me and the next three years passed in a rush of business deals, love and friendship. Don and I remained close. My desire to start my own window shade business only grew stronger as time passed, and as I tore December from 1969 and tacked a crisp, new 1970 calendar to the wall at home I knew this was the time.

I said my good-byes at Joanna Western Mills, departing to become a window shade dealer. Apollo Shade Company was born. My business was one child I nurtured and Lisa, my newborn daughter, was the other. I stumbled in unfamiliar landscapes on two fronts. Making babies does not teach one how to be a father, and making shades does not teach one how to run a company. "No job too large-No job too small". My motto worked (even though it was borrowed). Don Manna's lessons stayed with me, even though we didn't spend nearly as much time together since I started Apollo. Moving my family to Naperville, coupled with starting a business, did a fine job of chewing up my days. My hours for anything beyond my two primary responsibilities were reserved for my pillow.

Several months into my next 'grand adventure' my finances were low and my overhead high. Sweat beaded my brow; the hour of day didn't matter. On yet another customerless day, while staring blindly at a pile of bills, my doorbell (very similar to Ron's at Standard Oil) unexpectedly jumped to life. I hurried to the front of my store.

A well-dressed man stood at the counter holding a small metal bracket.

"Hello Sir. How may I help you?" I was eager to please him. I had faith in the lessons Don Manna taught me. 'Good service is something people are willing to pay for.' 'If you go the extra mile (because most people won't-or it wouldn't be called the *extra* mile) for your customer, you *cannot* fail.'

Answering in a deep, cultured voice he explained how he had been to three window covering shops and all three of them said they could not replace the bracket but they would be happy to sell him a whole new shade. He handed me the part. "Can you help me?" he asked.

I looked it over. A standard four-screw mount bracket. No problem-I had twenty in inventory. So did any self-respecting window shop.

"I can help you, sir. Please wait one moment." I quickly went in the back of my shop, grabbed the exact same part, just as quickly returning to the front.

"This is what you need. It is the exact same part. If you need help installing it I would be happy to do so. If not, your bill is two dollars even."

He had a pleasantly surprised look on his. "Why thank you young man!" He accepted the part, fished in his pocket and withdrew two dollars, which he handed to me. As I accepted the money he asked me for a business card which I happily gave to him.

"Hmm . . . Apollo Shade Co. How long have you been in business?" he asked.

"Today is exactly two months sir." The answer came as quickly and clearly as I could manage.

"Really? How did you come up with Apollo for the name? It's unusual."

"I want people to call me first," I answered. "In the yellow pages I noticed there are many companies that begin with AA. I want people to call me, but AA Shade Co. does not sound right. Apollo is still in the front of the telephone listings under 'window coverings'." I hoped I explained it clearly.

"Pretty smart!" he replied. "Well, again, thank you for your help. I may be in touch." He turned, leaving my shop. A two-dollar sale didn't help my day. Discouraged as I was Don Manna's advice still stayed with me pertaining to customer relations 'always be honest, always be fair, and always be nice.'

Two weeks later I received a phone call. I picked up the receiver.

"Apollo Window Shade, how may we help you?"

"Hello. Is this Barry Dujlovich?" a deep voice floated through the phone.

"Yes it is. How may I help you?" I answered.

"Barry, this is Mr. Parks. I was in your shop a couple of weeks ago. You sold me a bracket."

"Yes! I remember you. How are you Mr. Parks?" My heart rate increased. I had a good feeling. I recalled the expensive cashmere coat and heavy gold watch on his wrist.

"I am well, thank you for asking. I have a job to be done and I would like a bid from you. Can you be downtown tomorrow morning?"

Could I be downtown? Was he kidding?

"Of course I can be downtown tomorrow morning. Thank you very much for the opportunity Mr. Parks." I answered excitedly. He gave me directions and a time to meet then quickly rang off the line.

I met him as planned, and within thirty minutes I had a five thousand dollar order for shades and installation! My feet barely touched the sidewalk as I left his building. Mr. Parks, I quickly found out, develops office spaces in the city-very nice office spaces. But that was not where his *real* money came from. He also owned one of the oldest and largest printing press companies in the Midwest. At the end of the interview I couldn't resist asking one question.

"Mr. Parks, I'm *very* happy you called me, but I am curious as to why? You must have a regular shade company for your projects."

"I do-Apollo Shade Co. When I couldn't find the part I needed and all I got was the run-around from the other shade houses you were the only one to offer me the solution I was looking for. You're honest, and I appreciate that. You could have told me the same thing as the others but instead you helped me-even though it didn't help you. I develop a lot of buildings in this town and when I need shades you will be my first and last call—provided you don't screw up." He half smiled-and half didn't. "Now, if you'll excuse me, I have another appointment."

"Of course, and thank you again Mr. Parks." I was about to add something when his phone rang. Glancing up at me he waved his hand, invisibly propelling me toward the door as he smiled and mouthed a 'You're welcome.'

Mr. Parks was as good as his word and the jobs started coming in. Referrals from some of *those* jobs brought in yet *more* customers. My business expanded, and my need for materials grew proportionally. Don Manna re-entered my life in a new capacity. Before, I was an employee with a national firm but now I was a business owner, the same as Don himself, though on a much smaller scale. On more of an equal footing, our friendship flourished. We bought and sold parts and supplies from each other, and my many trips with him to Diversey Harbor were gratifyingly accident free.

Early morning turned out to be the only time of day we both had free to spend with each other. Hot coffee, good conversation and priceless advice were but three benefits I derived from our mornings. We discussed our market's direction, new products available and staffing problems. I also shared some things with him that occurred during my early days in business.

"Don, you will love this. Last week I installed shades at a unit in Lake Point Towers." He nodded. This was his turf, the high-rise, high-dollar luxury apartments built for Chicago's elite. "It was a twenty unit job." His eyebrows elevated a notch. A twenty-shade job is a darn nice job, and he knew it. A bubble of laughter spilled out as I went on. "So I parked my station wagon across the street on Olive. It looked like an illegal parking spot, but I needed to get my shades and hardware to the unit as quickly as possible. I was thinking about my wagon and not the job. I got everything inside unit sixty-two. The owners moved in this past Monday, so you understand I was under a serious deadline to complete the job. Once I was inside sixty-two, I decided to install the brackets immediately rather than return to the street and find another parking spot . . . I was in such a rush," I stiffed a giggle. "I installed them in the *wrong unit!*" We simultaneously burst out laughing. The waitress shook her head as she topped off our coffee. "I should have gone to *fifty*-two!" A new round of laughter followed as if a whole new joke had been told.

But it was not all laughter and funny stories. I complained bitterly to him about customers and the things they were capable of.

"I installed a full set of shades for a unit on Michigan Avenue."

"Uh-huh," his expression portrayed.

"It was a very nice place-many expensive works of art. I was installing the third shade in the living room-the view of the lake was very cool. I heard a noise in the hall. It seemed to be coming from a closet. I opened the closet door and you would not believe what I found!" I was getting worked up, reliving my indignation and shame.

"The owner was hiding in there, spying on you?" Don calmly asked.

"Yes! How did you know?"

"Barry," he answered in a calm, resigned voice, "you are dealing with *very* wealthy people. Some of those works of art you mentioned may cost fifty thousand dollars or more. How much was your bill for the work you did?"

"Two hundred eighteen dollars and fifty-seven cents" Even as I answered him my indignation faded. The rug woven of my self-righteousness instantly frayed beneath the weight of pure logic.

"I see," I said, dropping the subject.

Another morning started like any one of a hundred breakfasts with Don. It was Don's turn to gripe about customers. I told him jokingly, "Well Don, you could always sell me your business." In every jest, there is a kernel of intent.

"Hmm . . ." That was all I got for my tentative foray.

Another breakfast, another plate of eggs.

"I'll tell you what Barry. Two months ago you asked me if I would sell my business to you."

"No! I was kidding, of course Don. Please do not misunderst-"

"Barry, Barry, do you think I am a fool?" He smiled and folded his hands together in front of him on the tabletop. Disengaging his fingers from their woven stance he gently pushed plates, coffee cups, napkins, utensils and the sugar caddy to either edge of our small table leaving an unobstructed canyon of red and white checkers between us. Returning each hand to the other, his fingers remarried. "How does this sound?" He said this in a serious voice and I suddenly realized I was in the middle of business deal. My pulse jumped. "I will sell National Window Shade Co. to you. It will cost you two hundred and fifty thousand dollars. You will have my equipment, my inventory and my customer list. Most important, you will have my company name." He leaned back. Smiling he asked, "What say you, Barry Dujlovich?" The biggest decisions in my life seemed to be made with the shortest answers.

"Yes," I said without a blink. I offered my hand and he accepted it with his own.

A series of meetings with lawyers and accountants followed. The result amounted to Don financing a quarter of a million dollar loan with Apollo Shade's assets and my new house in Naperville as collateral. In the track of our friendship, now worn smooth by mutual trust, the deal went through without issue. I turned my five-year loan into a three-year loan. My desire to pay back the note early was two-fold; there would be less interest to pay and the sooner I paid the loan off, the sooner the business would be mine.

Sales were phenomenal. Why settle for one store when I could have two, or even three? My plan was faulty from the start. Learning a serious lesson in business I came to realize the monetary pain of expanding without proper capital to do so. My mini-empire of three National Window Shades wavered on unsteady legs. I made a decision to regroup, scaling back to my original one store business. Ever the wiser one (too late) I recalled Don's basic formula for success. 'Go after the money.' Digging deep into my memory I recalled the very conversation

"Barry, what would you prefer? To install one hundred window shades at a profit of thirty dollars per shade, or install five window shades at a profit of two hundred dollars each?"

I did the math quickly. My answer followed immediately.

"I would do the job with one hundred shades. The profit would be three thousand dollars instead of one thousand dollars. I would make more money."

"Barry, my friend." He paused, allowing my slowness to catch up. "How long will it take to install one hundred window shades?"

I calculated again. "Five days at a rate of twenty per day with two crews for install and an additional week would be needed to produce them." A glimmer glimmered.

"And how long would it take to produce and install five window shades. Hmm . . . ?"

"One day, two at the most." I answered. The glimmer had graduated to a beacon.

"Now my friend, how much is ten days of labor for four people as opposed to *one* day's labor's cost for *two* people?

The beacon illuminated a notch. A quick scratching on the chalkboard of my mind revealed a startling fact.

"I would only make two hundred dollars more on the hundred shade job," I humbly conceded.

"True, true. Think how many jobs you could do in those two weeks if they were *all* five shade jobs each, eh?" No mocking tone, no superiority-just a friend helping a friend. "Now Barry, if you can make one thousand dollars a day as opposed to three thousand dollars for two weeks work, what is the more profitable method of business?" The beacon became a blinding light. How well he taught me.

My family grew. My business grew. Recovering from my over-ambitious business vision, I took the five shade versus one hundred-shade parable to heart. My bank account swelled, my daughters (Pam, the latest addition) grew, and my wife became more a part of me than ever. Rolling into the nineties, I had the future by the tail when it turned around and bit me.

# CHAPTER XXI

## "Cerebral Vascular Accidents Happen"

Another long day, but a successful one I thought. Pulling into my driveway in Burr Ridge I did what I do every time I come home in the evening after a full days work. First I looked at the front of my house, an almost embarrassingly large one-story in an upscale subdivision. Then I admired the landscaping, the flowers and the perfect cut of my lush green lawn. As I pulled my car to the left to enter the two-car garage I looked to my right as I always did. The large peaceful lake rippled in the setting sun. The other perfect homes with perfect lawns sloped gently to the lake in oh so perfect fashion. My huge weeping willow swayed in the light evening breeze. Immensely satisfied with my home and grounds I stuck my keys in my pocket and went inside to see the *real* jewels in my world.

"Hello Honey," I said to Lee. Her back was toward me while removing a roast from the oven.

"How was your day Barry?" she asked, not deterred from her task.

I answered to her back. "It was a long one, but I finished the skylight job for McDonalds. It was thirty feet in the air and very tricky to install. But it's done! Did you pick up any beer?" I asked. Oh, I almost forgot to ask how her day was. "How was *your* day?"

"Beer is in the fridge, Barry. My day was wonderful. I went shopping downtown today and picked out *the* most perfect wrought iron outdoor patio set. You'll love it Barry".

Hmm . . . . I wonder how much *that* cost? Lee's taste, I noticed, developed at an astonishingly similar growth rate to National Window Shade's net earnings. I shrugged. What are you gonna do? I said to myself with a rueful grin. Lee turned from setting the roast on the counter. She beamed a smile toward me melting my heart tonight as surely as it did twenty-five years ago while recovering from my automobile accident. Lee was my American dream girl. My heart was lighter and smiles came easier to me for no other reason than her simply being near.

"For the inside porch, upper or lower outside patio?" I asked. I didn't really care. I knew whatever patio set she had chosen would be tasteful, functional and of high quality (and therefore expensive). Much like herself, I silently noted.

"The lower patio. The chairs and table are black with a scrolled floral motif. The neatest textured glass top came with the set. The salesman said when it rains the drops don't—"

"Hi Mom! Hi Dad!" My sixteen-year-old daughter Pam burst through the back door yelling out her hello's before she was even in the kitchen. She is like her mom I thought. And myself, I ruefully added, considering her height. The American branch of the Dujlovich tree was not blessed with great height. I topped out my clan of four at five feet eight inches tall. That was okay though. I loved my family, saying it silently to myself yet again. I never tired thinking of them. Lee drank daily from a spring of bubbling laughter and more than compensated for my lack of mirth. I laughed, but laughter did not swim just below the surface of my eyes looking for the slightest reason to come into being. Pam's and Lisa's hearts floated on a plane of lightness never darkened by the sight of death, the mutilation of human beings, the humiliation and pain of physical beatings. They are living the American dream, and their hearts pulled the heaviness of mine up to a comfortable (and livable) point somewhere in between. I was very proud of myself that I could give them this wonderful life.

"Hi Pam," Lee and I said simultaneously. By the time we said hello she was already bounding down the stairs to the lower level. This wasn't unusual so Lee and I continued our conversation with barely a hiccup.

Getting away from the miracle tabletop I told Lee I was very tired and I was going to sit outside and enjoy a cold beer.

"Fine Barry. Relax. I'll call you for dinner in twenty minutes." Lee answered. She handed me a beer and gave me peck on the cheek. Smiling inside and out I sat in a lawn chair facing the lake and thought about my day.

Dinner was announced, eaten, and then followed shortly thereafter with a gratifying snuggle between clean sheets and a fluffy goose-down comforter. Laying in the dark I planned my schedule for tomorrow in my mind. Two very important appointments I *have* to be at. So many things to do, so many . . . Sleep claimed me.

The explosions of a thousand bombs blasted me out of sleep. My head was being torn in two. My mind (a part *not* blown to bits) screamed at me to stop the pain. I couldn't. Shooting out of bed and staggering to the bathroom I stumbled to the floor. Dropping like a sack of flour I ended up on my side with my cheek pressed against the smooth, cold tile. My mind still shrieked for me to do something while yet another section freed my bodily functions from the prison of muscle control. My bathroom floor had no option but to accept a brownish splatter of roast, potatoes and beer. Chunks of vomit hung from my slack lips and my arms refused to obey my command to wipe them clean. Warm urine soaked my leg then spread in a puddle in front of me. My bowels let loose and last night's dinner sagged and squished against the back of my leg. I cried out, but no sound followed.

Lee was at my side. "Oh God oh God oh God oh God." The panic and terror in her voice ripped a hole in me. I tried to say anything to comfort her but all I had left were my eyes. That was not enough. "Barry! Barry! Oh God, Barry. Jesus, please, oh God Barry!" Her eyes were dying with me.

But Lee was once a nurse and her panic didn't last. A phone call and ambulance ride later the doctors had me.

The left side of my body was so much nothing. No feeling came to me. No heat, no cold, no sharp jabs or pinches registered. I knew nothing. I had no idea what was happening to me-only that it was very, very bad.

They cut into my throat allowing me to breathe. Medicated and shoved into a netherworld of sedatives, at some point a doctor gently nudged my right shoulder. My right eye opened to see him leaning above me. Lee stood in the background.

"Mr. Dujlovich, can you hear me?" He softly asked. "Blink your right eye if the answer is yes." A blink later he continued. "Mr. Dujlovich, I'm sorry to inform you you've suffered a cerebral vascular accident-a stroke. You've lost all faculties on the left side of your body. Do you understand what I'm saying to you?" Blink. "I'm very sorry. Most unfortunately our tests indicate you've experienced a brain stem stroke-most victims of this particular type of stroke don't recover. Every case is different though!" He added optimistically. "We will do everything in our power to reverse the damage. Physical therapy, medications and localized surgeries will help restore some of your faculties. Do you understand?" Blink. "Good. The most vital thing you can do at this point is to keep a positive attitude." He paused. "I speak frankly when I tell you your attitude will be the difference between your living and dying. I am turning your wife Lee over to you now, but I will be back. Again, I'm sorry Mr. Dujlovich." His duty done the doctor slowly turned from me. He looked at Lee while motioning her to come to the right side my bed and then he left the room, closing the door quietly behind him.

Lee did all the talking. "Oh Barry, I'm so sorry, I'm so sorry . . ." she retreated into sobs. "Please don't give up. We all love you. Lisa, Pam and I love you with all our hearts. Oh please don't give up. Nothing has *ever* stopped you. Don't let this be the thing to bring my Barry down." Giving up on words again she squeezed my right hand. I squeezed back. "I will be here every day Barry-every day."

Every day turned into six weeks. My nourishment bubbled through a feeding tube inserted into my stomach. I cried every day. My left eye should have participated in my self-pity fest but was unable to attend. My right eye cried for both. My nurse was supposed to keep my left eye closed but neglected to do so. As a result, the tear ducts failed and it dried out permanently. I ended up listening to the doctor explain how this happens in strokes, it was unavoidable, one of the conditions, etc. Were I able to speak I would have told him it was *not* unavoidable. The nurse failed to do her job, and in so doing, she cost me my cornea.

They sent me home a cripple. I could not walk, talk, scratch, or eat solid food. Nothing changed for months. Lee cared for me the first several months and then the crushing demands of bill collectors forced her to return to work as a surgical nurse. At that point I could barely manage to get to the bathroom. I still couldn't speak, walk anywhere or do anything.

National Window Shade and Barry Dujlovich are one in the same; hence my business suffered a stroke within several days of mine. The world, I realized, didn't care if I could not wipe my own ass. Bills are bills, and bills must be paid. The fickle finger of fate was not content with turning me into a silent, drooling imbecile, it was not content with taking my business to the edge of foreclosure, but seemed satisfied only when a fissure of discontent split my family into four separate islands of despair. One roof covered us all but we each lived remote lives, communicating with each other as necessity demanded, a far cry from the happy days of sunshine and laughter.

Pam, my youngest at sixteen, turned from everyone, finding an outlet for her grief and fear in her peers. Every passing day she slipped further from the bonds that had formerly kept us so strong. My humiliation at being able to do nothing about it crippled my heart as surely as the stroke crippled my body.

Lisa, God bless her, went to work at National Window Shade in an effort to keep the doors open. She found the strength to turn her fear outside of herself and possessed the intelligence to focus on sustaining our family business. Without her all would have been lost. Recently graduated from College she plunged into the business world headfirst emerging as the champion she is.

Lee returned to work, focusing on making money for the family while sinking into a severe depression that threatened to swamp her. Waves of despair lapped over her bow, rocking her to and fro, but never did they succeed in capsizing the strong spirit I fell in love with so many years ago.

*My* spirit, however, was not so strong. Weeks slid by without visible improvement. My tongue still sagged from the left side of my mouth like a forsaken piece of meat. Cleaning my own body proved to be almost impossible. Then, as time passed, it became a possible though exhausting chore. I could not sit out back on my patios. I couldn't make a meal for myself. I couldn't voice my rage, and the left side of my body was nothing more than a weighted corpse slowing down my right. Lying in bed from waking to sleep and back again the cancer of depression twisted its iron tentacles around the slightest glimmer of positive thought, leaving darkness where hope once existed. The dark glimmer tested the waters of my reason. It grew in strength as days of immobility became a listless pile of weeks. I couldn't ignore the logic one part of my brain hurled against its more positive minded half. The day came when the darkness won, and when it did I didn't run but welcomed my decision to commit suicide. The question was *how*. I had plenty of time to figure out the best method and spent many hours doing just that.

Examining the pros and cons of electrocution I tossed it back and forth at length, discarding that method. It seemed far too painful, not to mention sloppy. The chimes of my front doorbell interrupted my feasibility study on the effectiveness of standing at the top of my basement stairs and simply falling forward on my neck. Footsteps slapped the tile of my front foyer.

"Barry?" I couldn't answer. "Barry, where are you?" The voice grew louder making it's way down the hall to the back of the house. I recognized the strong voice of my long-time friend John Dvorak. My neighbor in Naperville for many years. We had shared hundreds of beers together on either his back porch or mine. Our kids had grown up together, roughing the perils of youth-all the healthier for their friendship. His head popped though the door to my bedroom. His smile faded, doused in the tears flowing unchecked down my cheeks. "Oh Barry, my friend." He didn't know what else to say. What *was* there to say? "Gee, you'll be fine in no time." "Come on Barry, we'll be eating at Tony's next month; drinking beer and laughing." John is a sensitive, intelligent man and he didn't insult me with obvious lies. Instead, he walked softly to my bedside, sat next to me and held my hand, doing his best to absorb my sorrow in silence. I motioned him to come close to my mouth. He leaned down, placing his ear scant inches from my lolling tongue. If he was repulsed, the emotion never made it to his eyes.

"Yes, my friend?" he quietly asked.

Gravelly stroke-speak fought its way to air. "Aihhgh wahntt khilll sehllf." I leaned back into my pillow, drained as much from the effort of speaking as the admission to another human being. He abruptly sat up, impaling me with a piercing stare.

"No Barry! In all the years we've known each other I've never heard such a weak and foolish statement from you! I can't say I understand, because I don't. Only you know the pain of your life. While killing yourself will certainly end *your* pain your act will only *cause* pain-a pain in those you love most-a pain that will never, ever fade inside them until they also die. You have never been a selfish man-until now!" He stopped speaking when he saw a fresh reservoir of tears running down well-worn tracks. Knitting his brows he continued speaking in the same uncompromising tone. "I recall a story you told me of a marine that wanted to kill himself. Do you remember it?" I nodded. "You told him his death would not be honored, and those he left behind would love him but curse him for his weakness. Do you remember Barry? Do you?" Another nod followed. His eyes and tone softened as he went on. "You need help my friend. I will come here more often to keep you company and on your next visit to your doctor you need to tell him of your depression so he can prescribe a medicine to combat it. You need to watch comedy on the television-*and you need to move around! Force* yourself! Fight *back!* You are a strong man, always have been. And, you are not alone." Further words of encouragement followed and toward late afternoon he departed.

I took his advice. My doctor prescribed Prozac and John prescribed Seinfeld. My emotional equilibrium returned after a time and soon thoughts of suicide seemed as forcign (and repugnant) to me as anything I've ever considered. Watching Seinfeld, I even scratched out a laugh, George Castanza is just too much. It was my first laugh in my post-stroke world.

The nuts and bolts of my life were slowly unraveling but I knew now I could at least face the road ahead. My loan company demanded the mortgage payment, and it seemed the I.R.S. spent more than I owed them on postage judging by the unbelievable number of mailings. My creditors demanded payment. My accountant advised me to file for bankruptcy. *That* I would not do. Don Manna didn't sell me his company to have me destroy its good name by filing for creditor protection.

"Your vocal chords are a twin unit," a doctor explained to me. "Think of them as flappers that rub against each other when you speak. When your stroke occurred your left flapper stopped flapping. Without nerve and muscle stimulation it can't operate the way it's supposed to." He paused to make sure I was still with him. I was. "Okay, here's the deal. Your right flapper is working perfectly, except there's no left flapper to rub against. Without the left flapper, the right side just waves around looking for contact. No contact-no sound. No sound, no speech. What we are going to do tomorrow morning is inject Teflon into your left flapper. The Teflon will force the left vocal chord to its former position in your throat. Your right flapper will have its partner again. In a short time you will have speech back. Now, if you'll excuse me, I have other patients to see." He took his leave but I barely noticed. I would be able to speak again!

The operation was a success and I started on the comeback trail. My attitude improved. Seinfeld continued to arouse chuckles, or at least an unhealthy sounding cousin. The Prozac continued to work its chemical magic. Countless hours spent in physical therapy culminated in me standing for one minute at a time, then two minutes. I have to get back to my business! I drove myself day and night to accomplish just that.

And I did it.

I went into my shop for an hour a day at first, then two hours, then half a day. Lisa was a miracle worker that saved my company, and as word spread in the business that I was back my creditors suddenly were so *very* glad to hear of my recovery.

The roller coaster that is life had crept along an hour at a time for two years. As my health recovered the roller coaster picked up speed, and in no time it was clipping through the months, then the years. Lisa stayed on, learning the business from the ground up. She never complained, a Dujlovich in the proudest tradition. I decided that if I ever retire my business would be hers. Hands down, no bull one hundred percent her baby.

I realized as years passed the consensus that doctors are all knowing is a myth. They know very little when it comes to strokes. I had one. *I* know what it's about. Through talking to other stroke victims I learned every stroke affects everyone differently. There are a number of myths related to strokes. The most prevalent one is that you lose feeling on only one side of the body. The left side of my body went dead, after time parts of it rejuvenated. I can feel parts of my left side as well as my right-just not *all* parts. Myth number two-recovery is impossible. One doctor informed Lee early on that I would never talk or walk again. Bunk! If you love your life enough and want it back-*you can get it back*! The human body is a biological machine. It hurts and it heals. Recovering from such a debilitating malady is not easy, *but it can be done!*

I learned to walk again (as long as I have something solid to lean on if needed). I learned to talk again (carefully, but I still talk). I learned to see out of my left eye again (after a cornea transplant performed by Dr. James Noth). I learned to say 'no' if something wasn't right. Life is too short to accept anything less than what I expect it should be. I re-learned that business is not the most important thing in life-family is. I learned that while friends wished me a speedy recovery, what they were really thinking is, "Thank *God* it's not me." I might have done the same. Good people are still people, and at the end of the day it's really all about the one looking back in the mirror. I learned that people handle grief in different ways-some retreat to drugs-some charge forth to work. Some pretended that my physical condition did not exist, and some (like my mother-in-law Lil Loess) emerged as unsung heroes; devoting time, energy, money and their healing essence to make another life better than it is. I learned that recovery from a stroke is not an overnight thing-it takes years, and if one has the will and desire to reclaim a life damaged (but not lost), it *is* possible.

I learned I cannot drink from a glass-the left side of my mouth will not conform and I make a mess of it, but I *can* drink from a bottle. Fortunately, beer is served in bottles. I learned that traveling to the brink of death (a priest administered last rights *twice* my first two days in the hospital) only made me fight all the harder for life. I learned that after my stroke my ability to dream during sleep vanished, but I didn't mind, because for me every day I wake up and see my family, every day I can get in my car and go to work and make window shades I am *living* my dream.

I learned life is the most beautiful gift granted under heaven and *nothing* is so bad that one should abandon this incredible breathing, heart pulsing, absolutely fabulous thing we call living.

# CHAPTER XXII

## "Only in America"

Today is a big day! I crossed out June fourteenth on my calendar. A red X joined thirteen others for this month. Over fifty years in America! So many things to do! My book's writer, Michael Goodreau and his fiancée' Linda from St. Charles, Missouri were in town to celebrate with me. Friends from all over Chicago would be arriving at my house early afternoon. Others from around the country had flown in to attend my party. Don Manna and his wife were coming as well as John Dvorak and his wife. When my eyes opened to greet the day I felt like it was Christmas. A long anticipated day packed with old and new friends, Croatian music, whole lambs grilled on an open pit and, not to be neglected, Croatian beer.

After picking Mike up from a nearby hotel we drove back to the house and collected Chris and Ray Goebel (Lisa's husband and father-in-law) as well as Chris's friend Andy. Chris is an honest, successful, secure man, and I thanked God again my daughter married him. I feel richer for knowing him and his father.

The five of us piled into a couple of vehicles and drove to a Croatian grocer off Cicero. My order for two lambs was ready to be picked up. Cases of Croat beer lined one wall, and by the time we left the stack was ten cases shy from when we entered. This was a celebration! I was throwing this party to commemorate my life in the United States of America!

Back at my house we hauled the lambs (at least fifty pounds each) down to the edge of the lake where two hollowed out spots filled with briquettes lay dormant, needing only charcoal fluid to bring them to life. It was a short wait, and in no time fire set about chewing them into dust. Our work was just beginning though. The lambs needed to be prepared for the spit.

I glanced at the rotisseries lying on the ground next to the bed of coals. So many memories. Twenty years ago when I started throwing these summer parties I rented similar units. I used to go to Croatian clubs in the city where they cooked lamb just like this. I wanted to cook the lambs at home but lacked the equipment. With one request and a number of dollars later I was the proud owner of two rotisserie units- the very same ones lying on the ground in front of me. This was my shindig so I promptly set the pace for the day.

"We need *Sljivovica!*" I looked around on the tables-no *Sljivovica*. "Chris, go get two bottles and shot glasses." Two minutes later he reappeared with them, and one minute after that we tossed back our first shots with a hearty proclamation of '*Zivili!*' from every drinker present. A cutting, twisting, sawing, bone-snapping hour later the lambs turned uncomplainingly above the now red-hot glowing pits. Our primary early morning task completed we energetically set about the task of transferring *Sljivovica* from the bottles to our stomachs. Burning embers radiated in my stomach this morning with the same ferocity as Joseph's private batch of fifty-eight years ago. A different color, a different label, but those were the *only* differences. I had one shot and felt blessed by God. I had two shots and I was glad to be alive. I drank three shots and felt so strong I could wrestle a snake! I hoped the snake was at least sixty-four years old so it would not have an advantage on me.

The day progressed. Croatian music floated to every ear and beyond us to the lake, then over its unobstructed surface. Lee appeared at my side.

"Barry, this is wonderful. I'm so happy for you! This is the best party yet!" She smiled every word into my eyes. Thirty-seven years of love flowed between us and I thanked God for the umpteenth time for sending Lee to me.

"It is Lee, it is." I answered. Looking out over my guests I felt inner warmth that visited on only the most special occasions. Don Manna hunched over, speaking with his wife. My son-in-law Chris (a firm believer in the restorative powers of *Sljivovica*) laughed uproariously with his audience as he delivered the punch line to a joke. Mike's fiancée Linda tossed back another shot of *Sljivovica* with Eileen, a good friend of Lee's. A hundred other friends congregated on my lawn in small groups or pairs all relishing the beautiful day. A cooperating sun held the temperature to eighty degrees. All in all, a perfect day I thought.

John Dvorak (picking at the last of the lamb) was right those many years ago. I *do* have a life worth living. Turning my gaze back to Don Manna I smiled inside and out when my eyes found him. Thanks to his wisdom and guidance my life is everything I dreamed a well-lived life should be. I have my family, my friends, my country and my business-the four corners of the well-constructed person known to the world as Barry Dujlovich.

Glancing beyond my guests, beyond the lake and well past the borders of this country we call America I looked back upon this great thing I called my life. Enjoying my sixty-fifth year of continuous breathing I prayed for many more. My health, while not (or ever to be) the same as before the stroke is getting stronger every day. Lisa & Pam are both married to wonderful men. Pam graduated from Southern Illinois University and has achieved her life long dream of becoming an Art Teacher. Lee is a picture of vibrant maturity. My business is flourishing beyond my expectations and I feel blessed my friends are here to celebrate my joy in being an American. My family gathered around me. Lil Loess, my mother-in-law, both my daughters, Lee and I stood together on the upper porch. An almost empty bottle of *Sljivovica* emerged which quickly found its way into shot glasses. We held our glasses aloft, and with a hearty '*Zivili!*' from every throat we downed our shots in unison. I drank to the day I stepped foot on American soil (for at least the ten thousandth time) and then asked a very practical question.

"Is there any *Sljivovica* left?"

# The Immagrant's Anthem

WHEN I SEE . . . . MY FELLOW MEN . . . .
AMERICANS . . . . JUST LIKE ME . . . .
WE SHARE A BOND . . . OF STARS AND STRIPES
A COMMON GOAL . . . TO BE FREE.

WE ARE ALL . . . . FROM SOMEWHERE ELSE
NOT NATIVE . . . TO THESE SHORES . . . .
FROM PLYMOUTH ROCK . . . . TO STATEN'S DOCK
WE LANDED HERE . . . . SEEKING MORE.

OPPRESSIONS THUMB . . . . IS LIFTED GONE . . . .
ALLEGIANCE RISING . . . AS ONE VOICE
THE LIFE WE MAKE . . . HERE IS OUR OWN,
UNITED, STRONG . . . WE HAVE THE CHOICE.

OLE' GLORY FLIES . . . ABOVE US ALL . . .
FORMER FLAGS . . . IN THE PAST . . . .
STANDING PROUD . . . . WALKING TALL . . . .
AMERICANS . . . . WE'RE FREE AT LAST.

Michael W. Goodreau

## What became of

Yela Dujlovich—Deceased.
　　Passed in Argentina, 1975

Mara—
　　Passed in Linz, Austria, 2005

Milka, Anka, Rushka and Regina—
　　Living in Argentina.

Milan Dujlovich—Deceased
　　Passed in Austria, 1995

Perinic—
　　Passed in Argentina, 2005

Mirko—
　　Alive in Argentina

Father Brkan and Sister Anka—
　　Left the Church and married.
　　Both Deceased in Argentina

Dominic and Jozo—
　　Unknown

Father Vasilj—Deceased
　　Passed in Chicago

Father Cuvalo—Deceased
　　Passed in Chicago

Edward Vrdolyak—
    One-time Chicago Mayoral candidate,
    Owner of successful Chicago law firm.

Marine Corps comrades—
    Unknown

Pat & Jim Campbell—
    Jim—Deceased
    Pat—residing in suburbs of Chicago, selling real estate

Cookie & Tom Custer—
    Happily married in western suburbs of Chicago

John Dvorak—
    Living in Naperville, Illinois

Donald Manna—
    Retired. Splitting his years between homes in Florida and Chicago.

## What Happened to . . .

Ivanjska—now in Bosnian territory.

Austrian camps—all leveled, not a trace left.

Sante Maria degli Angeli—given to the Italian Government by the Catholic Church.

Grottammare—became a seaside resort town.

Sea Isle City Catholic Orphanage—Closed by the Catholic Church.

The Croatian Commissariat at Drexel Boulevard—nothing has changed since I left.

*Danica* (Morning Star Newspaper)—still in publication.

St. Joseph's College, Oakbrook, Illinois.—Closed and annexed from Hinsdale to Oakbrook. Grounds currently in dispute between the City of Oakbrook, Illinois and luxury home developers. Litigation in progress.

National Window Shade Co.—Flourishing better than ever.

## One Immigrant's Observations

Dear Reader,

   These last few pages are not part of the story, hence reading this is optional. I consider the following as a written version of 'Soap Box' the program on Public Television created to allow the everyday person a chance to express their opinions on a variety of issues concerning the general public. Opinions are nothing more than an individual's thoughts on any given subject. The nice thing about them is that they can be endorsed or discarded. You are free to do so here.
   In the last several years numerous allegations of sexual abuse by Catholic priests have made the front pages of every newspaper in the country. Some of these men, who call themselves servants of God, are nothing more than pedophiles. It disgusts me that the Church has done so little to stop these crimes against God and the laws of this country. Pope Paul (may God rest his soul) and the Bishops have done nothing to solve this problem. The *only* thing they have done is attempt to reconcile the victims with money. Do they really think throwing money at victims will make the pain of sexual abuse disappear? They need to blow the dust off their bibles and settle down for a serious review of the scriptures.
   The Catholic Church is the largest landowner in the *world!* It sickens me that they close orphanages and churches while retaining private wine cellars, palaces of enormous wealth, and clothes of the finest silk. Have they completely forgotten how Jesus threw out the moneychangers in the temple? The depth of their depravity knows no bounds. I'm sure Satan is gleefully rubbing his hands together knowing he will eventually see many priests in Hell.
   I would like to see politicians in this country give up their meal allowances for one month and give the money to children starving *right here* in America. I'm not naïve so I know this will never happen, but wouldn't it be nice?
   America is a country of vulgar excess. Bigger cars, larger homes, fancier foods, nicer clothes. We have become a nation of false standards. More does not mean better-it just means more. America was not always this way. The commercialism promoted through television by large corporations has created a society that bases its values on material things. Something must be done or we are doomed as a society.
   It angers me to hear people complain about our government and the politicians that run it when they don't even vote! If you are too lazy to register to vote then keep your opinions to yourself! Do you complain about a car you haven't driven? Do you gripe about the fit of a jacket you've never worn? Don't whine about the process if you don't contribute to it by voting.
   There are people that come to the United States, work for years and then retire to draw social security. Instead of staying here they go back to the 'Old Country'. This, I feel, is not fair to America. They are willing to take the money and spend it but not *here* to the betterment of the United State's economy-the very one that made retirement possible.

It irks me that professional athletes are paid so much money. I grant they are the best in their sport and I applaud the level of excellence they exhibit, but do they really deserve multi-million dollar contracts? People work their entire lives in dangerous jobs performing their tasks with a similar degree of excellence, yet athletes make more in one year than they do their *entire lives*!

I am disappointed so many people use our nation's bankruptcy laws as a loophole to avoid their financial responsibilities, which are usually based on poor decisions. I feel if you incur a debt you pay it. Bankruptcy should not be used as cure-all to avoid paying one's debts. Our economy has suffered as result.

We need to conserve our resources better. I once saw a sign in a Chinese restaurant that read, 'Take all you want, but eat what you take'. Very practical.

The fabric of this country is woven of many cultures and many people. It is what makes us strong. All my life I've worked on speaking better English (and still do so to this day). I welcome immigrants, of course. But I strongly feel if you come to this country, learn the language! It disappoints me that people live here their entire lives and don't learn English. Not only are they missing out on all the opportunities that would open up for them they don't contribute to this country as they should. We all have a responsibility as Americans to help keep our country strong and united. How can we be united if there are entire segments of our population that can't communicate with us, or us with them?

I think every young man should spend at least two years in the military. I am proud I was a Marine. I was proud to serve my country. If you want the benefits of America be willing to fight for them.

I am sick of hearing people claim they are violent because their parents were. That is a cop-out. Violence is not hereditary. Every person decides to be violent, or not. There is no inner voice compelling them to beat their wives or abuse their children.

I can get in my car and drive anywhere in this country I want to. There are no border checks between states, no machine-gun toting goons demanding my papers. If you want to whine about your freedom being compromised go live in Russia or any of a dozen other totalitarian countries.

This is, beyond a shadow of a doubt, the greatest country on earth to live. Treasure it.